LIGHTS, CAMERA, ACTION!

Lights, Camera, Action!

CAREERS IN FILM, TELEVISION AND VIDEO

Josephine Langham

BFI PUBLISHING

First published in 1993 by the
British Film Institute
21 Stephen Street
London WIP IPL

British Library Cataloguing in Publication Data
Langham, Josephine
Lights, Camera, Action!: Careers in Film,
  Television and Video
  I. Title
  791.43023
ISBN 0–85170–343–7

Set in 10 on 11½ Sabon by
Fakenham Photosetting Ltd, Norfolk
Printed in Great Britain by
St Edmundsbury Press, Bury St Edmunds

CONTENTS

ACKNOWLEDGMENTS

The author would like to thank Maggie Sanson of Jobfit, Dinah Caine, Director of Skillset, the Broadcasting, Film and Video Industry Training Organisation, Kate O'Connor of Skillset, the Industry Lead Body for Broadcasting, Film and Video, Stuart Conway of High Peak College, Buxton, Derbyshire, Peter Gibson of the National Council for Vocational Qualification, Haim Bresheeth of the London College of Printing – the London Institute, Neil Grant of Bournemouth and Poole College of Art and Design, Mitch Mitchell of The Moving Picture Company, Irene Ibbotson of BBC North, Hilary Thomas of The National Film and Television School Short Course Training Programme, and Rod Hastie of the ITV Association. They all gave their time in personal interviews or long telephone conversations, answering queries either about the industry or about the impact of new developments in education and training. While every effort has been made to check the facts reported in this book, the opinions expressed remain the author's own.

I would also like to thank my husband Bill Byers Brown who, despite being busy with his own research, read the whole manuscript and shared the Macintosh computer with me, and Christine Upton who, once a week, prevented domestic arrangements from falling into utter chaos.

INTRODUCTION

Except for the favoured few who inherit fortunes or win the pools, most people have to earn a living. For all of us the cherished dream is to work at a job we thoroughly enjoy so that there is scarcely a barrier between the workplace and our leisure activities. For our work to be play, and our play to earn money, is probably one of the most deeply held desires of contemporary life.

Learning through playing has been one of the axioms of modern educational thought. Alas, this idea is concentrated in practice in the primary schools, so that for most people the transfer to secondary school is traumatic. Suddenly notes must be made, facts have to be learned, exams have to be passed and the golden age of playing, experimenting, enjoying *and* learning all at the same time fades into oblivion.

No wonder that when we finally kick the dust of school behind us we long to pursue the ideal of work as play in our adult lives. Since television and film have provided the main source of entertainment for adults in the second half of the twentieth century, it is equally unsurprising that many of us dream and fantasise about working in these two industries. As a result, entry to both has always been fiercely competitive and the vast majority of us have longed in vain.

There have been many reasons for this. In the past, many young people failed to finish the punishing horse-race which the British call their education system. Failure at school sapped confidence and interest and for most people there was an apathetic drift into jobs which were rarely enjoyed. The idea of choosing what we wanted to do was an unrealistic dream. The world of work was often dull and boring. Jobs were endured: real life began at the end of the day or week. With little education, and virtually no training, most people could find no way into interesting jobs in industries which were, and could afford to be, highly selective in their intake.

However, for the few who passed the finishing-post and went on to college or university, the situation was not so dire. They were part of an educated elite who were somehow entitled to 'an interesting career' as a reward for jumping the academic hurdles. Graduates were rare and favoured souls who usually got the plum positions, often enjoyed their jobs and, moreover, were well-paid for doing so. Even among this favoured few, however, jobs in the media were thin on the ground. Only the brightest and the best were selected, especially for the rarefied world of broadcasting.

Unfortunately the sharp division between the academic and the non-academic in British society (often class-based) has had over the years a negative influence on British economic success and productivity. A largely apathetic, unqualified, untrained workforce has been economically uncompetitive and Britain has slipped behind Western Europe, Japan and the United States in economic strength.

In the last decade, however, we have begun to wake up to the deficiencies which our education system has fostered and the debilitating effect this has had on economic prosperity. As a result there is a new emphasis on vocational training and, perhaps more importantly, on 'retraining'. 'Training' will no longer carry an implication of intellectual inferiority, and people who missed out on education after the age of sixteen will now have opportunities to seek qualifications later in life. In future the gap between the graduate and 'the rest' will no longer be so vast. If all goes to plan, practical work and on-the-job training will finally be given parity of esteem with the theoretical, academic education of the graduate elite. The result could be a highly skilled workforce, trained to do jobs they enjoy. This has enormous implications for all sides of British industry: perhaps the audiovisual industry more than most.

The *Concise Oxford Dictionary* defines vocation as a divine call to, or sense of fitness for, a career or occupation. While the divine element in career choices is perhaps not exactly compatible with modern ideas, the sense of fitness is very important. When jobs fit people and people fit jobs the sum total is an increase in human happiness.

Young people in the 1990s are just as drawn to the world of the media as they have always been. In the future, however, more of them should have the skills to work in film and television and therefore the capacity to make their dream a reality. The communications industry is a growth area. Indeed it has been suggested that, by the year 2000, up to 20 per cent of the European workforce could be working in the communications industry in its very broadest sense. Instead of the restricted entry of the past, which frustrated all but the extraordinarily able, the lucky, or those with 'good contacts', in the future there will be a variety of routes 'in'. There should be no reason why anyone who is really drawn to the industry, who feels that it fits them and they will fit it, and who is prepared to work hard, should be prevented from entering it for at least a part of their working life. This is the plus side.

But since life is not a fairy story there is also a negative aspect. The well-paid, protected and glamorous jobs of the past, the careers which usually lasted for life, are giving way to something new and different, tougher, more temporary, constantly shifting, with periods of unemployment as a fact of life.

Anyone planning to enter the film or television business in the 1990s therefore has to slough off traditional and increasingly outworn ideas about the industry. In the past decade film and television have experienced a period of dynamic and dramatic change fuelled by the new technologies. Film and television were once quite sharply separated industries. This is no longer the case: video has acted as a bridge between them so that professionals in all areas move quite freely between the three media and between the corporate, broadcasting, pop music, advertising and film sectors. Consequently it is now quite common to refer to film, video and television as a single industry.

This book looks at careers in film, television and video. It is principally intended for young people leaving school, college or university who are interested in working in the industry but who know little or nothing about it. It is also intended as a resource book for educators and career counsellors who wish to advise the many students who are interested in working in film and television but who have no first-hand experience to offer. It is also aimed at young people who have secured their first job in the industry but who are bewildered by the pace of change and frustrated by the lack of training opportunities; they may have heard of the National Vocational Qualifications but are uncertain what the NVQs might mean for them.

The film, television and video industry has undergone a dramatic upheaval in the past decade and many of the traditional work patterns are now in the throes of massive change. The book describes the various jobs in the industry in the context of the economy of the industry as a whole. Account is also taken of the proposed changes in education which will affect the routes in. The first part of the book, therefore, describes the state of play in the industry for those who want an overall picture and an understanding of what has occurred. However, readers who only want practical information on careers and 'the way in' should begin at the second section, which describes education and training. The third and fourth parts describe the processes of production and the actual jobs.

Good luck!

PART ONE
THE INDUSTRY

1

TELEVISION
What's Been Happening?

During the 1980s the film and television industries, which historically had been somewhat hostile and competitive towards each other, drew closer together. The economics of film and television became more closely intertwined and the border between the two became blurred: today film companies produce films for television, independent video companies produce television programmes and television companies finance feature films. In addition, with the decline of the unions and the ending of the closed shop, people working in film, television and video move freely between what were formerly three highly separated sectors.

The following three chapters will look at the implications of these developments for people contemplating a career in the audiovisual industries in the 1990s. The discussion will begin with television because, during the 1980s, it was the television industry which bore the full brunt of the many shifts in political and economic philosophy and it was also television which experienced the main impact of the new technology.

At the beginning of the 1980s the television industry enjoyed a unique position in Britain with a worldwide reputation for quality in content and technique. This was true for the public (BBC) and commercial (ITV) sectors. In the earlier 1980s most people would probably not have considered British television to be an 'industry' at all, certainly not in the sense of the chemical industry or the engineering industry. Television carried out a varied set of activities and was a 'mixed bag', partly in the public, partly in the private sector and partly in between. It consisted of a huge organisation, the BBC, which had long dominated British broadcasting, and a great variety of other commercial companies linked together as independent television (ITV). The majority of employees in television, to a greater or lesser degree, were sheltered from the full force of the cold winds of market reality. Producers and directors had little direct involvement with

3

finance as an aspect of programme planning. The name of the game was creativity: producing good programmes was the prime motivation. Financial responsibility was the task of upper management.

By 1991 much of this had changed. In that year the Broadcasting Act ushered in a franchise system for ITV, the initial intention of which was to sell independent television licences to the highest bidder. Although this was eventually modified by an emphasis on a 'quality' threshold (see below), the new system of granting ITV franchises meant that, in principle, British commercial television faced the full force of the market-place without legislative obligation to protect public service broadcasting, thereby confirming what had been a general trend during the previous decade. It even seemed likely that in the 1990s the BBC would be forced to follow suit in some form or another. The BBC's licence to broadcast comes up for renewal in 1996 and there has been much talk of a change in the system of financing the Corporation. To understand the dramatic implications of all this, especially for those employed or wishing to be employed in the industry, we must briefly examine British television in its historical context.

Public Service Broadcasting
In the 1920s, when broadcasting began as a mass medium, it was characterised by two different philosophical models. In the United States broadcasting was seen as a medium of entertainment to be paid for commercially through advertising. In Britain (and to a greater or lesser extent most other European countries) broadcasting was regarded as a public service, paid for by public funds (through the licence fee) and untainted by any form of commercialism. In Britain the government was involved in broadcasting almost from the first and legislated into existence the British Broadcasting Corporation (BBC), an institution which under threat of legal sanctions had to abide by certain basic principles.

The purposes of British broadcasting were repeatedly declared to be information, education and entertainment. Any inspection of BBC radio and television archives before 1955 (when ITV began) leaves an abiding impression of an upper middle-class institution more concerned with a lofty mission of informing rather than entertaining the British masses. For many years most BBC broadcasters believed they were in the business of 'improving minds' and they turned up their noses at American radio and television with its crude, commercial attitudes which resulted in poor programmes characterised by cheap quizzes and melodramatic soap operas! The British system was considered to be vastly superior and perfectly exemplified by its high-minded programmes and excellent production values.

4

Behind the British and most European governments' traditional attachment to the concept of public service broadcasting lay the belief that broadcasting had enormous power to influence people's minds. It was definitely not an industry like any other and it had to be carefully controlled and supervised. Governments feared the negative influence of broadcasting on their citizens and believed in its ability to mould public opinion and raise the general level of education.

After the Second World War, however, many business interests in Britain began to cast envious eyes westwards to the United States where commercial broadcasting, closely linked to the advertising industry, was making huge profits. A campaign began for the introduction of commercial television in Britain and in 1955 the monopoly of the BBC with its metropolitan bias was broken with the introduction of independent television (ITV), a commercial television system which had a regional base.

The introduction of ITV, however, was a typical piece of British compromise. Although the system was financed by advertising, the idea of television as solely a money-making industry was still unacceptable to most British people, especially to those in power. Various Royal Commissions and government legislation insisted that both the BBC and ITV had to provide a high-quality public service, and the commercial television companies were also put under an obligation to produce programmes which were educative and informative as well as entertaining. This public element in commercial television was supervised by an organisation eventually called the Independent Broadcasting Authority (IBA), and for the next thirty years a dual system (sometimes called the duopoly) of the BBC and the IBA, with a strong public service ethos, characterised British television.

Channel Four

The idea of public service broadcasting reached its apogee in 1982 with the introduction of Channel Four which, although it showed advertisements, was obliged under the jurisdiction of the IBA to take account of minority interests and transmit quality programmes. Channel Four was protected from the market-place: it was financed by levies on the advertising receipts of the ITV channels, which had the right to sell advertising time on Channel Four transmissions in their regions.

The establishment of Channel Four apparently confirmed the public service nature of the British approach to broadcasting. In fact, however, it also presaged a momentous change. Channel Four, unlike the BBC and the ITV companies, made hardly any programmes in-house; it commissioned them from outside. This was an enormous boost to the 'independents', small production companies which made 'films' (more usually videos), but historically had had great difficulty in selling them to the BBC or ITV.

Here a word of caution is in order: the term 'independent' can lead to considerable confusion since ITV is itself referred to as independent television. In the 1980s, however, 'independents' became the current term for describing small production companies which had no part in the transmission of programmes but which sold completed programmes to mainline broadcasters or co-produced programmes with them. Channel Four was the great stimulus to the growth of this sector because, as a commissioning company, it placed contracts for programmes with independent producers (it also placed contracts with ITV itself). *Brookside*, commissioned from Phil Redmond's company, Mersey TV, was a typical case in point. By 1984–5, 313 independent companies contributed 690 hours of television to Channel Four. By 1992, despite the recession (of which more below), there are calculated to be over a thousand independent companies producing programmes for British television.

Channel Four quickly established a reputation for innovative programmes which expressed radical political and social views. If asked, most people would have identified the Channel with the political Left rather than the Right. In fact, the principle behind Channel Four was an expression of the classical liberal economics which became politically fashionable during the 1980s. Channel Four challenged the cosy duopoly of the BBC and ITV/IBA and liberated British broadcasting from an organisational strait-jacket. In opening up the airwaves to the products of small companies it heralded a massive change in the system which had governed British broadcasting for more than thirty years.

Deregulation

Between 1982 (when Channel Four was founded) and 1992 the whole landscape of British television has undergone a vast and rapid upheaval. The reasons for this can be traced to two main influences: politics and technology. In the United States and Europe the 1980s saw the election of right-wing governments committed to a movement towards deregulation. This meant, in practice, freeing business from what was considered by economic conservatives to be the undue and excessive restraint imposed by government 'overregulation' and the restrictive practices of trade unions. This so-called 'Reaganomics' (after President Ronald Reagan of the USA) had a worldwide impact and led in broadcasting generally to the dismantlement of many of the public service regulations which had previously governed television. This had less impact in the United States, where broadcasting had always been less supervised and more commercial, than in Europe, where it led to dramatic change. In many European countries in the 1980s there was a stampede to adopt the free market model. The public service broadcaster's monopoly of the airwaves was broken. European countries which had never had any form of commercial television now permitted private stations to exist, and new television companies sprang up all over the place.

The first result of this was a boom in advertising. Television enjoyed a halcyon period of huge profits. Most of the private channels saw television as an entertainment medium and the days of the rather grey, preachy, government-run systems which had typified television in some European countries were numbered. Advertising money flooded in and by the mid-1980s the programming schedules of Europe's television systems had brightened considerably. With much more money slopping around, the future seemed rosy, especially for employment.

Conservative Policies

Mrs Thatcher and the Conservative Party came to power in 1979. The Thatcher government had many ideological strands but one of the most significant was a passionate desire to loosen economic regulation. The Prime Minister believed in a rugged free market individualism and was determined to push back the frontiers of state intervention. She was particularly hostile to what she referred to as the 'nanny' state which the mandarins of the BBC and the IBA exemplified. The state, she believed, meddled far too much in the affairs of the individual. Moreover, she was deeply suspicious of some British broadcasters who espoused liberal views and cultivated a 'lack of bias', an attitude which was out of tune with her own conviction politics.

The Thatcher government was also predictably hostile to any form of protectionism, especially as exemplified by trade unions, which were very strong in certain sectors of the broadcasting (and film) industry. With the Prime Minister gunning for the unions it was inevitable that broadcasting fell within her sights. The first round was with the BBC. In 1986 the Prime Minister ordered an inquiry (the Peacock Committee) into the financing of the BBC where many wet liberals were supposed to lurk. This aroused widespread fears in the Corporation about the maintenance of the licence fee. Peacock proposed abandoning the public service requirements of the BBC in a general sense: programmes which appealed to a minority audience (basically cultural ones) were to be financed through a pay-as-you-view system. The Committee also proposed that by 1996 the proportion of independent programmes on the BBC and ITV should reach 40 per cent; the government in November 1986 decided that 25 per cent should be the aim by 1990.

ITV, with its powerful unions, could not hope to escape from the government's reforming scrutiny and, in the end, it was probably ITV which bore the full brunt of the free market fervour. The 1990 Broadcasting Act abolished the IBA and the protective shield which it had erected to secure public service broadcasting on ITV. It was replaced by the Independent Television Commission (ITC) which has a much less interventionist mandate. The Broadcasting Act also altered the way ITV franchises were awarded. It was in her attack on the broadcasting unions, however, that Mrs Thatcher's economic philosophy was most in evidence.

A basic principle of the Thatcher government was a supreme confidence in the business ethic and the virtue of competition, which the Prime Minister saw as the basis of the world's most successful economic system, capitalism. Capitalism, for Mrs Thatcher, was an agent for good and the guarantor of liberty. One of her most widely quoted remarks, 'There is no such thing as society', summed up her hostility to mutually protective groups, especially those which acted together in such a way as to thwart the 'healthy' self-interest of the individual businessman or woman. According to this world-view, men and women pursuing their own self-interest would bring great economic benefits to the whole nation.

As a result, the Thatcher government consistently expressed a strong philosophical opposition to 'socialist' ideals, and particularly those which the union movement represented. According to this view, traditional British corporatism and craft protectionism, closed shops, union 'tickets' and all types of restrictive practices had been the main reason for Britain's lacklustre economic performance since the Second World War. Throughout the 1980s, therefore, the Conservative government launched a series of onslaughts against British trade unionism which left the movement reeling. New labour laws effectively broke union power. All this affected many British industries and the impact was very acute in television, notably in ITV.

At a meeting with representatives of the television industry in 1987, Mrs Thatcher declared ITV to be a bastion of the most severe restrictive practices. They had contributed to a fat-cat, mollycoddled industry which the government was determined to wean away from its cream. The government believed that ITV had been grossly overmanned and protected for too many years and that this had resulted in a virtual closed shop, soaring labour costs (particularly very generous overtime agreements) and expensive programmes.

8

Technological Change

In addition to the philosophical and political turmoil which hit British television in the 1980s, the industry also found itself disturbed by the rapid advance in the so-called new technologies. Television since its beginnings has always been the mass communications medium most closely linked to technological advance. Throughout its history the development of television has been furthered by many scientific disciplines, such as mechanical engineering, electronics, optics and acoustics. During the 1980s, however, the pace of technological change accelerated thanks to advances in semi-conductors, lasers, fibre optics and space technology. Semi-conductors gave rise to integrated circuits ('chips') and to microprocessors, and these devices rapidly achieved higher and higher levels of performance in television thanks to their capacity to store data, their computational speeds and their complexity. Digital data processing became increasingly important and this, combined with integrated circuits and microprocessors, quickly revolutionised every aspect of television technology including production, processing, storage, transmission, broadcasting and the receiving of audiovisual information. The end result was an explosion in audiovisual technology and, as we have seen, a spectacular multiplication of the number of television channels which could be transmitted (especially through cable and satellite).

In the past, television, with its terrestrial broadcasting transmitters and limited available airwaves, was easily controlled by national laws. It was regarded as a scarce resource. In the era of satellites, however, this attitude began to make no sense. Direct broadcast satellites and the services which cable could provide cut right across national boundaries and made regulation much more difficult and problematical. Technological change, therefore, provided an encouragement towards deregulation throughout Europe and further prompted the loosening of the noose of state regulation and the weakening of the concept of public service broadcasting.

Advances in television technology increased the versatility of the medium. A greater variety of production methods was possible and the process of making programmes was simplified. Costs of equipment were reduced and the whole industry became much more accessible. The result was a boom in the independent video sector; the technology of television was no longer the fiefdom of the experts at the BBC and ITV. Companies were formed to produce pop videos and publicity for the corporate and public sector. Every business wanted to market itself and the corporate video was the mark of a company which was doing well. This created an expanding video production industry with new opportunities for producers and freelancers: even experienced tele-

9

vision personnel with secure jobs began to 'moonlight' in the video sector to supplement their salaries.

The old system whereby an intellectual and craft elite, working within the framework of large institutions such as the BBC and ITV companies, monopolised a complex body of knowledge (lighting, sound, camerawork and so on), and therefore power, was eroded. So too was the protection from competition which the closed shop had ensured. Thus technological advance, combined with the deregulatory approach and anti-union legislation, split the industry open. The hey-day of the freelancer with energy and talent was at hand, and every-thing was possible – or that was how it seemed – at first. Then the recession hit.

The Recession

By the end of the 1980s the world economy had slowed down; the advertising industry was one of the hardest hit and the market model for television looked somewhat tattered. This was especially so in Europe, where a decline in programme standards and a slackening of the specifically European dimension of television (and film) under the impact of American imports became a matter for concern. As the decade ended, and the recession deepened, it was not clear that the money available for home-grown television production was actually going to increase. It seemed far more likely that the now heavily fragmented European television industry, of which Britain was a part, would be colonised by cheap American products; that the result of deregulation was going to be more of less – more 'internationalised', conveyor belt, factory-produced slick programmes and fewer stimulat-ing, innovative, exciting programmes which expressed a national or European identity.

The heady roller-coaster days of the mid-1980s were over and Eur-ope began to count the cost of deregulation: the dominance of the dollar via American imports and, in countries such as Italy, a sleazy and tawdry home-grown system which hit the lowest common de-nominator of public taste. No wonder the European Community began to take note, and no wonder many British legislators also began to view the future with alarm and to back-pedal on some of the more extreme free market views.

The Impact of the 1990 Broadcasting Bill

The Broadcasting Bill of 1990 was in many ways a reflection of all this. Although mainly concerned with ITV, its implications had effects on the BBC and the independent market. The Bill as originally drafted was very much an expression of free market views but, as the debate in

10

parliament and the country went on, some of the hardest free market edges were knocked off and replaced with what was called the *quality programme threshold*. While ITV franchises were to be auctioned off to the highest bidder, the principle that the market should be the *sole* arbiter of the winner was subverted. An exceptionally 'high quality of service' bid could outdo the highest monetary bid. This was at least a partial return to the principles which had governed British broadcasting throughout its history.

The Broadcasting Bill, however, did help the advance of the independent sector with its provision that 25 per cent of all new programmes shown on the BBC, ITV and Channel 5 after 1992 (when the Act comes into force) had to be supplied by independent producers. This provided independents with access to an additional minimum of 5,000 programming hours per annum. Independent production companies, mainly working in video but also in film, received a tremendous boost and looked like becoming a fast growing and influential sector of the UK audiovisual industry.

However, in also making provision for Channel 5 and for satellite and cable, the Broadcasting Bill gave impetus to the further fragmentation of television. This could have a very detrimental effect on programming by limiting the pool of revenue available. Money coming from advertising sales, licence fees or subscriptions will have to stretch further and there could be a corresponding decline in the quality of programmes on offer. The BBC, for example, with a smaller proportion of total broadcasting, could find the universal licence fee increasingly under threat. People who have many channels to watch may resent being forced to pay for the maintenance of the Corporation and its funding base could be attacked. The British tabloid press will be happy to load the cannons: newspapers have never had much love for television, which they see as their greatest rival.

Producers' Choice

Already the BBC has begun to respond to the threat from market forces and the independent sector. In the 1990s BBC managers launched a project called 'Producers' Choice', designed to increase internal competition within the Corporation. Producers are being given control of their own programme budgets and will be allowed to shop outside the Corporation for certain facilities. This is a revolution for the BBC and completely contrary to how it has functioned throughout its long history. The Corporation has always been a self-sufficient organisation. By April 1993, however, BBC producers will be expected to buy services they need (scenic design, costumes, studio space, graphics and post-production) from wherever they can secure

11

the best deal. BBC resources departments, which previously always supplied services, will in future only earn income if they can sell their services to programme-makers. BBC producers will be charged a share of overheads, such as accommodation and capital costs, in the same way that independent producers are charged. The only costs paid for centrally will be those for commissioning and transmission and for the running and promoting of the television channels. This will drastically reduce employment in the BBC. Those entering the industry must be aware of this – although, on the positive side, it could generate further expansion in the independent sector.

The Franchise Auction

The impact of the Broadcasting Bill has been particularly dramatic for ITV. The auction of the new Channel 3 broadcasting licences during 1991 caused considerable anxiety, and four incumbent TV companies (Thames, TVS, TSW and TV-am) lost their franchises. Eight of the licences, however, did not go to the highest bidder, as the original legislation had planned, because of the *quality programme threshold*. Eleven bidding groups failed to pass the threshold and were therefore rejected on these grounds, and three bids were rejected by the ITC because their quality promises were judged to be unsupportable given the cash level of the bid. The wide variation in the cash bids offered has caused considerable concern, especially in the case of those companies which bid huge sums (Yorkshire bid £37.7 million and Carlton Television, the newcomer which defeated Thames, bid £43.17 million), because, in addition to the annually index-linked cash sum, winners will also have to pay a fixed percentage of revenue – predetermined by the ITC. All this has engendered fears throughout the industry that financial problems will produce even more pressure to reduce costs, enforcing economies of scale which will have a depressing effect on programme expenditure, particularly in a period of declining revenues from advertising.

Impact on Employment

The above could also have a dramatic effect on employment and the skills (or lack of skills) which people moving into the industry will require. In the past television producers, even in ITV, were a protected species. Their main obligation was to make good programmes: it was for others to worry where the money was coming from. That protection has now gone. In the harsh climate of the 1990s the British television industry is likely to become more like the British film industry and to be persistently dogged by financial problems. It will no longer be enough to be a talented television producer: financial acumen will be as much in demand as creative and artistic ability – but more of that later.

It is also likely that many of the small companies which have sprung up over the last few years to produce films or programmes for television will not survive in the harsh financial climate of the 1990s. The ability to raise money from co-production sources and programme distribution, and operating overheads, will become increasingly important and, as the independent sector matures, take-overs, mergers and bankruptcies will become as common as they are in other British industries. Attracting investment will be crucial if a company is to survive.

Television (henceforth closely linked with film and video) is becoming an industry much like any other – except perhaps less stable than most. If in the old days producers made programmes to impress their peers, in future they will make programmes to impress their backers (that is to say, programmes that sell). The idea of the broadcaster as a figure apart, high on a pedestal above ordinary mortals, well-paid, admired and virtually untouchable, has gone for ever. In future most people working in television will no longer be employed in secure jobs. The development of more terrestrial channels and the growth of satellite-delivered services both direct to home and via cable headends for onward distribution, plus the likely impact of High Definition Television (HDTV), will inevitably open up more opportunities for employment (this will be discussed in more detail in Chapter 3), but most of the new employees will be freelancers working across the film, television and video sectors. The traditional culture of the television (and film) industry will be irrevocably altered and employees will be subject much more to what could be wild fluctuations in the marketplace. Newcomers to the industry should be aware of this. But before we look at the future in more detail we must examine what has been happening in British film.

2

FILM

The Shape of Things to Come

Prior to the 1980s film production was an industry apart, with its own culture, traditions and working practices. It held itself aloof from television, which it saw as a competitor for audiences. In the 1950s the popularity of television had almost killed the British film industry and many old film hands really despised and resented the 'Little Box in the Corner'. Film people regarded the BBC as too establishment-oriented and television in general as down-market without any true cultural value. The fact that the British film industry was often in financial difficulties increased the sense of alienation.

During the 1980s, however, the film and television industries drew much closer together. As we have seen, political, financial and technical pressures brought about a revolution in television and this in turn altered its relationship to film. There had always been some overlap between the two: many productions for television were filmed, the BBC had its own film studios out at Ealing (now closed because of financial cut-backs) and a number of film companies produced commercials for ITV. Although the film industry did not experience the same degree of upheaval during the decade, many changes did take place and particularly in the feature film sector.

Feature Films
'Features' are those films intended for release in the cinema. They usually run between 90 and 110 minutes and generally tell stories. Documentary films intended for cinemas are a relative rarity in the 1990s, although they used to be popular, especially in the 1930s. The basic fact about film which everyone who wishes to enter the industry has to grasp is that it is a very expensive medium indeed (especially as compared with video), but it has a special mystique because of the beauty and accuracy of the images it produces and the hands-on immediacy of its editing techniques. It is the visual quality of film which cinematographers and directors enjoy, a quality which the

14

video image until recently could not even approach. For many years the practised eye could tell immediately if a television programme had been recorded on film or video.

Costs of feature film-making can be very high indeed. The 1990 Walt Disney production *Dick Tracy* cost $46.5 million to make. To recover such sums a great deal of effort has to go into marketing and distribution, because profits are recouped at the box office (and increasingly on the video sell-through and rental market). Television programmes (at least until recently) are not financed by the numbers of people who watch them, but films are. So, in addition to production costs, $48.1 million went into the promotion of *Dick Tracy* in the USA and another $13 million overseas. In view of these sums of money it is not surprising that very few British feature films are being made at the present time. Money has always been a problem for the British cinema and one of the persistent cries of the industry has been for some form of government intervention, through tax breaks and so on, to protect British film from American domination. These pleas have usually fallen on deaf ears.

The British government has always been far less bothered about film than television. Film, although a mass medium, does not engender the deep fear in politicians which broadcasting can evoke. Film, in its theatrical setting, does not enter the home directly and it does not deal, at least directly, with political matters. Parliament has therefore never been much concerned about its impact. Indeed, non-interference (even malign neglect) could be said to characterise the attitude of most British politicians towards the home feature film industry. Campaigns to protect the British film from American competition have met with the lukewarm response which marks the British attitude to most cultural issues – an attitude incidentally which has often been in sharp contrast to other European countries, notably France and Eastern Europe.

The American Giant
The experience of the European cinema industry, including the British, cannot be separated from the impact of American film. While European *broadcasting* developed along its own particular path watched over by anxious politicians, European *films* have always faced a monumental struggle with the American giant. In the very early days of cinema history the Americans quickly established an expertise, assisted by the natural benefits of weather and light which Hollywood in California provided. The advent of the 'talkies' probably helped the non-English-speaking European cinema to survive, but the difficulties for the British film industry were only compounded. The sharing of a

common language made the British particularly vulnerable to the American cultural invasion, of which film was a case in point. Since the British government was usually uninterested in protecting its own, the American entertainment industry met with a free run, a situation which persists today.

Nevertheless the story was not entirely bleak: British cinema did survive over the years thanks to the unsung heroes who were passionate about keeping it alive. In the 1930s, for example, British filmmakers carved out a splendid reputation for high quality documentaries and British technicians were admired for their consummate professionalism. In the 1940s and early 1950s the British feature film industry beat off some of the American competition, and the lively Ealing comedies enjoyed vast popularity. By the 1950s, in fact, films were being produced which actually reflected the reality of British provincial and working-class life and the cinema was becoming a genuinely popular art form. In 1955, however, came the establishment of ITV and a shift of audiences from the sober programming of the BBC. Television suddenly became a 'popular' medium of entertainment. Even the stately BBC gave way to the trend and began to woo (rather than instruct) viewers, with the result that all over the country cinemas closed as the British stayed home in droves, glued to the novelty of the Box in the Corner. By the end of the 1950s the British feature film seemed in terminal decline, with no hope of recovery in sight.

One of the interesting features of the history of British cinema, however, is the frequency with which the industry has been written off and the equal frequency with which the supposed corpse has revived. In 1963 *Tom Jones*, a British film financed by the American studio, United Artists, was an international success. Other famous 60s successes included *A Hard Day's Night* (1964), *Nothing but the Best* (1964) and *Morgan* (1966). Britain in the 60s was 'swinging' and one of the main beneficiaries of the new fashion for all things British was film. Soon 'the name's Bond, James Bond' was a phrase which reverberated round the world, and British cinema became a popular international success. (For a discussion of this period see Robert Murphy's *Sixties British Cinema* [London: BFI, 1992]).

These so-called British, big-budget films were, however, almost always financed by American money. Although the film industry in Britain was superficially doing well and employment was booming (many American companies had realised that production costs were low and the workforce highly skilled), it lost its financial independence and most of its essentially British character. The themes, the actors and the technicians may have been British, but the money, treatment

16

and marketing were American. British cinema by the late 1960s had become part of a transatlantic movie culture. It had lost the authentic British voice which films of the late 50s and early 60s such as *A Taste of Honey*, *The Loneliness of the Long Distance Runner* and *Saturday Night and Sunday Morning* had expressed.

During the 1970s there were good British film-makers around who were not totally tied to American financial apron-strings. John Schlesinger, Richard Lester, Ken Russell, Ken Loach, Peter Watkins, Ridley Scott and Alan Parker were all making low-budget British films. Some of these film-makers had come up through television and others through advertising, where the technical excellence of British film craftsmanship and invention still flourished. On the whole, however, the work of British film-makers did not appeal to mass audiences, who were brought up on a diet of American films, though they were popular with a minority audience of the young educated middle class, who wanted something more from the cinema than pure entertainment and had a feeling for film as an art form. By the end of the decade, however, some of these directors, weary of the financial struggle which working in British cinema demanded, had emigrated to America in search of the 'big bucks' necessary to make films which would appeal to an 'international' audience.

In the early 1980s the British picture seemed to enjoy something of a revival with the huge worldwide success of films such as Hugh Hudson's *Chariots of Fire*. The early 1980s saw a boom in British film-making and hopes were suddenly raised for the expansion of the industry. The collapse of Goldcrest, a prestigious British film company, put an end to this period of optimism and seemed to confirm that British film-making was doomed. Financial insecurity seemed to be endemic – at which point enter Channel Four.

British Cinema and Channel Four

1982 saw a surprising new twist in the convoluted history of British cinema. Channel Four, the new commercial television channel with its guaranteed income and its minority remit, had a dramatic impact on British film and can be credited with creating a mini-boom in British cinema. Television, the historic enemy, was, it seemed, galloping to the rescue of British film as Channel Four's commissioning editors began to put money into the industry. A deal was negotiated which permitted films financed by Channel Four to have a six-month showing at the cinema, after which they could be transmitted on the small screen.

For years television had been viewed as hostile to film; now it became its patron and a whole series of successful, low-budget and well-received films were produced, including *Letter to Brezhnev*, *The*

Ploughman's Lunch and *The Draughtsman's Contract*. The film industry perked up tremendously and began to make quality films for television as well as for theatrical release. American 'made for TV' films might still dominate the market-place, but the British, it seemed, thanks to far-sighted managers at Channel Four, had found a novel way of offering an alternative to the American presence on the small and large screens. British film-makers were beginning to carve a niche in British television's minority channel; British television was putting money into the British film industry: a beneficial symbiosis was apparently under way. Everything looked set for a revival of the British film industry.

The Recession
By the late 1980s, however, optimism had faded again. Why? There were two reasons: American dominance and the world recession. It soon became apparent that deregulation and the emphasis on the market had actually benefited the giant of the film entertainment industry, the United States. Despite the efforts of the British Finance Consortium, founded in 1985 to support British film-making (and funded by the government, Cannon, Granada TV, Rank and Channel Four), as well as the establishment of private investment corporations specifically to raise funds to finance British films, American influence steadily increased throughout the 1980s.

By the end of the decade this had become a matter of grave concern, not only in Britain but also in those European countries which took film more seriously. It was suddenly apparent that the indigenous European film and television industries, despite their early buoyancy, had been adversely affected by the internationalisation of the money markets and the decline of public service broadcasting. Unemployment in the European audiovisual industries began to grow alarmingly. As far as the entertainment industries were concerned, it was suddenly abundantly clear that the main beneficiaries of the free market had been American business interests.

The European Dimension
Trouble with the American film industry was not a new phenomenon for Europe, as we have seen, but it became more acute in the late 1980s and seemed likely to worsen as the increasing number of private television channels provided even more markets for cheap American films and programmes. Some European countries had over the years developed aid schemes to protect their film industries against American encroachments, but these too had fallen out of favour in the period of deregulation. Suddenly the European Community awoke

18

to the realisation that its film and television industries, important elements of its cultural identity, had become the prey of American business and were indeed largely unprotected against the American colossus. The fashionable idea that entertainment was an industry like any other suddenly sounded rather hollow as European film companies went under and people woke up to the cultural threat this represented. Europe might be a giant in general economic terms, but the highly efficient and profitable American entertainment industry was the market leader. In comparison with America, Europe's film industry was a dwarf and a rapidly shrinking dwarf at that.

During every year of the 1980s the American share of the European cinema and television market increased. In fact, from 1975 European film production has declined by 40 per cent, despite the fact that superficially, with the increase in television stations, the market should have expanded. By the end of the 1980s almost 60 per cent of cinema films shown in Europe were of American origin. In Germany and Poland the American market share was 80 per cent and even in France, which maintained a relatively healthy film industry thanks to a traditionally interventionist government policy on cultural matters, the American share of the market was over 50 per cent. The United Kingdom showed a similar trend and between 1989 and 1991 experienced the lowest level of theatrical film production since 1981.

The American film industry had two advantages over its European rivals. It benefited from a huge internal market and from a worldwide English-speaking audience. In most European countries 80 per cent of indigenous films were only exploited within their national boundaries and consequently were hardly ever able to recover their costs. American movie-makers were able to recover their money within their own borders, and beyond that everything was profit. In 1989 the export surplus of the American film industry was $2.5 billion yet, except for a very few so-called *succès d'estime* (such as the award-winning Danish film *Babette's Feast* or the French films *Jean de Florette, Manon des sources*, and *Cyrano de Bergerac*), European movies hardly ever penetrated the States at all. Less than 1 per cent of European (including British) films were distributed in the American market. In television the situation was similar: in 1989 the European countries paid out more than a billion dollars in television royalties to the US and estimated royalties for 1992 were twice that. The much vaunted international *programme flow* (which free marketeers talked so much about) largely flowed one way: from America to Europe.

The success of American cinema was not simply due to the films themselves and the size of the internal market but also to the commercial way they were produced and the uncompromising way in which they were marketed. From the beginning of the idea for a film, from inception to release, every Hollywood production was subjected to the strategies of the market economy. Film as art form was an accidental pay-off: film as profit-making activity was the main concern. 'I make films,' Alfred Hitchcock once said. 'If it turns out to be art that's fine with me.' In addition, the Americans developed an extraordinarily effective distribution and marketing system: 60 per cent of American movie costs can be devoted to marketing, while the figures for European films vary between 2 per cent and 30 per cent. On top of this most of the worldwide film distribution companies are American-owned.

This, then, is the picture of the film industry in Europe: one of American domination with the native European film industry struggling to survive. Is the picture, therefore, all bleak? Not quite: one of the positive results of the recession at the end of the 1980s has been a realisation that, as far as Europe is concerned, deregulation and market forces might not be the ideal solution for the cultural industries of which film is a major part. This is particularly the case on the Continent where, as a reaction to what has been going on, a certain amount of reregulation has begun.

The national cultures of Europe do seem determined to resist domination by the strong technological cultures of the USA and Japan. The European Community, in particular, has become very concerned by American domination of the film and television industries and has launched a whole series of initiatives and introduced regulations to protect the European market. The European Film Distribution Office (EFDO), the European Script Fund, EURO-AIM, EFDO's MEDIA project – all these reflect the new dynamism. The EC has also given its support to European initiatives in sales, distribution and co-production. There are also moves towards an intensification of Community aid for large-budget films which can be exported. *Laissez-faire* economics have proved dangerous for the European film industry; moderate interventionism now seems to be the name of the game.

The British Connection
Even the British government, the arch upholder of the free market system, may have begun to moderate its approach and to have woken up to the potential importance of the British film industry as Europe moves towards economic and political union. Politicians are realising that Britain occupies a key position at the crossroads between Europe and the USA, and that the skill of British technicians and the facilities of British studios have been utilised for a number of American blockbusters, especially in science fiction, thereby making a sizeable contri-

bution to the British economy. As an English-speaking country, with access to a potential US market of 245 million and a European market of 325 million, the opportunity exists, once the recession is over, for the UK to become a major film and television base. The government is, it is rumoured, finally beginning to realise that it may pay economic dividends if the film industry is supported and, perhaps in the light of this, some modest assistance was offered in the budget of March 1992. It must also be said, however, that the recession may finish off all such hopes. We shall have to wait and see.

Another cause of moderate optimism centres on the fact that the audience for films is growing. The popularity of cinemagoing as a leisure activity is increasing and in Britain the decline in cinema audiences that took place in the 1980s has been reversed. This is especially the case for the 15–24 age group who, having formed a habit of cinema attendance, may continue to go in the future.

The Future

Assessing the overall picture, therefore, it looks as if the demand for feature films will increase, although the outlet will no longer be mainly cinemas but also television. Feature films are expensive to produce and their exploitation on television, video, and via satellite, cable and pay TV will be an increasingly important factor in the economic viability of the industry. Feature films have become a key element in the schedules of satellite and cable television. In their turn the video and television industries are very dependent on the publicity which a film generates in the theatre. (It has been said: 'If the cinema did not exist, the video industry would have to invent it.')

British television, including the BBC, is continuing the trend initiated by Channel Four and is investing in British film and filmmakers. Television managers are moving beyond purely monetary considerations and are involving themselves in creative decision-making in order to protect their investment. As a result, the economics of film, video and television, as pointed out in Chapter One, have become so closely intertwined that it is now quite correct to think in terms of one industry rather than three.

Feature films will survive and so will jobs in the industry, but it will require energy and far-sightedness to resist the Americans. If something is not done today, in twenty years time all films could be American in the same way as today most video recorders are Japanese. Workers in the British film industry will be working in branch plants of the American industrial entertainment complex. Jobs may be there but an authentic British (and European) cinema will have gone. This is, however, the worst scenario. It is more likely that film production

21

in Europe will increase in the 1990s, thanks to the European Community's commitment to a policy of moderate protection. It will, however, be an extremely tough battle.

Advertising

One area of British film-making which retains its national character is advertising, an area where in the past the film and television industries met. British commercials are often of a very high quality and were (and are) traditionally recorded on film because of its visual superiority. Generally, more money is spent per second of screen time on a commercial than on a feature film. To be fair, however, that is somewhat a function of the fact that often the same size of crew has to be assembled even though a commercial is much shorter.

There has always been a great deal of talent around in British advertising and this is reflected in television commercials, which have an international reputation for originality and humour. Many producers and directors in this field are now treating commercials as mini-dramas (the Nescafé Gold Blend saga for example) and are honing their story-telling skills in ways which are more characteristic of the feature film.

Companies specialising in film commercials are exceedingly professional and the technical standards extremely high. Many young, talented film-makers with feature film ambitions start in the advertising industry. (Film-makers with international reputations also make commercials: Peter Greenaway, Federico Fellini and Woody Allen are just three examples.) Unfortunately this section of the industry has been particularly hit by the recession and the resultant decline in advertising budgets. It must be assumed, however, that the sector will recover once the recession is over and, in April 1992, there are said to be some signs that a slight increase in advertising budgets is already taking place.

Summing Up

For many years television and film were exceptionally difficult industries to break into. The moving-picture landscape in the last decade, however, has changed dramatically. The market is more open and newcomers now have more chance. To a large extent this has been the result of technological advance, which promoted the video revolution. This, together with the advent of cable and satellite television, has brought the barriers down. It is time to examine more closely the impact of the new developments.

BROADENING THE LANDSCAPE
Video, Satellite and Cable

In Chapter One we looked at the impact of technological and political change on the traditional landscape of British television. Chapter Two surveyed film, which did not experience the same upheaval as television, but did, from the point of view of employment, move towards more integration with the television sector. This was largely because of the decline of union power and the problems posed by the increasing strength of the American film industry.

This chapter will examine some of the newcomers to the industry and the impact they have had, and will continue to have, on the broad employment picture. Video technology, satellite and cable have all contributed to a change in the nature and pattern of employment in film and television over the last few years. This has drastically altered the outlook and the working environment of the two traditional sectors. There will be further changes in the future, especially if plans for the introduction of HDTV are successful.

The Video Revolution
Video was the big story of the 1980s and, as we saw in Chapter One, it rapidly brought about a change in certain aspects of television production. Lightweight cameras and instant playback facilities revolutionised news coverage in television. Where picture quality was less important than topicality and immediacy, electronic news-gathering (ENG), or video recording, quickly replaced film as the favoured method of news-gathering. The old method, whereby cans of films were dispatched, usually by motorcycle, to laboratories for development in time for editing for the evening news, disappeared almost overnight. Film camera crews attached to news production in television companies had to swap to video (which actually was very simple to use) or else retire.

In employment terms, however, video made its greatest immediate impact on the non-broadcast section of the industry. The great virtue of video is that it is quicker and cheaper than film to use and the technical equipment is lighter and more portable (though its actual technology is far more complex). Once the quality of the image improved enough to rival (although not equal) film, independent entrepreneurs saw possibilities in video and independent production companies sprang up to exploit new business opportunities.

At the start of the video expansion most of the companies were very small, many of the staff were inexperienced and, because of low profit margins, freelancing on very short-term contracts became the main mode of employment. Initially these video 'freebooters' in the non-broadcast environment were looked at askance by the well-trained and heavily unionised employees in broadcasting and film. But the advance of the non-unionised freelancer in the small video companies has been quite unstoppable and has eventually spread to the older industries. By 1992 virtually 60 per cent of all employees in the film, television and video industry were freelance, and this percentage has been growing all the time.

The great attraction of video as far as employers were concerned was that it did not require large crews and this cut costs. One person could do several different tasks and, since unions made little headway in the independent sector, there was no strict division of labour according to function. What came to be dubbed *multi-skilling* developed. Instead of separate people being employed to write scripts or do research or handle lights, cameras and so on, everything could be done by one person. This, aided and abetted by government policy, was to drive the first nail into the coffin of the old specialised craft unions which had dominated film and television (at least ITV) for so long.

In its early days the independent video industry was not involved in creating material to show either in a cinema or on television. Basically the two highly prestigious industries were closed to outsiders. The BBC and ITV tended to look down on non-broadcast video production as a 'mickey mouse' sector, full of inexperienced, second-rate 'amateurs', notable only for their lack of professional finesse. Most independent video companies produced an inferior product in broadcasting and film terms (and remember that both British film and television were known for their high technical standards) and, as far as mainline production was concerned, were therefore irrelevant. Small-time video producers and their employees would never, it was thought, darken the doors of any established British film or television studio. They were merely involved in the decidedly inferior and rather sordid commercial activity of making half-baked productions for the assorted clients who commissioned them.

Who were these clients of the non-broadcast sector? They were

24

record companies wanting to publicise a singer or a song; local authorities wanting to extol the virtues of their area or give out health information to the public; multinational corporations that wished to promote products, illustrate their contribution to scientific research or provide safety instructions for their employees. In any event, whatever or whoever they were, as far as mainstream broadcasters and filmmakers were concerned, they were of no importance at all. Certainly the work of video companies who serviced such clients could not be compared to the important business of broadcasting high-quality, public service programmes of information, education and entertainment to the great British public.

In fact, the pop music and non-broadcast corporate sectors quickly proved to be huge money-spinners, especially by the mid-1980s. Companies, corporations and local authorities were beginning to fancy the idea of advertising themselves through a prestigious up-to-date medium and were beginning to put big money into promotional videos. Moreover the significance of the video sector was not purely commercial: training videos (especially interactive training videos), a neglected sector of British educational provision, quickly became a growth area. John Cleese made a fortune through humorously teaching people about management techniques.

Fairly swiftly, technical and production standards improved in the non-broadcast sector, particularly since, unlike broadcast programmes, a corporate video was destined to be seen over and over again by highly critical and often expert audiences. Scientists invited to watch a chemical company's video were unlikely to be fobbed off with generalities or poor production techniques. Polished presentation and up-to-date information were essential, and the old days, when a boring elderly managing director in a conservative suit spoke direct to camera, were left far behind. Professional presenters, graphics, 'paintbox' techniques (another offshoot of the microchip/computer revolution) soon made their mark.

Although some video companies became multi-million dollar businesses, the employee base was usually still kept very low, with staff used on contract for individual productions. Consequently it was (and still is) much easier to break into the non-broadcast video world than into television or film and, in some ways, it provided an excellent training-ground for all facets of production. The mainly freelance staff had to be capable of turning their hands to anything and, in pop video companies especially, directors and producers were sometimes very young indeed, often in their late teens and early twenties, a situation unthinkable in conventional film or television. Moreover pop video producers proved to be inventive and imaginative, undercutting some

25

of the more conservative and traditional ideas of the rather stuffy light entertainment producers at the BBC and ITV. Pop videos took the teenage market by storm and made conventional television seem old-fashioned.

Gradually the fact that a lot of money could be made in video attracted the attention of the creative and technical staff in mainline films and television. The improving technical quality of video production also changed minds. The best corporate productions began to compare favourably with films and broadcast television and many 'professional' film-makers and television producers and directors began to freelance in the independent sector. Working in video was no longer regarded as 'slumming it'.

The walls between the various sectors of the audiovisual industry were beginning to crumble. In February 1988, 1,400 people attended the first Video Communication Festival, organised by the newly formed International Visual Communications Association (IVCA); and it became clear, even to the dinosaurs of the film and broadcasting world, that the video industry might be around for a rather long time, and was actually becoming respectable. More significantly, it was also finding government support: small entrepreneurial companies of the independent type fitted in well with a prevailing Thatcherite philosophy which was hostile to restrictive practices in the film sector and in ITV and also to the public service ethos of the BBC.

By the end of the decade, independent video companies were making programmes and video 'films' for television. Former employees of the BBC and ITV and the film industry migrated to the independent production sector, often attracted by the lack of bureaucracy and the entrepreneurial atmosphere. This trend was encouraged by the government's insistence on the so-called 25 per cent quota. Legislation was introduced which guaranteed that by 1993 at least 25 per cent of programmes on the new Channel 3 and the BBC would have to be made by independents. Although the independent sector has been badly hit by the present recession, some sources estimate that in 1992 the whole independent video sector could be worth £1 billion, with a turnover in the non-broadcast sector of somewhere in the region of £200 million.

Today there are many independent companies producing material for broadcast and non-broadcast purposes. For newcomers to the industry the openness of the independent sector has triggered endless possibilities. The video revolution has broken down the union barriers and broadcasting elitism which once seemed insurmountable. For years film and television were extraordinarily difficult to break into: video has made the technology, and therefore the industry, much more

26

accessible. Many people can now enter the industry through the non-broadcast sector and those with experience cross between film, television and video as they gain in knowledge and technical expertise.

The Waning of Public Service Broadcasting

The decline of public service broadcasting is also likely to benefit the non-broadcast sector. In the future BBC and commercial television will probably make fewer educative and documentary programmes. Specifically educational programmes could indeed be pushed completely off the mainstream channel and into the educational video market. Educational video may then become a boom area for many independent companies as encrypted learning and satellite educational channels increase and as educational programmes on broadcast television diminish. In addition, the pace of change in all employment will by the year 2000 make training and retraining a vital aspect of educational provision (this will be discussed in more detail in Part Two). Every individual with a desire to succeed will have to cope with a world in which technological change puts an increasing onus on the employee to learn new techniques and to constantly update his or her skills. Educational videos have already become an important means of teaching people. Producing the software for increasingly sophisticated interactive training systems will in the future provide an outlet for people working in the video industry and will probably, therefore, be a rich area of employment.

The Workshop Sector

One interesting non-commercial area which has provided many opportunities for newcomers, and has also been an excellent source of training over the last decade, is the so-called 'workshop' sector. Workshops actually encompass both film and video, but the ease and cheapness of video in particular stimulated an expansion in this 'alternative' sector. 'Independent workshops' are small production groups, many of which were established in the early 1980s as a result of political pressure for more open access to broadcasting. Workshops are usually non-profit-making and often have a specific political, social or sexual orientation. They were set up to give space to those film- and video-makers who wished to challenge the attitudes and ethos of the mainstream industries, and are usually subsidised, often by the unions, the BFI or Channel Four.

Many of the existing workshops are involved in training people who would not normally have access to film and video equipment so that they can make videos and films for themselves and their organisations, many of which are voluntary. Many people have become enthusiastic

27

about film- and programme-making through their workshop experiences and some of them have entered the commercial side, often initially in the non-broadcast video sector. This has brought a broader outlook to more conventional areas of the industry.

The Impact of the Home Video Software Industry

In addition to the production of videos for broadcast and non-broadcast purposes, the video revolution has had another very important and largely unforeseen effect. This is the impact of the home video recorder on public interest in feature films. Ownership of video recorders boomed in Britain in the early 1980s. Although initially this probably had a negative effect on cinema attendance, it provided a secondary source of revenue for films, and the growth of the video rental market has almost certainly helped to develop an appetite for films among young people. At first the major distributors of films were wary of video; increasingly, however, they began to appreciate the financial benefits which could accrue from its exploitation and have gradually moved into a video market which has become an ever more significant element in the calculation of profits.

Although by 1992 the video rental market has begun to decline (this may be temporary), the sell-through market (the purchase of films over the counter) has increased: the public's interest in film is, it seems, being maintained. Cinema admissions in Britain have risen, albeit rather slowly, and it does appear that the feature film industry and the home video feed on each other to their mutual benefit. This is difficult to quantify, but many young people who purchase films on video watch them over and over again and there is a growing impression that this has produced an interest in film techniques. The development of the laservision market in the United States, where classic films are reissued on videodisc with additional material such as interviews with directors and actors about the making and editing of the film, is an expression of this trend. From this point of view the impact of video on the film industry may have been very positive. The real effects of this, however, lie in the future, and are difficult to predict.

Satellite Television

Another sector which since 1989 has had an impact on employment in the traditional British film and television industry is satellite television. Technically, when people talk about satellite (and cable) television they are talking only about a *delivery* system. Careers in satellite and cable television, therefore, often have more to do with sales and marketing than with the actual production of films and programmes, the *raison d'être* of the traditional industry. In fact, for old-timers in

28

film and television, satellite and cable television are not really bona fide sectors at all, because the focus of activity has shifted from programme- to profit-making. Traditionalists see satellite (and cable) as brash new phenomena, illegitimate offspring of the new technology and the market-place, feeding parasitically on the creative talents of the traditional workforce. This attitude does not endear them to satellite and cable employees who, in their turn, view traditional employees as elitist, feather-bedded hacks out of touch with modern reality. (The tone of the debate can be rather bitter at times.)

BSkyB, which dominates the British direct-to-home satellite market, is a particular target for the enmity of the traditional broadcaster and film-maker. The company is in broadcasting to make money and this point of view is ultimately reflected in its programming and policies. For business-oriented people, BSkyB represents the broadcasting model of the future. Its supporters are excited by the limitless business opportunities and untold riches (as yet unrealised) which the company offers.

Satellite and cable television bring into focus the distinction between broadcasters who are channel operators and broadcasters who are programme producers. Channel operators are concerned with 'packaging', scheduling, transmission and marketing of programmes but not usually with their production: most programmes are 'bought in'. Satellite and cable, on the whole, *consume* programmes and films which have already been made for other outlets. Programme producers are concerned with the creative activity of programme-making, which inevitably dictates a different set of criteria and motivations. (Although the publisher-broadcaster mode of some of the ITV stations and Channel Four is not production-oriented, there is a strong interest in programme-making because of the channel's commissioning activity.) The clash between satellite and cable broadcasters on the one hand and traditional programme-makers on the other is a clash of cultures which derives from their different perspectives.

The start-up costs for satellite broadcasting are extremely high and, partly for this reason, the development of a satellite service in Britain has been immensely fraught, a situation which has given considerable pleasure and solace to its many critics. At the beginning of 1990 it looked as if there might be two competing companies broadcasting direct-to-homes via satellite: Rupert Murdoch's Sky Television and British Satellite Broadcasting (BSB). Sky Television was first into the field and launched its four-channel network in February 1989, using the Astra satellite. BSB, its rival, had a more up-market image and very glamorous headquarters in the Marcopolo building, south of the Thames. Its services, relayed via the Marcopolo satellite, were originally scheduled to be launched in the autumn of 1989 but the start had to be postponed to the spring of 1990, a fatal delay. Its receiver, the so-called 'Squarial' (because of its shape), encountered design and production problems. This delay gave Sky time to build up an overwhelming lead, assisted by publicity in the Murdoch-owned press.

1990, however, was not a good year for investment in any business venture, and especially not one on the scale of satellite television. BSB and Sky were launched as the recession began to bite and advertising revenues began to fall. It was a nightmare scenario for a new television venture. Satellite dish sales failed to take off, despite a marketing blitz; BSB began by losing £30 million a month while Sky lost £10 million a month. Finally, amid much controversy over the issue of monopoly, in November 1990 Sky Television and BSB 'merged' into BSkyB, a merger which had not been cleared with the IBA.

The new company, however, still faced financial difficulties. To counteract this, the staff of the two combined stations were cut from around 4,500 to fewer than a thousand and the nine existing channels were rationalised into six. Programme resources were also cut from £5.1 million to £2.9 million. Opponents of satellite immediately charged that the result was a decline in programme quality, that the emphasis was on what was cheap to do rather than what was worth doing. Over the next eighteen months BSkyB struggled on, losing money all the time, but dish sales gradually began to take off. By 1992 BSkyB had reached 2.9 million homes (13 per cent of total) and dish sales were about 70,000 a month. In March 1992 BSkyB was technically in the black (except for paying off interest on loans) and was beginning to win favour in the City. In the same year BSkyB announced plans to spend £175 million on programming, two-thirds of which were to go on its two movie channels. (In comparison, ITV planned to spend £540 million on programming for *one* channel during 1992.)

BSkyB movie channels are paid for by subscription and are encrypted so that only subscribers can have access. Four-fifths of sales income comes from subscriptions to the two movie channels. Seventy per cent of people who purchase dishes subscribe to the movie channels and 80 per cent of those take both. This has helped to boost revenue. The movie channels on satellite television may also act as a stimulus to the film industry in rather the same way as the home video-recorder has made young people more knowledgeable about, and interested in, the cinema. It is difficult to say at this point: the satellite movie service has been in place for less than three years, so it is impossible to judge what its effects may be once the recession is over. Advertising income is another source of funding for BSkyB, and this too is increasing.

30

Besides the movie channels, BSkyB provides three free services: Sky One, its entertainment channel; Sky News, a twenty-four hour television news service; and Sky Sports which, as its name suggests, is dedicated to sports. The basic purpose of these channels is to bring in subscribers to the movie channels where most revenue is generated. The recently launched Comedy Channel is also available to movie subscribers. In addition to Sky television, Astra dish owners can receive satellite stations such as MTV, The Children's Channel, Lifestyle and Screensport, plus a variety of other stations broadcasting in German, French, Dutch, Spanish, Italian and Japanese.

The future of satellite television is still a matter of controversy. Some experts think it will become really profitable by 1994 and there is certainly now much optimism in the City. Others point out that many people in Britain say that they will never get satellite television or that they will wait until cable brings it in unobtrusively (see below) with the added benefit of cheaper telephones. Some media consultants suggest that satellite will control a fifth of all television advertising by 1998, but others are more cautious and query whether advertisers will be so interested in television as a medium once the audience has become fragmented. There is certainly some evidence that advertisers are becoming disillusioned with television now that the era of mass audiences for a very restricted number of channels is over. This may mean that BSkyB will have to spend more on programming if the company is to attract new viewers and advertisers. This in turn may help to increase employment.

The development of satellite and cable television, however, has undoubtedly been assisted by the present crises in the terrestrial channels. The BBC, with its Charter due for renewal in 1996, is now a nervous institution, particularly since the Conservative government's plans for the Corporation are not clear. Channel 3 will also certainly take some time to settle down in its new economic environment. Some companies will struggle under a heavy financial burden because of the high prices they have paid for the franchise. The 1990 Broadcasting Act was intended 'to level the playing field' between terrestrial and satellite channels. It looks as if it may have had some measure of success in this!

Whatever the future and profitability of satellite television, however, it has had an impact on the general employment picture. BSkyB has provided an alternative theatre and 'culture' of work rather as the video industry did in the 1980s. There has been ruthless cost-cutting at BSkyB, but the company does employ technical, engineering, journalistic, administrative and sales staff and, although most of its programming is bought in, BSkyB does produce its own programmes. Sky

31

News, for example, employs journalists, presenters and scriptwriters.

Compared to traditional broadcasting companies, programme production at BSkyB is extremely informal. Multi-skilling is everywhere and there is little evidence of the traditional, rather hierarchical broadcasting 'culture' of the BBC or ITV. The atmosphere at Sky is breezy, with less stress for entrants on experience and more on commitment and enthusiasm. It will probably be easier for inexperienced newcomers to break into satellite television than it has ever been for them to break into the BBC, ITV, Channel Four or the film industry. Many of the staff at BSkyB are quite young. The company takes on what it calls 'script-runners', who are similar to runners in the film industry (see Chapter Four). Runners do chores and are given the opportunity for hands-on experience: they can then work their way up into other jobs. BSkyB will also sometimes offer work experience and work placements to young people during school and college holidays. Employment opportunities in satellite television, however, will inevitably depend most on the market-place and on the rise and fall in profits.

Cable

Satellite television is one illustration of how the industry has become more 'permeable' for outsiders; cable is another. Cable, like satellite television, is basically a delivery system (although it also produces some programmes). Cable too is paid for largely by subscription. In addition to television and radio, cable can provide interactive telephone and communications services such as home shopping, home banking (tele-banking,) security and alarms services, electronic mail and remote meter reading. Cable made great headway in Canada and the United States from the 1970s onwards (thanks largely to the transmission problems created for terrestrial broadcasting by the huge geographical distances), and it was much vaunted in Britain in the late 1970s as the system of the future. Cable was supposed to be the harbinger of the 'wired society', gaining much support in government circles. But, for various reasons, cable penetration in Britain proceeded at a snail's pace for most of the 80s.

1989, however, saw a huge influx of cash from US and Canadian cable and telephone services (when restrictions on non-UK shareholding in cable companies were dropped) and, by the beginning of the 1990s, the progress of cable had quickened considerably. By 1992 cable franchises for areas covering two-thirds of British homes had been granted and it is now expected that over half the population will have cable available to them (should they choose to pay the subscription) by 1996.

There are different types of cable systems available. 'Broadband' cable (sometimes referred to as 'wideband') is the one that matters. Broadband cables are the modern, multichannel, interactive systems now being installed in most areas of the country. They can provide a full range of new television channels, telecommunications and interactive services. In 1992 forty-nine broadband cable systems are operational and they are the base on which the optimistic forecasts for the cable industry rely. (Readers should note that 'narrowband' is used in opposition to broadband but is a relative term without explicit definition. The telephone system is sometimes referred to as narrowband to distinguish it from the system which is also capable of carrying television signals. At other times the old television cable system is referred to as narrowband because it is capable of carrying only four to six channels as opposed to the new broadband systems which can carry thirty or more.)

'Local delivery franchises' are similar to cable franchises, though the licensees may utilise not only broadband cable but SMATV (satellite master antenna television). SMATV are smaller systems servicing only specific blocks of flats; these systems have been built to deliver a range of satellite television channels to the homes connected to them. In addition there are 'broadcast relay cable systems', sometimes called 'communal aerial systems', and these do not have to be licensed. They exist to provide broadcast television (BBC and ITV and Channel Four) to a number of homes from a master aerial. 'Upgrade' are old cable systems installed initially for relay purposes and then upgraded to provide new programme services. Upgrade cable services have a limited capacity.

At the present time cable supplies twenty-three British-based television channels fed into cable 'headends', the control centre of the cable system, and then delivered via coaxial cable to British homes. In addition to the usual broadcast channels, available services include: Sky One, Sky Sports, Sky Movie Channels and Sky News. Other channels available include: MTV Europe (a rock music channel), Indra Dhnush (Indian programmes), Discovery Channel (the natural world), Mind Extension University (educational programmes from the USA), channel E (adult education from Manchester University), Lifestyle (Women's Magazine), Bravo (an old film channel).

Cable subscribers are not limited, as are British satellite subscribers, to what is available on the two Astra satellites or Marcopolo. Most cable companies pick up and relay services from other satellites. Broadband cable systems therefore carry many other channels such as TV5 (francophone programmes), Worldnet (US Information Service), RAI (Italian television entertainment), CNN (twenty-four hour news from the USA), Sat1 (German commercial television), Moskva (Russian television service), Eurosport (sports programmes).

Although cable, even more than satellite, is about delivery rather than programme-making, most cable companies do have small-scale studios where local programming is produced. Many of the broadband cable systems run a local channel for news and information plus special features: this provides considerable community access and minority programming. (Westminster Cable's Arabic Channel is one example.)

Local programming may well be the surprising success story of cable, although it is comparatively insignificant from the point of view of revenue (unless local advertisers use it extensively). Local programming on cable proved to be very successful in North America, supposedly recreating something of the community atmosphere of the proverbial 'conversation around the village pump'. People like seeing themselves and their neighbours on television. When Granada Television ran its so-called Television Village experiment in 1990 (in which it provided the village of Waddington with access to all available television channels), it was the local programming which proved most popular. In the last week of the experiment only 3 per cent of viewers were not watching it.

Most of the jobs in cable involve marketing and sales and it is mainly people with these skills who will find employment in the sector. However, in North America, and this is likely to happen in Britain, many people became involved in producing local television programmes on cable. The community element of local cable programming may prove to be a useful training-ground for people who wish to know more about how a television studio functions.

The Role of the ITC

Before leaving satellite and cable it should be pointed out that the Broadcasting Act of 1990 gave the new Independent Television Commission (ITC) responsibility to license and regulate all non-BBC television services, whether terrestrial, cable or satellite. In its first year the ITC was principally concerned with terrestrial television because of the importance of the Channel 3 franchises. Over the next few years, however, the role of the ITC in the development of satellite and cable is likely to be increasingly significant. The 1990 Act ensured that for the first time every programme service provided from within the United Kingdom was licensed. Previously, programme channels carried on cable systems were regulated by the Cable Authority (which ceased to exist on 1 January 1991 when the Broadcasting Act brought the ITC into existence).

Looking to the Future: the Role of HDTV

We have looked briefly at video production and satellite and cable television and the way these have affected the traditional film and television industries. Mention should also be made of the possible impact, especially on employment, of HDTV, or High Definition Television.

HDTV is an entirely new system for the production, transmission and reception of television pictures of a very high quality. As such it represents a major challenge to the industry as it exists today. For years only television engineers and technicians were interested in HDTV, but now the imminent introduction of HDTV has become a definite possibility. In Japan, an 8-hours-a-day HDTV service has recently been launched; in Europe and the US, HDTV is expected to reach many homes by the middle of the 1990s.

HDTV provides an improvement in technical quality and televisual experience. The picture is wider, clearer and contains more information. The detail and clarity of the high resolution image (the result of 1,250 line definition rather than the conventional 625) obviously make it of interest to people who respond to the quality of the image (in the same way certain visually oriented individuals always prefer film to video). HDTV will pack a much more dramatic punch: viewers will have a greater sense of immediacy and involvement in what is happening on-screen, as if they were 'inside the picture', an experience more akin to seeing a film in the cinema than watching television today. HDTV will be further enhanced by improved sound quality. Certain types of programme will be especially suited to HDTV: films, drama, sports, and 'spectacles'.

From the point of view of economics, the problem with HDTV is that, in addition to the home receiver purchased by the consumer, a whole range of new hardware will be required for recording in studios, including cameras, mixers, monitors, tape recorders, editing machines, character generators, special effects machines, production mixers, paintbox systems, slide stores, scanners, and telecine machines. This will mean a major and costly retooling for the industry (although it has to be said that broadcasting studio equipment is constantly updated anyway because of rapid technological advances). It is difficult to see where the revenue will come from to offset the expense. For most television companies it will be rather like the switch to colour from black and white television. In the UK this resulted in no increase in revenue for ITV, yet to maintain its audience it had to adopt colour when the BBC did. By contrast, the BBC was able to increase its revenue by increasing the fee for a colour licence. (In fact, it has been suggested that HDTV could create a bonanza for public service broadcasters if the government agrees to the raising of the licence fee for HDTV.)

There have been many predictions about the impact of HDTV, but the truth is that no one really knows. Some experts think that people will not be prepared to pay for new sets, others think it will be extremely popular and compare it to the successful introduction of compact disc technology in the record industry. Some suggest that it will help to finish off the film industry because producers will abandon film in order to shoot in HDTV. Others argue that, on the contrary, HDTV will boost the film industry because, when compared to conventional television, films will reveal their true quality on the receiver sets. It is impossible to say, but the present television screen is certainly unsuitable for movie display – it is the wrong shape for one thing. This will no longer be a problem with HDTV.

Newcomers to the industry should be aware of the possible impact of the introduction of HDTV and the effect this will have on the job market. On the whole, it should increase employment opportunities, but many complex factors are involved.

Summing Up

In the past decade the British film, television and video industry has experienced a period of massive upheaval. Technological change, political attack, the decline of union power, the rise of the independents, have all blurred the lines between the various sectors. From the point of view of employment the industry has been transformed. Opportunities have expanded and will continue to expand; at the same time, however, career security has diminished and unemployment has increased. The recession hit the advertising industry particularly badly, and ITV has also been damaged by the franchise auction and the projected unemployment in companies which lost the franchise race. The recession has halted the expansion of the independents (despite the legislated 25 per cent rule) and even the monolithic BBC is facing organisational change that will cut jobs.

In the 1990s the industry will be easier to enter thanks to video, satellite and cable and there will be more mobility (especially within Europe), but employment terms, salaries and perks will be less attractive (except perhaps for the extremely talented or the unusually skilled). The whole industry will be more diverse, insecure and hazardous. Freelancing will become the main method of employment and permanent jobs may be a thing of the past. In addition, thanks to the pace of technological change, constant retraining will be necessary.

Anyone who wants a career in film, television or video in the 1990s, therefore, must understand the new structure (or lack of structure) in the industry and the implications of the changes for employment opportunities. A career in film or television or video in the 1990s (and beyond) means possessing the emotional stamina and flexibility to accept the uncertainties and enjoy the roller-coaster atmosphere of an industry which will always be subject to rapid technological change.

Many people in the industry today are perplexed and disturbed by the way in which established working practices have become out-moded, and they are fearful of what the future holds. What happens in the communications industry today, however, will happen in other industries tomorrow. The employee of the future will have to enter the workforce expecting change as a fact of life and be prepared to retrain periodically. He or she must also be prepared to move in and out of jobs as employment opportunities wax and wane. The film, television and video employee is in the vanguard of that change. The question is: how can the individual secure some protection in a very exposed climate?

It is time to look more closely at the education and training landscape as the industry moves towards the year 2000. First, however, we must focus on the industry's very real crisis in training.

PART TWO
EDUCATION AND TRAINING

4

THE CRISIS IN TRAINING

By 1992 training had emerged as one of the main problems facing the industry. How are the increasingly prevalent freelancers to secure the necessary skill base which will maintain the industry's high standards? In the past the BBC and ITV trained their own staff but their role is diminishing in the totality of broadcasting. In the film industry the unions had protected the skill base but this too was eroded with the decline in union power. It is clear that there is a severe and growing skill shortage. Old training systems cannot keep up with the pace of change. How then is the industry to train people for the future? What does the industry really require? What sort of people will the industry need? New systems must be developed, new approaches explored.

For young people entering the industry today the future has many possibilities. The decline of restrictive practices has loosened the dead hand of tradition and there will be more opportunities available. It is the old who find change difficult; the young accept it. The audiovisual industry, however, has become more complex, so the young should prepare themselves well.

The 1980s witnessed important changes in the British approach to education and training. Politicians began to realise that in the 21st century employees would have to be highly educated and possess marketable skills in order to cope with the pace of technical change. In response to this the government embarked on a series of reforms in education and training designed to prepare the British workforce for the brave new world of the year 2000. New systems, new qualifications, new methods of assessment have been introduced. The next section of this book will discuss these developments in more detail, looking in particular at the effect of the changes on higher education and vocational training and at how the new ideas are having a practical impact on the broadcasting and entertainment industries. But first some explanation is in order of the terminology in education and training.

Until the age of sixteen formal full-time education is compulsory in Britain. The minority who choose to go on after sixteen used to have two very different paths ahead of them: they could opt either for education or for training. Education usually meant academic courses – theoretical in approach, and open-ended in the sense that they are (or were) in many cases not directed towards a specific goal (a job of some sort), and competitive. The subject-matter in education is broad and general rather than narrow and skill-based. Students who opt for full-time education usually do A levels and then, if they are accepted, go into 'higher education' – which means a university or college to gain a degree.

Training is separate from education and is sometimes referred to as vocational training. It implies learning which is practical, work-related in the sense of the job market, and has definite goals in view, usually the acquisition of a specific craft or skill. It is often short-term; one-day training courses are not uncommon. Training courses are generally referred to as 'further education'. On the whole, training is not competitive but directed instead towards the acquisition of 'competence'. You can either do the job or you can't: there is no competition with other candidates to secure higher grades. Traditionally higher education is full-time and training both full-time and part-time.

In Britain there has always been a sharp distinction between the two. Post-sixteen students were sorted into appropriate learning slots and considerable class snobbery attended the chosen path. Higher education was for the clever and the few, training for the less intelligent and more numerous. Those acknowledged to be clever rarely opted for vocational courses because these courses had more than a whiff of inferiority about them: training was down-market. The only real exceptions were degrees in medicine and law; even engineering at degree level was regarded as somewhat inferior. In short, training in Britain lacked prestige and was usually deemed 'lower-class'.

Britain's economic competitors did not share this bias. In West Germany vocational courses (and engineering) were held in high esteem and it has often been pointed out that this is not unconnected with the country's economic success. The link between skill-based knowledge and the high quality of services in countries such as West Germany and Japan eventually impressed itself upon the attention of British legislators. Evidence accumulated that effective training increased a state's productivity and profits. Rather belatedly, the British have begun to come round to this point of view. The increasing impact of technology on Western society has meant that a much higher proportion of the workforce must be highly skilled. This will even more be the case in the future: an untrained workforce equals

42

widespread unemployment and low productivity – in other words, economic disaster.

In 1984 the British government commissioned a report entitled *Competence and Competition*, which emphasised the lack of training and skills within the UK as compared to other European countries.[1] In 1988, 63 per cent of the British workforce had no vocational training at all: this compares with 38 per cent of the Dutch, 26 per cent of the German and 53 per cent of the French workforces. More than 70 per cent of British workers who will be in the workforce in the year 2000 are already in employment and most of them are unskilled. They are totally unprepared for the market of tomorrow.

The government needed to act and act quickly, and in the last decade the improvement of the vocational skills of the British workforce has become an important part of public policy. This will be discussed in detail in Chapter Six. Suffice it to say here that employers, employees, educationalists, trainers and the government all agree on the need for action to improve the nation's skills, and that throughout the 1980s an effort has been made to increase access to further and higher education.

People now talk of 'education and training' in the same breath and accept that the separation in standing and prestige between them has had an injurious effect. Of course there is still a residue of innate conservatism. Britain is singularly resistant to institutional change. It has been suggested that if Britain is really serious about educational reform and a higher evaluation of training, then A levels should be abolished altogether. It is argued that it is ridiculous to make the A level system the academic gold standard when an increasing number of entrants fail the exam and 80 per cent of British children never even get admitted to the course.[2] It seems unlikely, however, that any British government will have the insight and courage to do this in the foreseeable future.

Despite the A level stumbling-block, however, it is true to say that for the first time in Britain the characteristics of college- and university-based higher education and of work-oriented further education and training are beginning to converge. Higher education is increasingly oriented towards the workplace and the workplace is in turn more alert to the need for some form of qualification system for skill-based tasks.

Education and Training in the British Audio-visual Industry

British film and television have always been a mystery to those seeking to work in the industries. There are five main strands to working in television and film: creative production (for example, director, wardrobe designer), technical (engineer); craft/technical (vision mixer, camera operator); journalistic (journalist or researcher); and administrative/management (production manager). In the past it was always difficult to break into film or television, particularly at producer or manager level. Opportunities for employment were scarce, mainly because until the 1980s there were only three places where film and television people were employed: first the relatively small film industry where experienced unionised staff worked on feature films and commercials, then the BBC, and finally ITV.

How then did people train to enter the film and television industries? How did they get the knowledge to qualify for work in the business? The answer is that they mostly didn't: in the arcane way of many British institutions there was virtually no formal method of education or training which was recognised by the industry for a job in film and television. Training did not precede entry into the profession; rather, it followed it. The main problem was always 'getting in'.

Film

Getting into film was especially difficult. Degrees cut no ice, indeed they were largely irrelevant. The film industry and the universities had nothing to say to each other: you were either in film or out and having a degree made no difference. Further education, with, for example, a City and Guilds qualification, was a little better for the craft grades but not much. The main way in was either 'luck' or 'pull', and 'insiders' had it easier. On both the craft and the production side the main way in was through 'contacts': a mother or father who worked in films in any capacity was a definite asset. A word in the ear here, a tip-off about a vacancy there, was the way the industry worked. There was hardly anywhere specific to go for practical information and for many years no independent or academic institutions provided education or training acceptable to the film unions, except for a few art colleges offering foundation courses in film and programme production.

A craft job in the film industry was almost a family inheritance, handed down from father to son (rarely from mother to daughter). Of course people complained about the outrageous unfairness and the Catch-22 situation: without a union card people could not work and without a definite job there was no union card.

The restrictiveness meant in practice that many people (even sometimes those with Oxbridge degrees) entered the film industry as
'runners' or 'gophers'. This was (and is) a 'dogsbody' job. It involved
doing errands for the production team and only the incredibly persistent were taken on and survived. It meant long hours, low pay and hard
work. It was a grind and it could lead nowhere, but it offered the
potential recruit an opportunity to gain knowledge of the industry at
the ground-floor level. Runners often ended up doing tasks quite unre-
lated to film-making. They could, for example, find themselves taking
the director's car to the garage to be repaired or his coat to the
cleaners. Running errands showed willing and was thought to be
character-forming, and it allowed people in the industry to assess the
suitability and aptitude of the would-be recruit. As many people
in film can testify, having the appropriate skills or training are all
very well, but the qualities which matter most are dedication,
determination and imagination (this will be repeated often in this
book), and these attributes are difficult to quantify in any examination
system.

'Film people are different' is a truism, although defining their peculiar quality is difficult. It certainly includes an obsessive fascination
with film and a willingness to work long hours. In a world of fanatics,
academic degrees and vocational qualifications were beside the point.
What mattered in the industry was enthusiasm and, certainly at all
craft levels, being a union member. If you had a union card then you
could certainly do the job. In the rather macho world of film-making,
paper qualifications could even be a handicap.

Union Membership

For many years the main aim of the would-be recruit was to get into
the appropriate union. The main film union used to be the ACTT
(Association of Cinematograph Television and Allied Technicians),
which effectively operated a closed shop in the film industry (and also
in ITV). It recruited about 1,800 members a year with a total membership of about 21,000. If you wanted to work you had to be a
union member; an application to join a union had to be signed by a
group of members who were willing to support you. Initially the new
employees with a union card had to stay on the same grade for two
years.

This created in the young trainee a high degree of loyalty towards
the union sponsors and encouraged from the outset a corporate and
communal feeling about the union and the job. After two years the
trainee could move to new employment or go freelance. It required
patience to progress through the union grade structure and the whole

system fostered a sense of brotherhood (less often sisterhood!) Rampant individualism was not admired; in any case, it was inappropriate since the technology of film and, in its early years television, called for team effort.

Best Trained Technicians in the World
There is no doubt that the whole system was far removed from the ideal of equal opportunities and indeed was irrational, restrictive and unfair. The fact is, however, that it worked very effectively. The slow pedestrian grind through a union apprenticeship produced some of the most skilled technicians in the world. Film is an extremely expensive medium and mistakes can be disastrous. Trainees started at the very lowest levels where they could do no harm. Promotion was slow and most people were exceptionally well-trained in how to do the job above them before they were ever promoted to do it.

The union structure, for all its faults, ensured excellent on-the-job training. No further education college or film studies course could offer better. Top jobs in the film industry (producers, directors, cinematographers) usually went to people who came up through the system. Very talented directors might move across to film from the stage or television (and vice versa) and many of these would have degrees, sometimes in drama in the case of theatre directors. As far as the film industry itself was concerned, however, academic qualifications were meaningless.

Television
In television the situation was different: formal education could be very significant and a degree mattered, especially at the higher levels. The conventional high road into programme production was via the BBC, which was part of the British cultural elite. To get into the BBC management or top levels of production, a degree was (and still is) very useful indeed. Recruits did not need to know much about television, since the Corporation itself would train them, but the creative side of programme-making was felt to be the domain of the exceptionally clever. A degree, especially from Oxbridge (preferably in something esoteric), indicated intellectual superiority and a common point of entry for the graduate trainee was as a 'researcher'. BBC News Traineeships, for example, were much sought after and the scheme received thousands of applications every year for very few places, most of which went to high-flying graduates.

The Corporation was not totally degree-oriented, however. One route in as a producer was (and is) via journalism. Working on a newspaper often led into radio, and radio, especially in the regions,

46

could in turn lead to a post as a researcher or journalist in television. From there, if the recruit had the ambition and the energy, he or she could move up through the internal training schemes of the Corporation to producer level. Entry into sports broadcasting was more idiosyncratic, since many reporters came in via their own enthusiasm for a particular sport.

BBC Engineering was similarly prestigious and highly competitive, although in the early years a degree was not necessary. The Corporation was expensively equipped and stood at the forefront of technological experiment and research. BBC engineering entrants were usually school-leavers on the science side with excellent A level passes (usually in physics and maths), and with very good references. An interesting development in recent years (and would-be recruits should take note) is the increasingly high level of ability demanded on the engineering side of television. As broadcasting equipment has become more complex and sophisticated, engineers have to be well-qualified in electronic communications. Degrees are now more common in some of the technical areas of the industry since engineers have to understand theory as well as possess practical skills.

On the whole engineers at the BBC were, and are, a special breed. They have a separate career and training structure within the Corporation and they can be quite scornful of more obviously 'creative' types. Few engineers were impressed by the idea of producing and they were rarely interested in moving over to the creative programming side of broadcasting: it was the technology which fascinated them. BBC engineers were provided with the opportunity to work with equipment at the cutting edge of the communications industry. Retraining on new equipment was part of the normal career process and job satisfaction was high.

Other technical/craft posts in television, such as camera operator, sound engineer, and lighting specialists, were filled by recruits who had had some form of technical training at the tertiary level. They usually did not have degrees but held instead a BTEC qualification or something similar. Exceptional candidates would be taken on for a six-month probationary period, after which they would be considered a trainee within a particular specialism. The BBC would then train them through their own internal courses.

There was a strict hierarchy in television, but an ambitious recruit could move, thanks to the various BBC training courses, from the lower technical levels through to the higher, and then on to the creative side as a producer or director. In the early days directors with this type of background sometimes had an advantage over the non-technical recruits from the universities because practical skills were then a more important component of programme-making. There was, however, a persistent bias in BBC management to promote people with degrees and it was therefore harder to come up purely through the craft route.

Other positions in the BBC (support staff and so on) were similarly sought after and were recruited through outside 'competitions', but generally only the brightest and the best got in. Once in, all sorts of opportunities were available for those who wished to advance. In the past most people entering the professional grades were white Anglo-Saxon males, but women graduates were often recruited at the secretarial level, and a few of them did clear the hurdles and make it through to producer level (especially if they had charm or good looks, a situation which, while it was unfair, was typical of an industry which placed a premium on physical attractiveness). However, women rarely became directors: this used to be regarded as a technical position for which they were not suited. Even more rarely did they break into the higher echelons of BBC management because they came up against what has been called the 'glass ceiling': senior management posts were assumed to be a male preserve. Recently, thanks to considerable pressure, the BBC has made a concerted equal opportunities effort, but it was not the case for most of its history. The ethos of the white Anglo-Saxon, Oxbridge-educated, middle-class male permeated all levels of management at the BBC.

For many years the system resulted in a highly skilled, professional but rather narrow, inward-looking workforce. (Narrowness was usually vigorously denied, but there was an out-of-touch quality about the BBC which did not help it when it came under political attack.) A job at the BBC had extraordinary cachet: 'I work for the Beeb' was a remark likely to cause an envious intake of breath at parties. That it also might have given some members of the Corporation a rather exaggerated idea of their own importance was unfortunate.

The BBC and television training were for years virtually synonymous. Its internal schools had an international reputation and people from broadcasting systems all over the world came to take courses. In management, engineering, journalism and so on the training was of a very high quality and one of the basic principles, whatever the level or speciality, was that employees were given an overview of the whole complex process which producing BBC programmes entailed. This was combined with an emphasis on 'on-the-job' training and formal teaching.

By contrast, training in ITV in the early years did lag behind the BBC. Since the BBC trained staff beyond its requirements, however, qualified people moved from the Corporation to the higher salaries of

48

the commercial sector, which was often accused of 'poaching' the best people. The 'production process as a whole' nature of the BBC training system colonised ITV (and to a very small extent the feature film industry) and the outward flow of creativity probably provided at one time about half the senior posts in the rest of the industry. It also contributed to the consistency and uniformly high quality which characterised the British audiovisual industry for many years. This is part of what is meant by British broadcasting 'culture'.

As ITV grew in stature and wealth, however, its training programmes also expanded. They were usually organised on a company basis with companies specialising in certain areas: for example, Thames Television had a technical trainee scheme, ITN had an editorial trainee scheme, and Granada had a course for trainee researchers (which was advertised externally every year and led to thousands of applications for perhaps six places). ITV also developed a close relationship with Leeds Polytechnic and Ravensbourne College of Art and Design, both of which were well-equipped and ran courses in television. Many ITV employees were sent to Ravensbourne for updating and retraining. In addition, the IBA had formidable engineering responsibilities, so its engineering department, based mainly at Crawley Court near Winchester, became a byword for technical excellence.

For many years the technology of television was complex; operators of equipment had to be highly skilled because the mistake of the uninitiated or the inexperienced could be expensive. No wonder, therefore, that the BBC and then ITV were prepared to pay for in-house training rather than trust it to an unknown agency. The system was inward-looking and autonomous (and very frustrating to those who wished to train in television yet who could not find employment with the Corporation or the ITV companies) – but it worked. If it irritated outsiders who failed to break in, if it appeared cliquish and elitist, the main argument used in its defence was the high quality of the programmes. It was judged by its results and British television was the world leader.

The benefits and job satisfaction in television were high. Union power was entrenched in ITV and although this made it difficult for people to get jobs, it did ensure that people in the craft areas were highly competent. Life in the media in any capacity bore no relation to life on the assembly line. The work was highly skilled with a glamorous component and would-be recruits clamoured constantly for entry. This produced a somewhat smug attitude in those who had the jobs and perhaps an overweening pride (and greed) in some sections of the industry. The unions were extremely powerful; union agreements produced inflated overtime benefits which were reported in the right-wing press with hypocritical indignation (journalists on newspapers were not exactly paupers). Nemesis, however, in the guise of Mrs Thatcher, was at hand.

The television industry had already come under attack in the 1970s. At first this was mainly from radicals on the Left and the main manifestation was a campaign for more 'public access', which meant more programmes made by non-BBC, non-ITV staff reflecting working-class, ethnic minority and community concerns. Critics questioned why it was taken as a God-given right that only employees of broadcasting organisations could make programmes. They accused the BBC particularly of being monolithic, self-contained and difficult to penetrate. Over the long haul the left-wing attack may have gradually weakened the Corporation because, in the 1980s, the BBC proved unequal to the task of repulsing the more orchestrated and effective right-wing onslaught on its unwieldy bureaucratic structure and its finances. As a national institution, the BBC had been inclined to believe in its own immortality, an attitude which left it ill-equipped to deal with the changes which occurred in the industry in the 1980s and with the animus directed towards it from the Right.

As we saw in earlier chapters, in the 1980s the industry underwent a period of upheaval. Video technology made the industry more accessible and permeable and craft unions no longer had a monopoly of the knowledge that gave them power. The Conservative government launched a concerted attack on all restrictive practices and ITV was particularly vulnerable. With deregulation, and the advent of satellite and cable, the number of broadcasting channels increased. (In Europe in the last ten years the number of channels has grown from 39 to 120; by 1995 this is expected to reach 250.) The 25 per cent quota encouraged small companies to spring up all over the place and this meant that the BBC and ITV were no longer so dominant. The Broadcasting Bill thrust ITV firmly into the market-place and the BBC found itself under attack over the cost of the licence fee.

Financial pressure on all sides led to cutbacks and training was a major casualty. Training was an easy target for cost-cutting managers at the BBC, more concerned with short-term solutions than long-term benefits. Similarly ITV, faced with a drop in advertising and with the franchise auction, had little energy or money to 'squander' on training. The government's onslaught on the unions meant in practice that there was no longer any group or body which took standards of craftsmanship to heart in film or in the industry at large. By 1990 the mysterious and haphazard training system in British film and television was falling apart. Some provision still existed but it was insuf-

50

ficient to cope with the scale of the problem. Training, virtually unnoticed, had fallen off the agenda. Suddenly, the industry awoke to a skill shortage.

It was the burgeoning of the small independent companies and the expansion of the freelance market which brought the problem into focus. Many new recruits had no training at all and had to pick up skills and knowledge as they went along. It is difficult to convey how much of a shock this was to old-timers with a tradition of a rigorous and thorough apprenticeship behind them. The old craft unions that had insisted on high-level skills no longer had the authority to insist on anything, and the craft technicians who knew the industry through and through were retiring and not being replaced.

What was alarming was that in some areas standards did drop. The British were beginning to lose their reputation for craft skills. Production mistakes which formerly would never have been tolerated cropped up more frequently on the small screen. The cracks were showing. Many retired television hands looking at live programmes could be heard to mutter, 'That would never have happened in the old days', and they were right! Suddenly, and very suddenly at that, the industry which had considered itself the best in the world found it had young untrained personnel and a severe shortage of the high-calibre staff which it had come to expect and rely on. The training 'system', illogical and irrational as it was, was rapidly unravelling and there was nothing new to replace it.

Something had to be done – but what? Training was expensive and it required organisation. There was no longer any dominant agency which could provide a training service: the unions had lost their teeth and the BBC and ITV were under severe financial pressure. It was time for the industry to look beyond itself. It had to turn its attention to the new thinking about training which, as we noted at the start of this chapter, was beginning to penetrate government circles. There were, after all, courses in film and television provided by higher and further education. Perhaps they should be taken more seriously? A major transition was under way.

Notes

1. *Competence and Competition: Training and Education in the Federal Republic of Germany, The United States and Japan,* a report prepared by the Institute of Manpower Studies for the National Economic Development Council and Manpower Services Commission, London, MSC, 1984.

51

2. Employer quoted in interim report by Sir Christopher Ball, *Learning Pays, the Role of Post Compulsory Education and Training*, London, Royal Society of Arts, April 1991, p. 41. This is a powerful argument in favour of training, pointing out the economic advantages which could ensue if Britain developed an efficient training system.

5

MEDIA DIPLOMAS AND DEGREES
Are They Any Use?

Young people who want to enter the industry often ask: *Should I take a degree? Will I have a better chance?* Well, yes – and no. The answer has to be: it all depends. Since 1990 there has been a shift in the way education and training are viewed by the audiovisual industry. There has also been a shift in the way that 'higher education' views training. This chapter will examine the situation in detail.

The American and European Model
In some ways the problem with education and training in the audio-visual industry in Britain in the late 1980s was unique. Other European countries managed the change in employment patterns brought about by the decline of public service television, and by deregulation, more smoothly. One of the main reasons was that their skill training provision was better organised and more widespread.[1] In the United States also, where many more people went to university, students who wished to get into the industry did degrees in film, media studies or journalism and part of the degree often involved an element of training. People with degrees in media studies in American universities did not expect to enter the industry at the top level: many of them went into the craft and non-professional areas. In Britain people who wanted to get into film rarely went to university, and those with degrees who went into television had rarely followed any relevant or useful course. At university they were likely to opt for classics, politics, modern languages or English literature.

The Traditional Inferiority of Media Studies
It was a fact of British life that industry and university were worlds apart. Since education was seen as totally separate from training, the universities had little interest in industry. This was particularly so for the audiovisual industry. For many years British institutions of higher learning did not offer media or communications studies at degree level

at all. Such courses were viewed as frivolous and 'American'. (Consequently, television, one of the most important mass media of the twentieth century, was, until recently, scarcely examined or studied by British scholars.) Film was slightly more acceptable, since it could be regarded as an art form, but graduates recruited by the BBC were still likely to know more about 'Beowulf' than Ingmar Bergman.

Journalism was a similar case in point. Television news relied on journalists, but for years British universities regarded a journalism degree as a peculiar American aberration. Until recently there were no undergraduate degrees in journalism offered by any British university or polytechnic, although a number of polytechnics did offer journalism courses as part of a three-year course in communications or media studies. Only in September 1991 did the London School of Printing, City University and Lancashire Polytechnic all begin to offer the first British BA degree in journalism.

Industry Suspicion of the BA

The blame for this bizarre attitude, however, cannot be laid entirely at the doors of higher education. Film, broadcasting and newspaper personnel were all for different reasons equally suspicious of media degrees. Workers in creative and technical areas were unimpressed by ivory tower academic study. For years journalists believed that the best way to train was to start at sixteen as a cub reporter with minimum qualifications and 'work your way up'. Indeed the proposed new BAs in journalism have been regarded with much suspicion. Keith Hall of the National Council for the Training of Journalists has declared that the impetus for such courses has not come from the industry and that graduates won't be regarded as having the training required. Brian Hitchen of the *Daily Star* was reported as saying: 'BAs in Journalism? They don't turn me on ... I've only met one graduate in journalism who was any good. Most of them are appalling. There's only one way to learn journalism and that's starting at the bottom.' (Quoted in Nick Turner, 'Newshounds on Course', *Guardian*, 30 September 1991.)

Film people at all levels had similar attitudes and sniffed at impractical theorists from academic institutions. 'They don't even know how to thread a Steenbeck' was a familiar cry. Graduates who entered the BBC showed a similar disdain for media degrees. Any academically 'respectable' degree (in Sanskrit perhaps or theology) proved intellectual worthiness. This then merely had to be 'topped up' or 'finished off' with professional in-house training. In short, the working world of British film, television and journalism was just as wary of educational qualifications in media studies as universities were suspicious of media studies as a valid intellectual discipline. The industry was (and still is) strongly biased towards 'on-the-job' training.

This was all very well when the industry did take on some training responsibility. The problem is now that the old informal training structure has gone and anyone wanting to enter the industry who expects effective on-the-job training is likely to be disappointed. Neither the BBC nor ITV can afford to train on a massive scale any more and, since there are fewer permanent posts in these institutions, so there are fewer people trained by them. If it used to be difficult in the past to get a staff job in the BBC or ITV (Channel 3 after 1993), it will be even more of a problem in the future. Training will still be offered to core staff, but an increasingly large percentage of workers will be freelancers who generally will be expected to have received their training elsewhere.

The crucial question, however, is *where?* The answer is that it will probably be through private and industry-sponsored schemes, but these are unlikely to be of the systematic broad type which the BBC offered or the rigorous apprenticeship of the craft unions. Private training schemes will pop up all over the place to meet demand, but most of them will be short-term, the users will have to pay, and they will be of varying quality. Inevitably, therefore, given this situation, more weight in the future will be placed on the courses offered by colleges and universities. Those who intend to go into the media industry should take account of this. The collapse of training provision in the industry has necessarily shifted the balance further towards the media courses provided by higher and further education, which are moving in to plug the gap.

University Media Courses

Higher education in Britain has traditionally been devoted to the pursuit of knowledge for its own sake. There was always a sort of snobbery about technical courses which dirtied the hands. Anything which smacked of vocationalism in higher education was regarded as illegitimate. Even within media studies courses the technical/vocational aspects of the curriculum were generally underplayed. Critical awareness was stressed above practical knowledge. Courses which took students into a studio and exposed them to the actual equipment were not highly regarded; too much (or even any!) emphasis on technical knowledge was considered intellectually limiting.

This attitude is finally beginning, slowly and painfully, to change. In the last ten years there has been a shake-up in higher education thanks to the government's emphasis on the market-place. The end result has been the erosion of academic elitism. The conversion of polytechnics into universities and increasing student numbers are two aspects of the trend. More and more higher education is consumer-led; institutions of higher learning will no longer be able to afford to ignore 'popular' courses in a world where they have to 'bid' for students. The government has used the funding weapon as a means of implementing change: the more students a university takes on, the more money it gets. While the 'reform' has its critics, what it means in practice is that the universities (including the former polytechnics) are having to offer courses which will attract 'the customers' – students.

What many customers want are media studies. Communications and media studies courses everywhere are oversubscribed, since there are not enough of them available. Those courses which do exist are flooded with applicants. In the new market-led higher education system it is inevitable that media courses of all sorts will burgeon. As higher education responds to the market-place, and to the impact of high technology on employment, it will have to accept that young people want knowledge *and* jobs. Degrees with a technical component put students in a more powerful position in a competitive labour-market.

The Media Degree, Its Market Worthiness

School-leavers who want to enter the audiovisual industry but want to do a degree first are therefore likely to find that in future a 'relevant' degree will have the edge over a degree in a more academic area. This is especially the case for courses which include a practical component. With BBC and ITV training cut back, and union power in retreat, would-be employers will be looking for students who already know something about the practical side of the industry. In market terms, over the next few years anyone who wants a job in the industry will find that the stock value of a degree in film, television, media or communications studies will increase vis-à-vis other degrees, particularly if it has a practical component.

Practical Advice on the Media Degree

Just as the audiovisual industry was in the vanguard of change in employment, so the evolution of media degrees in universities and polytechnics heralds a shift in approach in higher education. Most degree courses will probably ignore the vocational element for some time to come (as long as they can, if some academics have their way), but media degrees will not be able to do so. They are being driven towards a more vocational bias by the crisis in training in the industry at large. Indeed, as higher education and industry move closer

56

together, the impact of one on the other will or should be an increasingly significant phenomenon in other industries and degree courses as well. In the market-place money speaks: if students demand to study film, video and television then universities, if they want to stay in 'business', will provide them with the chance. This means a major change in the ethos which has governed higher education in Britain for more than a century.

However, a word of caution is in order: the change in higher education is not all positive; there are pitfalls to avoid. As higher education moves into the market-place, the onus is on the prospective student to be consumer-conscious and well-informed. One of the great strengths of higher education in Britain has been a rigorous control of standards: Britain's universities were notably uncorrupt. When only a very small percentage of people went on to university, and when the staff-to-student ratio was small, standards were very high. The awarding of degrees was very carefully supervised and there was a consistency about the courses offered and the levels which had to be reached. A degree from any institution of higher learning in Britain had a universal value.

The significance of this can be understood by looking at the United States, where there was little overall supervision. In some notorious cases small American colleges (usually in the South, it is said) would award doctorates and degrees to candidates regardless of their ability. Since the courses were not cheap, there was more than a whiff of 'buying a degree' about them. It was always necessary to know where an American degree came from: a doctorate from Charismatic Christian College of Nowhere, Tennessee was obviously not to be compared with one from the Massachusetts Institute of Technology. In the future, no matter what the politicians and the academics say, when student numbers increase in British universities, there will be some slippage in standards and supervision. In the race to grab students some institutions and departments will offer courses which may be inferior in quality. There will be more 'cowboy' courses around.

Some canny students ('customers') will see an advantage in this if some degrees offer an easy option. However, be warned: the industry will become alert to those institutions which have high standards. In a world where degrees have a vocational component, employers will quickly suss out the courses which produce well-qualified students. It is perhaps overstating the case to suggest that some media courses will be rip-offs, but students will have to be increasingly discriminating about the degree courses they choose to embark upon. There will be a much greater variation in what is on offer and there will be some poorly financed and under resourced courses. Despite the ballyhoo about the free market, it is as well to note that shabby goods are one of the less attractive features of the increase in consumer choice.

Practical Advice

What practical advice, then, can be offered to the school-leaver who wants to study for a degree with the aim of ending up with a job in the industry? First and foremost, degrees which actually study film, television or modern communications will be increasingly valuable, and especially if they have a practical component. This is part of the fall-out of the crisis in training and the shift to a more vocational element in higher education.

Secondly, school-leavers will have to become knowledgeable about the courses they wish to embark upon. In a tough, economically competitive climate, where training may be difficult or very expensive to find after graduation, students should not start a three-year under-graduate course with the vague hope of getting into the industry. Some of the courses may qualify them for nothing. They must be prepared to ask pointed questions about course work, equipment and tutors.

Many people employed in higher education have no first-hand knowledge of the film and television industry. They know the theory but have not practised the art of film- or programme-making. This is perfectly acceptable in a theoretical course, and higher education must never be solely about fitting people into the labour-market. However, if a course has a practical component and the vocational element is what is attractive to the student, then the people who teach it should know what they are talking about. A lecturer who teaches students to write scripts for television, but who has never managed to sell one himself, should be treated with caution.

So what type of questions should prospective students ask? Some of the following may provide an idea:

How many students are there on the course?
What is the staff-student ratio?
Is there any hands-on training?
Are there work placements, and if so where are they?
Have the staff teaching practical components first-hand knowledge of the industry?
Have previous students found jobs?
Is the equipment in the department reasonably modern?

The last question is important because film and video equipment is very expensive and higher education is not wealthy: this is especially the case in the art colleges and arts faculties where most media studies are based. Higher education institutions are unlikely to be able to afford the equipment of a really up-to-date television station, but they should have access to technical information about the newest technology and the existing equipment should not be ancient. There has been some research on interactive video systems as a means of retraining people in television: similar software packages may be a viable option for colleges and universities in the future. CD-I holds out particular promise in this area. In addition, if the government's educational reforms are successful, there should be more employer-led industry involvement in college-based courses, particularly in terms of money and personnel, and this also should help.

The Broadcasting, Entertainment, Cinematograph and Theatre Union (BECTU, the new amalgamation of the ACTT and BETA) certainly recognises the importance of the practical and theoretical as crucial components when accrediting courses. Central to the union's criteria is that the course should be as relevant as possible to the demands and requirements of the industry. In addition, however, they also want a theoretical component which includes an understanding of technological development, industry trends, and current and future practices, as well as an appreciation of the social, cultural and political context of the media. The courses should incorporate 'a critical understanding of the influence the media have on public attitudes to issues of race, gender, sexuality, class disability and political beliefs.' BECTU currently accredits seven colleges:

The National Film and Television School
The University of Westminster
Bristol University
Bournemouth and Poole College of Art and Design
West Surrey College of Art and Design
The London International Film School
The London College of Printing (part of the London Institute)
(see the Appendix for addresses).

Some of these offer degrees, but others offer diplomas or vocational qualifications. The significance of union accreditation is that qualifications from these colleges and universities entitle the holders to an automatic union ticket with their first job. Since the unions are not as powerful as they once were, this is no longer so vital. However, union accreditation does mean high standards and all these institutions have excellent reputations for the combined theoretical and vocational provisions which they offer. Since this is probably the way media studies will go in higher education, it is appropriate to list them here. No doubt, as media studies become more vocationally oriented at universities and colleges, more courses will be recognised in this way.

Summing Up

Media studies, in their combination of both the theoretical and the practical, technical and academic knowledge, are tailor-made for the educational and training climate of the future. Their time has come; purely academic degrees will be of less significance except in terms of university research. The point of the government's reforms in higher education is to increase the practical work and industry-related component. In future one cannot simply have a good degree and expect training to be tacked on in the workplace: it won't be. Proven skills in technical and practical matters will be more highly valued as the inequality between vocational and academic training diminishes.

Other Degrees

This chapter has concentrated on the shift in the perception of media degrees and on their increasing significance. There are, however, other areas of study which will be of value and importance to the industry. As we have seen, communications are an increasingly significant asset in a country's economic viability. Policy issues will therefore play a large political role. In the 21st century those who have studied communications policy will have an advantage. Law degrees which consider transfrontier issues will be useful, as will degrees in politics, if they encompass media policy. Degrees in drama or art and design have always been valuable in the industry. As we shall see, drama training can be useful for film directors and, of course, for performers. Art and design degrees, especially when they have a work-related component, will help people find employment in areas such as costume, make-up, graphics, and scenic design. One rather new development is the need for computer experts, right across the board from animation to management.

However, it is degrees in financial services such as accountancy which will be in particularly short supply. As we noted above, in the past television was partially sheltered from the market-place. This is no longer the case. Finding the money, securing the loans, persuading the backers to release more funds will all become part and parcel of the making of programmes for television, just as it has always been for the making of feature films. While making money might not seem as obviously exciting and creative as making films, it will become of major importance to creative survival. There will be no shortage of jobs for those with the right financial qualifications.

Further Education and Training

There are all sorts of further education colleges offering courses in the craft and media area leading to qualifications varying from a BTEC to

Royal Society of Arts or City and Guilds awards. The principle which applies to degrees will probably also affect these qualifications: the crisis in training will increase their usefulness in securing a job (although at the time of writing the recession is so severe that even people with experience are finding it difficult to get work). After all, if the industry is not training people as it used to do, it has to look elsewhere. When employers want a new recruit they will want someone who has received some form of training; if this has been acquired in further education, then so be it. Again, just as in degree courses, financial skills are very much in demand. The industry needs people who know how the Inland Revenue functions and about VAT. Knowledge of contract administration, performing rights and payments will also be much in demand.

At the present time there is a revolution going on with the introduction of a new system of vocational qualifications which puts a premium value on on-the-job competence (rather as the unions used to do). This will affect the courses offered in further education and the whole education, training and employment picture. Anyone leaving school, college or university and wishing to enter an industry must understand the implications of what could be a massive sea change in the British attitude to vocational training. Employers need to understand it too. The next chapter will examine the issue of vocational training.

Note
1. In the end, it may be decided that the British managed the conflict between deregulation and public service television better than other countries, but it was touch-and-go all the way and the unforeseen fall of Mrs Thatcher in 1990 probably contributed most to the survival of a modified public service ethos.

6

THE BRAVE NEW WORLD OF VOCATIONAL TRAINING

In the last decade the government has introduced widespread reforms in education and vocational training which have been closely related to the perceived needs of industry and commerce. In schools the introduction of the National Curriculum, with its emphasis on science and technology, has attracted much attention, and in higher education the provision for widening access (although without a pro-rata increase in resources) has won approval. It is finally being recognised that British education, excellent as it is, is in many ways more suitable for the nineteenth than the twenty-first century, and steps have been taken to remedy the situation.

In addition to mainline educational reform, however, there have been a host of other initiatives and schemes which aim to improve the provision and quality of training both at school and in further education. Chapter Five touched briefly on the inequality of esteem between education and training and the injurious effect this has had on British economic success. The cornerstone of the government's attack on this problem is the proposed introduction of a post-sixteen training qualification, the National Vocational Qualification (NVQ); in Scotland, the Scottish Vocational Qualification (SVQ). The development of the N/SVQs is the culmination of the government's efforts to bring education, training and employment closer together. This was the central aim of two government papers, *Working Together: Education and Training* (London, HMSO, Cmnd 9832, July 1986), and *Review of Educational Qualification in England and Wales* (London, The Manpower Services Commission and the Department of Education and Science, 1986). If N/SVQs succeed, they could be the most important reform of the British education system since the 1944 Butler Act.

On the whole both the political Left and Right approve of the new emphasis on training, although the government has been criticised for not providing sufficient funds for the job to be done properly. A more fundamental philosophical criticism has come from those who have suggested that the government's enthusiasm for training springs, not from a concern about developing human potential, but rather from a materialistic view of the workforce as human fodder to stoke the industries of the future. In the year 2000 and beyond employers will need skilled workers to slot into jobs to keep their industries profitable: the Conservative Party, the argument runs, being the party of employers, is prepared to provide this.

Critics see the 'reform' of the universities and the emphasis on training as part of a right-wing plot designed to destroy the traditional ideal of education that knowledge is important for its own sake. The government, they suggest, does not want to produce a thinking electorate (which undermines its power), but a workforce of skilled zombies tamed to consumerism. Certainly British higher education has produced highly critical, analytical people who have irritated politicians by questioning society and government. As universities and colleges move closer to the job market and numbers expand, some observers believe that the critical, intellectual elite which dominated the universities will be reduced to an impotent rump. This, they say, is exactly what the government is seeking.

Whatever the reasons behind the reforms, training is certainly now a major priority on the political agenda and anyone currently entering the job market must understand what is happening in higher and further education and come to grips with the changes: they are going to have a major impact on employees in the workplace of the future.

The route into higher education has almost always been clear, straightforward and well-understood (at least by teachers, academics and the middle classes). Most people recognise that 'a degree means something', even if they are not sure exactly what. In contrast, the provision of further education and training has always been chaotic, confusing and complicated. It is doubtful whether the vast majority of ordinary people in Britain have ever really understood how the training system worked. The routes towards vocational qualifications have been incomprehensible to many young people and also to those who, having found higher education closed to them, have been utterly confused by the alternatives on offer.

The accrediting bodies in further education are various and include: BTEC (the Business and Technology Education Council); the RSA (Royal Society of Arts) Examination Board; and the City and Guilds of London Institute. While absolutely excellent, the considerable incoherence in the pattern of these courses, and the qualifications they offer, has created problems. The diversity of provision has acted as a barrier and has discouraged many young people from going on to further education. 'Where is it all going to lead?' has been the usual question, and when there has been no real link-up with the working world there has been no truly satisfactory answer. As a result, many young people simply left school at sixteen because there seemed no point in staying on. Had the vocational courses on offer actually seemed straightforward (in the manner of a degree course route), or had they qualified students directly for employment, or even set them on an alternative route to higher education, this would have been a different matter. The system has, however, never functioned in a such a clear-cut way.

The government's answer has been to try to tidy the whole area up and create order and simplicity out of the chaos. Unfortunately, because so much has to be sorted out, over the past few years there has been a proliferation of initiatives which has contributed to further confusion. We are assured that in the end all will be well and training will be sorted out, but it has meant that the pace and scale of change has produced its own problems. One needs almost an official qualification in 'new training initiatives' to understand the twists and turns in government policy on employment and training, especially as it affects young people in the post-sixteen age group.

Employer Involvement

One of the major principles to keep in mind is that a fundamental part of the government's dogma is that education and training are no longer the sole prerogative of the educators; that employers should be increasingly involved, and that the educational institution and the workplace should be closer together. This is the pivot of government policy and at the present time (1992) we are smack in the middle of a period of change.

A word of caution: one of the major obstacles to an understanding of what has happened, and what is happening, in education and training is the bureaucratic delight in acronyms. We will therefore look at some of the most important of these and attempt some clarification. In addition, policy changes all the time and organisations come and go. Some of these bodies therefore alter their names (and acronyms) with changes in policy emphasis.

Word Games: TEED, TECs, ITOs, TVEI, COMPACT, CPVE, EHE

Those 'in the know' love to fling about acronyms – to the immense confusion of everyone else. Most of the new training initiatives are funded by the Training Enterprise and Education Directorate (TEED), which is a section of the Employment Department (ED). Obviously the ED is very concerned with training, but funding also comes from the Department for Education (DFE) and from the Department of Trade and Industry (Dti), both of which have money for education, training and industry-linked initiatives.

The Training and Enterprise Councils (TECs) are relatively new. They were set up in 1989 and consist of eighty-two independent companies throughout England and Wales which have multi-million pound contracts with the government. Their purpose is to forge a partnership for business information and training and they are intended to take over the local work of the government's Training Enterprise and Education Directorate. Part of the TEC remit is the development of links between education and industry. (Some suspicious people see the TECs as Trojan horses paving the way for the government to snatch education and training funds from the hands of local authorities.)

Industry Training Organisations (ITOs) were developed recently to establish training strategies within particular industries. There are at the present time more than a hundred ITOs in existence representing all sorts of industries. Some ITOs date back to 1964 (when they were known as Industry Training Boards), before the new era of emphasis on training was established. Film and television came late to the idea, possibly a reflection of the fact that until the late 1980s training in the industry functioned satisfactorily, if rather eccentrically. The ITO for the audiovisual industry used to have the unwieldy title of the 'Broadcast Film and Video Industry Training Organisation' (BFVITO, on which, see below), but has now adopted the same title, 'Skillset', as with the industry lead body.

The Technical and Vocational Education Initiative (TVEI) was one of the first training/educational reforms introduced by the Conservative government in 1983. It has been extended but some TVEI initiatives will be finished by August 1993. In a sense, it paved the way at school level for what has happened elsewhere. TVEI is not actually a course but rather represents a philosophy of education, the aim of which is to orient schoolchildren to the world of work and to provide them with information about where they are going in the future. Schools, the argument runs, have existed in a vacuum: they have been quarantined from the real world. This isolates children who have no conception of what happens when schooldays end. Suddenly at the age of fourteen they are faced with the crunch: what are they going to do when they leave school? How are they going to spend the rest of their lives? How are they going to earn a living? TVEI aims to orient the 14–19 age group towards their future in the workplace. It is also an attempt to reshape the education curriculum to include vocational elements with a technical bias so that education will be more relevant to employment. TVEI tries to enhance students' technological awareness and knowledge. (A large proportion of TVEI schemes include media studies because media studies fits in well with the philosophical concept.) It is expected that the TECs will eventually take over TVEI-type responsibilities.

COMPACT is a scheme which forges actual links and exchanges between industries/employers and schools. Employers guarantee jobs with training to young people who reach an agreed standard of education. Students at school go on work placements and employers are given the opportunity to provide input into the educational curriculum. The overall aim is to strengthen employment opportunities for school-leavers by allowing them to gain direct knowledge of working environments and of the skills associated with particular jobs. COMPACT is run by local education authorities. Kensington and Chelsea Local Education Authority has forged links with the BBC as part of its COMPACT scheme and is providing schoolchildren with information about, and experience with, the working world of television and radio.

Other training/education initiatives have included the Certificate of Pre-Vocational Education (CPVE), Professional Industrial and Commercial Updating (PICKUP), and Enterprise in Higher Education (EHE), a national programme helping higher educational institutions to develop in an enterprising and business-conscious way. During their studies, university students are brought into closer contact with the world of business, often through work placements (part of the trend discussed in Chapter Two).

National Vocational Qualification
The jewel in the government's crown, however, is the post-sixteen provision of the National (and Scottish) Vocational Qualification system. This is the most significant breakthrough of all and it has momentous implications for those proposing to enter the workforce now and in the future. The basic aim of the NVQs is to change the whole of the British qualification system from school through to further and higher education and right into the workplace. It proposes to weave education and training into a coherent and rational pattern.

How the System Works
In 1986 the government set up the National Council for Vocational Qualification (the Scottish equivalent is SCOTVEC, which was established somewhat earlier) to oversee the new system. The National Council for Vocational Qualification is headed by Sir Bryan Nicholson (appointed in 1990) and has twelve members who have been set a number of tasks. The Council's mandate is to establish the NVQs in a coherent national framework which facilitates open access (meaning

that anyone can try for an NVQ) and progression (people can move up the various levels). The Council accredits awarding bodies but it does not award NVQs itself. It also has to ensure that the NVQ qualifications will be relevant to the needs of industry. As we have seen, the involvement of the employer is an important axiom of government policy and employers are a key element in the new structure. They will be actively encouraged to invest in the training of their workforces.

The Council's major responsibility is to secure standards of so-called occupational competence and to ensure that the new vocational qualifications are based on these standards. It is upon this idea of competence that all other aspects of the N/SVQs rest. Consequently a complete framework of vocational qualification for all occupational sectors, 'from pest control to ballet dancing', has to be designed and set up. (This includes the film, television and video industry, but more of that later.) Each industry must agree on the job descriptions and national standards required for their workforce. Industry leaders therefore have to set up Industry Lead Bodies (ILBs), which analyse what the particular industry does and the various jobs and tasks which workers carry out. The ILB for the audovisual industry is called Skillset and the one for performers generally is The Arts and Entertainment Training Council. The Lead Bodies must also take proper account of future needs in the industry, especially with regard to technology, markets and employment patterns (this is of particular significance to the media industry).

Competence is the key word and bears repetition. It means the ability to perform a whole job to the performance level expected in employment. A competence statement is *not* a narrow skill and knowledge specification: it must match the job performed in reality and includes the ability to adapt to new situations. It encompasses not just technical ability but other aspects such as the capacity to organise, plan, innovate (if required) and to respond to non-routine events. It may also include, if these are part of the job, interpersonal skills, that is, dealing with people such as colleagues, clients, customers, subordinates and superiors.

The revolutionary aspect of the N/SVQs is the proposal to increase recognition of learning acquired through experience at work. N/SVQs are not courses or curricula but qualifications. They are not a training system but awards which will encourage employers to provide training and employees to seek it out. The criteria for the award of an N/SVQ have nothing to do with the manner in which the person achieved the required level of competence: the candidate achieves an N/SVQ by demonstrating competence in a given role against the standards set by the industry. This does not mean, however, that people arrive at the

67

standards required without undertaking training. Indeed the N/SVQs might require more from learning programmes than existing qualifications do. They are not intended to undermine the role of colleges, but rather, it is hoped, even to enhance them. RSA, BTEC and City and Guilds all support the N/SVQ programme and are revising their own vocational courses in line with the occupational standards published by the various industries.

As N/SVQs become more universal they are expected to lead to a growth in the demand for post-sixteen education and training and also for adult learning opportunities. N/SVQs, in addition to providing a simpler system of vocational qualification, will also offer an alternative route into higher education. Britain will then truly become a 'learning society'. It is increasingly being accepted that an educated workforce pays off, economically, socially and personally. The logic is: educated societies are more successful; educated people are better off; it is the technologically skilled societies which do well.

The problem besetting the British educational system is that most people have their last contact with it at the age of sixteen. People have their one shot at being 'educated' at school and if they miss the boat for further training they have missed it for ever. This has been disastrous both for the individual and the country. Thanks to N/SVQs, people will be able to seek education and training throughout their lives. This at least is the theory.

It is important to realise that plans for N/SVQs run parallel with the government's plans to expand university places (discussed in the previous chapter). The name of the game is to encourage more people to seek out and experience 'education and training'. Upholders of the moribund British class system have often put forward the idea that the so-called working class did not really want to be educated. In fact, evidence suggests that the demand for post-compulsory education and training is a function of supply. The experience of the Open University, and the expansion of polytechnics and colleges of higher education over the last decade, have suggested that British people do want to learn if they are provided with the opportunity, if they are not humiliated in the process (here A levels are a stumbling-block) and if the entry route is clear and comprehensible. N/SVQs should assist in this by motivating people to seek out courses which will then provide them with the opportunity to acquire qualifications that are simple, universal and flexible.

Some people fail to see the necessity for work-based qualifications, and particularly for a system which is as all-embracing as the N/SVQs propose to be. Qualifications, however, are psychologically important because they give people a sense of self-respect and make them more ambitious. Many people in Britain feel they 'failed' at school and this puts them off education and training for life. With N/SVQs, if someone is already doing a job to the right standard, as set down by a particular industry, then he or she can immediately get the credit towards an N/SVQ. Certain supermarket chains, for example, have linked into the N/SVQ system for retail marketing so that their cashiers are now able to earn an N/SVQ. There are already over 300 N/SVQs in place and many industries (such as the audiovisual one) are moving towards setting up more.

Initially the N/SVQs specified four levels of achievement, with Level One the basic and Level Four the most complex:

N/SVQ Level One shows competence in the performance of a range of work activities. These are mainly routine and predictable or are tasks which provide a broad foundation primarily as a basis for progression.

Level Two shows competence in a broader and more demanding range of work activities and involving greater individual responsibility and autonomy than at Level One. As a comparison, N/SVQ Level Two is at the level of five GCSEs at grades A to C. It includes tasks which are complex and non-routine and, in some areas, it may include supervisory competence.

Level Three is equal to a BTEC National Diploma or a portfolio of two A levels plus five GCSEs (at grades A to C).

Level Four shows competence in the performance of complex, technical specialised and professional work activities including those associated with design, planning and problem solving. Competence in supervision or management will be a requirement at this level. Level Four is equal to a BTEC Higher National Diploma and to the Diploma in Higher Education (Dip. HE).

In addition, there is an N/SVQ Level Five presently being developed which is likely to include the BA/BSc honours degree.

The government intends that the N/SVQ framework will cover all major occupations in British industry for Levels 1–4 by the end of 1992. One of the great attractions of N/SVQs will be their portability. They will, in fact, represent a logbook of work experience.

It should be noted that, in association with the NVQ system, the government is also proposing to introduce a system of general National Vocational Qualifications for students in schools and colleges. The GNVQ will receive a phased introduction in ninety educational institutions in the autumn of 1992 and will cover five areas: business; art and design; health and social care; leisure and tourism; and manufacturing. The GNVQ will be initiated at Levels Two and Three and will be based on a 'statement of attainment'. The

GNVQs will be comparable to academic qualification at A and AS level and also to occupational NVQs.

Some cynics think that the N/SVQ system will never work in Britain because, despite the rhetoric, skills will never acquire 'parity of esteem' with academic knowledge. If this is true, then the future looks ominous for the British economy. The fact is that we have to have a better trained workforce or our competitors will outstrip us. Academic qualifications are extremely valuable, but in Britain they have led to the denigration of practical skills. If N/SVQs help to counteract this, they will serve their purpose and fulfil an invaluable role.

Benefits
Only time will tell if the N/SVQs will be successful, but research does support the view that a workforce which has qualified in some way is more efficient because it is more self-confident and motivated than one which is not qualified.[1] In addition, the system has a built-in flexibility: employers will be able to update skill requirements as jobs come and go (the average British company only lasts five years), while employees will go on earning qualifications to adapt to new circumstances. Everyone agrees that there will be a sea change in the way training and personnel development will be carried out. Murray Butcher, a Divisional Manager at City and Guilds, has described it as a new culture, where 'training should become an integrated aspect of every workplace, as common as the telephone and as frequent as the weekly pay cheque.' (Quoted in: Arts and Entertainment Training Council, *Training Matters*, No. 3, December 1991.)

What about degrees versus N/SVQs: will it be worth going straight into higher education or will it be better to go into further education via the N/SVQ route? The question cannot really be put like that. Degrees will always be valuable to the individual, and, if they have a technical component, increasingly valuable for the employer. They also indicate a certain intellectual competence. What the N/SVQ system should mean, however, is that the vocational and technical route will no longer be looked down upon and the overwhelming prestige of the degree could very well diminish vis-à-vis a more practical training. Also, N/SVQs at Levels Four and Five will provide alternative routes into higher education for those who want it, and this will mean the end of the one-shot chance at higher education. There should be no need to compare other qualifications to the degree: they will all be part and parcel of the education and training provision. N/SVQs will be very beneficial for people who have missed out on education and training and who previously have never been able to qualify in anything, even though they are highly competent.

Industries which are strongly skill-based have always valued standards of competence. In the audiovisual industries, and especially film, union recognition was always more important than any theoretical knowledge because it was being able to do the job which mattered. It is now time to consider in detail the possible impact of the N/SVQs on the film, television and video industry.

Note

1. See Geoff Mason, S. J. Prais and Bart van Ark, *Vocational Education and Productivity in the Netherlands and Britain* (London: National Institute of Economic and Social Research, November 1990). This compared biscuit factories in the Netherlands and in Britain and showed that the British often had the more expensive and modern equipment but were less efficient and productive than the Dutch. In Britain the workforce was untrained, while the Dutch workers were trained and committed to the job. On the whole this meant that the Dutch factory functioned efficiently and that the Dutch could handle problems well, for example the equipment breaking down.

7

THE NVQs
What Will They Mean for the Audiovisual Industry?

The proposed revolution in training will probably have a major impact on film, television and video. As we have seen, at the end of the 1980s training was in crisis. The industry which relied on 'on-the-job' training suddenly found that the system was falling apart. In response to the emergency, in 1988 a consortium of interested parties commissioned the Institute of Manpower Studies to conduct a study called 'Skill Search'. This was a landmark because it analysed employment patterns, training and skill shortages throughout the industry. The 'Skill Search' report, which was published in January 1990, surveyed about 8,000 broadcasters and freelancers.

The Freelance Economy
'Skill Search' identified a clear trend towards freelance employment. It estimated that 50 per cent of the industry would be freelance by 1992. (In fact, this prediction has been outstripped: in 1992 more than 60 per cent are freelance.) There were many contributory factors: the government's insistence in the White Paper on Broadcasting (which paved the way for the Broadcasting Bill) on the 25 per cent quota, which led to the growth of the small independent sector; the recession, which made many employees in the film industry redundant; the tightening of financial belts at the BBC and ITV; and the effect of the franchise auction, which has led to increased unemployment in companies such as Thames. The trend can only accelerate over the next few years. Some of the new franchise holders for Channel 3 are not producer/broadcasters on the old ITV model but publisher/broadcasters like Channel Four. Carlton Communications, for example, which will take over from Thames in 1993, expects to be very lightly staffed and will commission programmes from independents relying on a freelance workforce.

All this has meant changes in the workplace, especially in television. The days of a 'career' in broadcasting, in the sense of a lifetime job, have gone forever for most people. Working in broadcasting is now similar to working in the film industry where, at certain levels, free-lancing was always much more common and where people were hired on contract for a specific short-term period. Freelancers have to adapt to a constantly changing market, and 'Skill Search' emphasised that workers of the future will have to be willing to retrain as often as the demands of the industry require.

The problem for employers in the new era is how they can evaluate a prospective employee's competence in the absence of any officially recognised training system. One of the exquisite ironies in the film industry at the present time is that employers who detested and resented union power are now actually asking prospective employees if they hold a union card because a union card is a guarantee of competence. In the new open market many employers have had their fingers burned through allowing inexperienced and inadequately trained (but cheap) staff to touch expensive equipment. The union system, while it was cumbersome, unfair and restrictive, did train people very well. N/SVQs acknowledge the importance of the on-the-job competence which was so much a part of the union philosophy.

A Plan of Action
In the face of the 'Skill Search' report, which stressed the shift to the freelance market and the problems with training, what was the industry to do? The obvious solution was to link into the government's new training system, the N/SVQs. In 1991, rather belatedly, an Industry Training Organisation (ITO) was formed. As we have said, the role of an ITO is to establish a training strategy for an industry.

Skillset – Industry Training Organisation
The ITO for the audiovisual industry is the Broadcast, Film and Video Industry Training Organisation (BFVITO), now called 'Skillset', and the groups involved in its foundation were the Advertising Film and Video Producers' Association (AFVPA), the BBC, Channel Four, the Federation of Entertainment Unions (FEU), ITV, the International Visual Communication Association (IVCA) and the Producers' Alliance for Cinema and Television (PACT): in other words, a power-house of industry employers. BFVITO's skillset role is to assist employers with decisions connected with the resourcing of training. One of its main activities is to liaise with the industry lead body.

Skillset – Industry Lead Body
'Skillset' was part of the industry's response to 'Skill Search'. The industry was prompted to begin the process of establishing N/SVQs,

and Skillset is the Lead Body serving this function for the film, television and video industry. It was set up before the Skillset Industry Training Organisation (BFVITO), in the summer of 1990, and is currently concerned with an industry-wide project to create the necessary framework for the government's new training qualification scheme. It is supported by representatives from each of the employer groups: BBC, ITV, Channel Four, AFVPA, TPA, IPPA, IVCA, the BFI and the trades unions (BECTU, NUJ and EETPU).

One of Skillset's first acts, together with TEED (see above, Chapter 6, p. 64), was to undertake research to establish occupational standards for the film, video, television and radio sectors. The result was a so-called 'mapping' report of jobs, an essential first step in the process towards an N/SVQ system. It established a functional definition of the industry: *to inform, educate and entertain people by capturing images and sound and delivering them at a distance.*

Mapping the Industry

The report mapped the whole industry: broadcasting employees, independent companies and facility houses, freelancers, specialist sectors (both commercial and corporate), radio and film processing. With the N/SVQs in view it took on the task of identifying the range of occupational roles, the broad functional groups and the existing occupational standards and current qualifications appropriate to each sector. In other words, it was the beginning of an attempt to systematise job descriptions in the industry. The research focused on 'sector specific' occupations and skills in areas such as: camera, lighting, sound, production, post-production, engineering, make-up, wardrobe and television journalism. The study included interviews with UK terrestrial broadcast companies, and a postal survey of 1,800 independent production companies, 3,000 broadcasting employees, 2,900 freelancers and 600 television journalists!

800 Job Titles

Employers, trades unions and trade and professional associations were asked to submit a complete list of job titles and staffing structures or membership grades. The result, from different parts of the industry, was a list of over 800 different job titles! Obviously some sort of rationalisation was in order and a working party was set up to review jobs and designate common functions based on knowledge of job content. The aim was to identify jobs which might be the same but which had different titles in different sectors. The exercise showed that the various sectors of the industry were moving closer together and that it made sense to integrate both job titles and the various terms used in production.

Skillset and N/SVQs

Rationalisation was also obviously beneficial for any link with the new government training qualification framework. In April 1991 the consultants Transcend Technology were appointed to assist Skillset with the development of industry standards, specifically in relation to N/SVQs. Working groups consisting of representatives of employers and employees, the corporate sector, unions, radio, film, television and video were established to analyse job descriptions and to set up standards of competence. The groups represent:

Art and Design	Make-up and Hair Dressing
Camera	Post-production
Costume	Production Operations
Direction	Projection
Graphics and Animation	Research
Journalism and Writing	Set Crafts
Laboratory	Sound
Lighting	Special Effects

A Formal Training Framework by 1993

Management and engineering jobs are also part of the industry, but the N/SVQs in these areas are emerging from the management and engineering industrial sectors, of which broadcast, video and film engineering and management will be sub-categories. In July 1991 the working groups were briefed and trained for each sector. The draft standards were published and distributed for consultation with the industry and other interested agencies in May 1992. In the summer and autumn of 1992 it is expected that assessment methods and delivery systems will have been developed and by the end of the year pilot standards and assessment methods will then be in existence. Skillset Vocational Qualifications will then be submitted to the National Council for Vocational Qualification and to SCOTVEC for modification. The industry will then for the first time have a formal training framework to implement which will be comprehensible, accessible and part of the national system. It will mean that those who enter the industry as freelancers, perhaps through a small video company, will, if they can do a job, be able to be assessed by the industry for an N/SVQ or a credit towards an N/SVQ. All bodies awarding vocational qualifications will have to make sure that these are in line with the occupational standards of the industry. Skillset has defined the fundamental purpose of the industry as being: *to create, provide and disseminate radio, film, television, video and electronic productions for general and specific audiences.*

Arts and Entertainment Training Council
The Arts and Entertainment Training Council (AETC) is the Industry Lead Body for setting standards of competence for artists and performers and it is slightly ahead of Skillset in this task. Basically Skillset is to decide upon the standards of competence (that is to say, the qualifications) for awarding N/SVQs for all jobs which go on *behind* the camera, while the AETC is concerned with standards for those who work *in front of* the camera. The detailed research on standards development for the AETC is being undertaken by five 'sector committees' representing: music; performing arts, including dance, opera, mime, circus, and variety; creative writing; visual arts; management and administration.

The key purpose of the arts and entertainment industry as defined by the AETC is: *to create, present and promote artistic activities in order to entertain, stimulate and educate.* Among other industries which have Lead Bodies relevant to film, television and video are:

DESIGN – Industry Lead Body for Design.
TECHNICAL – Arts and Entertainment Technical Training Initiative (AETTI).

Academic qualifications were never significant in the film or video industry: it was the track record which was important. There were rarely any professional entry requirements except to be a member of a union. The N/SVQs, if they succeed, will suit the temperament of the industry very well because of their on-the-job orientation, but they are in an experimental stage and it is not known how successful they will be. However, since even television, which was more oriented towards very high academic standards for entrance, has become more accessible in recent years (as the independents have become a more significant proportion of the industry), it is likely that the technical/vocational bias of the N/SVQs will make them more acceptable.

The problem is that we are in the middle of a period of transition. Higher and further education are converging, but have not blended yet and it will probably take some time for the N/SVQs to achieve the parity of esteem which the government wants. It is impossible to predict the extent to which the vocational content of existing courses will match the requirements of the industry-dictated N/SVQs. The only advice that can be offered to prospective employees at this point

76

is to be aware of what is happening in the industry and to become familiar with the standards of competence as these are issued. Also take encouragement from the fact that some form of cross-industry standards of competence are being established.

A Note of Caution

There is scepticism in the industry about the government's seriousness regarding training and the effectiveness of the N/SVQs. Many people do not believe it will be possible to structure a universal training system across the whole industrial sector. They point out that the industry has survived very well without paper qualifications and question what good they will serve. Critics also insist that in any case the audiovisual industry is not an industry like any other. They point out that N/SVQs were first developed for industrial sectors such as construction, engineering, hotel management and catering (where N/SVQs are well-advanced). While many talented people (and old-timers) accept that it may be possible to set standards of competence for technical skills, they are almost insulted by the idea that it is possible to dissect any of the artistic, creative jobs in the industry and make up a training programme which will lead on to an assessment of competence. Creating a feature film or video or television programme, they say, is not a measurable activity.

There is some truth in this, but we should be wary of the word 'creativity', since it can be used in many senses. When creativity means producing something which is clearly new and unique, which does not fit within the bounds of what society expects, then vocational training has no place. Pure creativity, in the sense of a totally new way of looking at the world, is not open to assessment.

The production of a film, video or television programme, however, while it is a creative activity, is not totally new and unique every time: much of the production process is routine. There is certainly a creative aspect in many of the routine jobs because they can be done badly or well and this will affect the final product and its creative soul. Although it may be difficult to specify the criteria to make a judgment of good or bad quality, it is nonetheless possible. Some of these criteria can be set down and regarded as preconditions of competence.

Initially there was considerable doubt regarding the effectiveness of the Arts and Entertainment Training Council in making provision for the N/SVQ framework, on more or less the same grounds as those applying to Skillset. This is now more muted as the AETC workshops have produced functional analyses of the various jobs in the industry. Even critics have admitted that the whole process of job and industry analysis has been a useful exercise. A recent edition of *Training*

Matters (an information journal published by the AETC) quotes the actor Alfred Molina: 'There's nothing mystical about the acting process. It's technical. It's like making a meal. You've got the ingredients: you just have to put them together.' (No. 4, March 1992)

Other criticism of NVQs has centred on the fact that possession of the necessary skills to do a job will not necessarily guarantee employment in the industry, that there are other intangibles which people in the industry value. It is argued that working on a film is not at all like a routine factory job: the hours of work are irregular and circumstances are often uncomfortable, so qualities of character are important. Qualities mentioned include persistence, a capacity for hard work, calmness under stress, the ability to ride the ups and downs of the industry, imagination, the ability to take rejection. How, it is asked, can the N/SVQs possibly take account of this and other abstract qualities such as flair?

The answer is of course that they can't. But, leaving aside the rather patronising assumption that factory workers need no special qualities, not everyone in film, television and video is exceptional (even if some think so). For the vast majority of employees, qualifications can provide self-esteem, confidence and recognition, all of which redound to the benefit of the industry. N/SVQs won't solve every problem in any industry, but they will solve some. Of course possession of N/SVQs will not ensure a job: that depends on all sorts of factors (personality, the general employment picture, luck). It was ever so, but at least in the future would-be employees will have an industry standard for assessing the ability to do a job.

From another point of view, assessing competence in the workplace is probably less radical in the audiovisual industry than anywhere else, since it has been always been an aspect of the way the industry functions. Film certainly only ever cared about performance (and union membership) and the performance side of the job has always been very exposed to public assessment. While N/SVQs might not be perfectly adapted to the entertainment industry, they can provide a framework. For an industry with a training vacuum and only piecemeal provision available, sometimes of a very inferior kind, this could have a revolutionary effect.

Summing Up
Chapters Five and Six have looked at the way education and training are changing in Britain. Traditionally, academic qualifications have been at a very high premium in our society. In the year 2000, in a world full of technology, a purely academic qualification will probably be less highly valued. There will be more emphasis on understanding

technology and an ability to do the job, and most jobs will require skill and technical competence. If the N/SVQs work, people will not finish their education at sixteen or twenty-one, but will be part of a society which is continuously learning. Retraining will become a constant fact of life and the N/SVQ system will help this along. This is not an option but a necessity: as the workplace and the technology change constantly and rapidly, a system or a person that fails to adapt will come to grief.

The traditional academic route, the degree course, is changing to meet this situation. Higher education is incorporating training and expanding its numbers. 'Enterprise in Higher Education' is providing students with a taste of work experience. Further education is being simplified and vocational training will take place within the framework of the workplace. This whole process has begun and will continue. At the present time there are no N/SVQs in place for the entertainment industry, either in front of or behind the camera. By 1993, however, most of the standards of competence should be known and colleges which deliver training will have to work closely with employers. Assessment will be carried out in the workplace or through realistic simulations. Young people wishing to enter the industry will have to investigate more closely the N/SVQs and understand the implications of the new system. Old hands may find that N/SVQs provide a stimulus for retraining in a world where jobs come and go.

All this lies in the future, albeit the very near future. In the meantime, what are would-be recruits to the industry to do? There are currently a few training schemes which accept people without qualifications. These include Jobfit, CYFLE, the Scottish Film Technicians Training Scheme and a course run by the North East Media Training Centre.

Jobfit

This is a basic training scheme for production and technical grades of the film and video industry. Supported by Channel Four, Thames Television and the unions, Jobfit was founded in 1985 and was initially only concerned with film training. However, the demand in the industry for technicians skilled in both film and videotape has recently led to the establishment of a pilot scheme in videotape training. This is supported by independent companies, IVCA (the professional association for visual communication users) and TEED. Jobfit hopes to integrate the video scheme with the film training in the near future.

Jobfit is a UK-wide freelance training scheme for new entrants. The course takes two years and involves college-based training and work placements. Since its beginning about eighty or more students have passed through the course, some as young as eighteen and others in their thirties, though most are in their early twenties. One of the great strengths of Jobfit, unlike many training schemes available, is that it provides trainees with a broad understanding of the industry (the principle which BBC training always stressed for television), which other more narrow training courses do not supply. Moreover Jobfit has carried out a vigorous equal opportunities policy which has meant that it has trained a large number of women and people from ethnic minorities. Jobfit advertises nationally in the press for applicants and anyone can apply. Competition is inevitably fierce, so it is as well to take note of advice later in this book about how to prepare and apply for such courses and jobs. After their Jobfit course is finished, trainees join the freelance market in junior technician grades, and at least eighty per cent have found jobs. It is the intention of Jobfit to work closely with the N/SVQ system.

CYFLE
CYFLE was set up to meet the needs for Welsh-speaking technicians in the freelance film and television sector in Wales. Again training is for a two-year period during which trainees are attached to various productions. Trainees have had attachments in camera, sound, editing, floor management, make-up, wardrobe and design, direction and production assistance. The scheme is sponsored by S4C, TAC (Welsh Independent Producers) and the trades unions.

Scottish Film Technicians Training Scheme
The Scottish Film Technicians Training Scheme is organised by the Scottish Film Training Trust, which was launched in 1982. At that time it was the only registered charity in the UK devoted solely to training people in the professional skills of film and video production. The Scheme takes on about five trainees a year who go on various attachments during which they receive on-the-job training. Ninety-five per cent of the Trust's trainees are currently working in the industry. The scheme has been under review for three years and, at the beginning of 1993, will be established on a more secure basis with the length of training time extended from one year to eighteen months.

North East Media Training Centre (NEMTC)
This Centre is based in Gateshead in Tyne and Wear, and provides a two-level, eighteen-month course specifically designed to produce people who are capable of making an immediate contribution to the television and film industry. The course comprises both hands-on

80

practical work and theoretical study. Components include: production management, direction, studio and location work, sound, camera and editing. There are currently thirty-five people on the course, which is directed towards people in the North East but not exclusively confined to them.

Retraining
For people seeking retraining there are short course schemes available such as the National Short Course Training Programme organised by the National Film and Television School and courses provided by Ravensbourne College in Kent (Ravensbourne has considerable experience working with ITV employees). Trade organisations, such as the British Kinematograph Sound and Television Society (BKSTS), also offer technical courses, as does the Broadcasting, Entertainment, Cinematograph and Theatre Union (BECTU), the Royal Television Society and the Producers' Alliance of Cinema and Television (PACT). One of the most interesting initiatives, however, is the Freelance Training Scheme established in October 1991 by ITV and Channel Four. The fund consists of £300,000, which will be used to subsidise the cost of new courses as well as the methods of training, for example open learning. (The BBC is not putting money into this scheme, although it backs Skillset, because, according to newspaper reports, it is already putting millions of pounds into its own training schemes.) Given the scale of the problem vis-à-vis training, these excellent courses and the Freelance Training Scheme are but drops in the ocean. Contact names, addresses and telephone numbers can be found at the end of this book.

A Word of Advice
At the present time, with the N/SVQ vocational system still not in place and with the industry in recession, the would-be candidate for employment faces an even more difficult situation than usual. The best course of action of all, if you really have talent, is to get hold of a video camera and make your own tape, or join a community video workshop which can provide you with hands-on experience. There are many independent workshops which provide experience and training.[2] The great advantage which media students graduating from college possess over other candidates is that they learn how to make programmes or mini-films which they can then hawk around to possible employers. This is still one of the best methods of getting into the industry. Camp on the doorstep, put your foot in the door, do anything to get someone to look at your work. If you are talented, someone in the smaller companies may take you on. Don't expect to

be made a director straightaway or to be paid well: many companies are run on a shoestring. Say you'll do anything – and mean it.

If you have the right temperament, a freelance career in film, video and television can be interesting and exciting. If you are someone who wants to know exactly what you will be doing in the next ten years, then this is not the right industry for you. Probably few other industries will suit you either, since change is going to be the one sure thing that, in the future, we will all encounter in our working lives.

Notes

1. Final report by Carol Varlaam, Patricia Leighton, Richard Pearson and Scott Blum, 'Skill Search': Television Film and Video Industry Employment Patterns and Training Needs (Brighton: Institute of Manpower Studies, Sussex University, January 1990).
2. For information on all training courses in video and film, see Directions, A Guide to Practical Training Courses in Video and Film, published biannually by the British Film Institute's Planning Unit.

PART THREE
PRODUCTION: WHAT IT'S ALL ABOUT

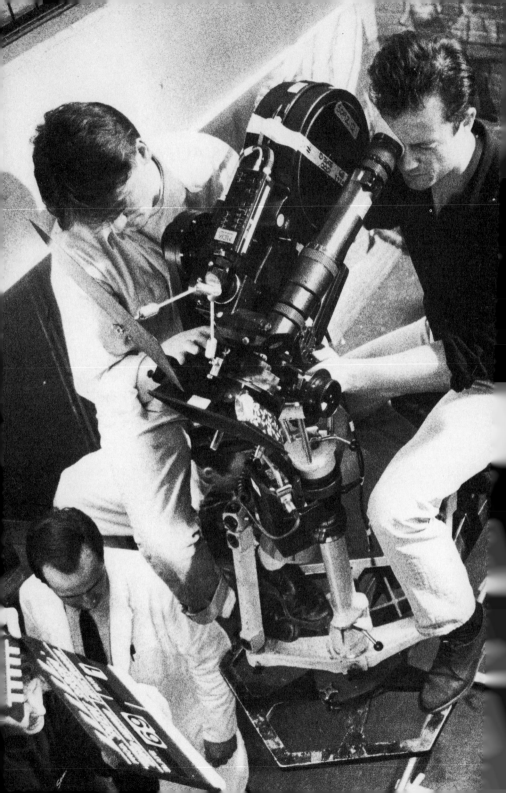

8

SO YOU WANT TO BE IN FILM OR TELEVISION?

The most important question of all is why do you want to enter the industry. You should try to answer it as a very first priority. If you wanted to be a doctor, you would probably be able to explain yourself easily, perhaps something along the lines of wanting to help suffering humanity. Wanting to be in film or television is altogether different. Some of the reasons you may be ashamed of: they may seem trivial. You want to enter the industry because it looks glamorous or fun and you meet famous people? Perhaps it's the excitement: you see yourself as a television journalist reporting from a war front? Or you want to earn lots of money and have heard what newsreaders and Terry Wogan get? Perhaps you think it looks easy to appear on camera — after all you only have to look good and read the Autocue. You may like the idea of being recognised: if you do, then obviously you want to work in front of the camera, because no one recognises producers, directors or editors on the street (even though they are the most important people of all).

It is important to come to an understanding of yourself and your motivation. Film and television are entertainment media. Our most delightful fantasies are wrapped up in the images they convey. Imagination is an essential part of human life and is probably the most vital element in all film and programme-making, so you have one appropriate talent. But, as you spin your dreams about your future, try to separate reality from fantasy. There is no shame in wanting to be a star — stars have usually wanted to be stars — but the odds on success are poor. Be realistic about the chance of success. It's easier for a man than a woman and a man has a longer shelf-life in the industry. (How many women over sixty read the news? Equal opportunities still has to hit the screens.) We all build castles in the air and many of us nurture the old Hollywood dream of 'being discovered'. In the meantime, build yourself something on solid ground to be going on with while you wait. If you want to be a star you are not being realistic, but then the stars were not realistic either.

Character
Success in the entertainment industry is as much to do with temperament and character as talent and good looks. Everyone will tell you this and they tell you because it's true. If you want to work in film or television you are entering a dynamic, high-pressure, roller-coaster world. When you *are* working, the hours could be long, the circumstances uncomfortable, job security minimal and the pay, at the lower levels, abysmal. This is increasingly the industry of the freelancer and you will need patience, persistence and, most important of all, a very thick skin.

As profit margins get lower and financial risks greater, employers are increasingly hard-nosed. If you are not up to scratch, little mercy will be shown. You will need to be able to take humiliation and criticism and to bounce back. Some directors can be very bad-tempered when something goes wrong at an expensive location or on the studio floor. Big money is involved, which puts everyone on edge. This is a temperamental industry and the emotional temperature in a television control room can get very high indeed. Can you stand being yelled at totally unjustifiably? Directors don't want explanations: they want results. *Resilience is essential for survival.*

Do you enjoy working with a team or are you a loner? Producing a film or a television programme is a group activity. This does not mean that there is no place for the individualist and the introvert in the industry, but you have to know your own character to know where you are best suited. It is easy to recognise our strengths, to know in what ways we are talented or gifted; it is more difficult to know our weaknesses and faults, yet these can be just as crucial.

Creativity
Perhaps you are not quite sure why you want to be involved in the industry. Perhaps you can't really say what it is which attracts you, but you know it is there and it drives you on. It may be that it is almost too profound for you to acknowledge. You may have a view of society which you want to convey and feel that you could express it best through the medium of film, video or television. Somewhere inside you is a gut feeling that you have your own particular voice which seeks expression and that the visual image rather than writing is a more natural medium for you. You feel that working in the industry will provide you with the opportunity to express what you have to say. This desire to communicate one's own particular vision is an essential

86

ingredient of all creativity. *Make its acquaintance.* Try to find out, and articulate, why working with film or video attracts you. Try to write it down on paper. (This exercise will stand you in good stead when you go for an interview.)

There is a multiplicity of reasons why people want to enter this industry. Probably the only inappropriate reason is looking for a secure job with a pension. If that attracts you, look elsewhere. There was only ever limited room for that in the past and now there is no room at all. This is an extremely high-risk industry and it is likely to become more so. Unions warn of the dangers inherent in what they call the 'casualisation' of the industry, both in terms of employee safeguards and in work quality, and they are right. Be warned, but, if you want to accept the risks, press on.

Preparation

You want to enter a workforce where the competition is especially fierce and where your fellow employees are often very talented, highly ambitious and driven. It is no use vaguely thinking it would be nice to do 'something interesting' in films and hope that this will see you through. Competition even for courses to begin to learn about the industry is intense. Academic and technical courses at every college and every university receive a deluge of applicants every year. If you get as far as an interview you've overcome the first hurdle, but you will never get any further unless you are well briefed. Before you even step into the interview room, be sure you know how films and programmes are made. You can be certain your fellow interviewees will know.

People who work in film are especially passionate about their work: not to say obsessive and fanatical. They live, breathe and eat the world of the cinema. Most of them have been like that since they were young. Would-be film-makers today are mad about film or video, both watching it and making it. They watch films all the time and most of them already know about camera angles and technique. Outsiders often say that film people are 'different': they say it because it's true. Don't for a moment hope that you can turn up for an interview for a course or a job relating to film airily expecting the interviewer to tell you what the industry is about. You will be expected to know. Not everything, but something.

The best-known British directors at the present time include Ridley Scott, who made *Thelma and Louise*, Alan Parker (*The Commitments*), Roland Joffé (*City of Joy*), Nicolas Roeg, who is currently making a film called *Chicago Loop*, Ken Loach, who made *Riff-Raff*, which won the main prize at the 1991 European film awards, Peter

Greenaway (*Prospero's Books*), Derek Jarman (*Edward II*), Terence Davies (*The Long Day Closes*). If you want to get into any British film school you should know all the work of these directors, both past and present. This brings us to the second major question in this chapter.

What Do You Know About the Industry and How it Functions?
The first part of this book presented an analysis of the present state of film, television and video. Many school and college leavers will try to skip this as the hard bit. In fact, if you want to get anywhere today, you would be well-advised to become acquainted with the major issues. The first piece of advice is to read the section on the industry trends and then get hold of the media pages in certain newspapers and copies of the trade journals listed in the Appendix. Keep up to date. Know what is going on.

After that, get down to practical details. Television especially is all-pervasive in this society, but do you know anything about how a programme is made? Do you know how a film is made? Do you ever imagine what is going on behind the camera? Do you ever think about the preparation which making a film or television programme entails? When you are sitting in the cinema engrossed by a film, or are watching a television programme at home, do you understand how they have been put together? How much do you know about cuts and editing? Do you, in fact, know what an editor actually does? Do you appreciate the difference between film and video? In the next chapters, this book will tell you something about all these matters. Use it as a starting-point and then seek out more information.

The Constructed World of Film, Television and Video
Films, commercials, television programmes, pop videos, whether fictional or factual, are all 'constructed'. There are very few occasions where a camera records a variety of scenes and the pictures are then transmitted or projected without any change.

To understand the significance of construction in the moving picture industry, consider for a moment the 'unconstructed' family video. This has a very limited audience because it is invariably numbingly boring, except of course to the participants. The audience of a home-made video are usually the people recorded by the camera. They are waiting to see themselves: not a vision with universal appeal. The home video rarely has a theme, there is no story-line and no argument. No one has planned the shots or organised the participants. If feature films, television programmes or commercial videos were made on the same principle there would be no industry since no one would ever watch them. Off-the-cuff shooting rarely produces a watchable result: it is in the 'crafting' of a film or programme that the art of picture-making resides. It is the combination of many highly talented (and well-trained) people working together to construct a production which makes it 'professional'. A multiplicity of finely honed techniques and skills in numerous craft and design areas lies behind the professional entertainment which films, programmes and videos provide.

It is this ability to communicate effectively, so that the audience is seduced into continuing to watch of their own free will, which is what the *communication* industry is all about. The audience wants to watch a feature film because the producer/director has orchestrated a group of people doing many different jobs to produce images and dialogue which engage its interest. The simple images are the result of a complex process called *production*.

The way a film or a television programme is constructed depends on the people involved making certain choices. They are guided by what they believe makes a good film or programme; this belief is based on their own ideas and perceptions and on experience, since they are inevitably influenced by the knowledge of what has worked well before.

People working in the various production areas have an individual viewpoint arising from their personal expertise. The camera operator, in a film or on a news shoot, may choose to take certain pictures rather than others (in television studios, however, camera operators are strictly controlled by directors); the scriptwriter selects specific words to describe a situation; the editor has arranged the pictures in a certain order and has thrown away those frames which do not accord with his or her idea of 'good' editing. Other camera operators, scriptwriters or editors would have made other choices and the end result would consequently have been very different. If the funds were available, it would be an interesting experiment to provide two experienced directors and crews with the same story-line and then give them a free hand. Two very different films or programmes would probably result. In short, choice and decision-making by a wide range of professionals lie behind the creative process of film and programme production.

In the following chapters we will look at the various jobs in the industry and see what the people in them actually do. You can then decide where your own interests and talents lie. In the past the boundaries between job areas in the industry were clearly defined because the technology was unwieldy and complex. Each element in the production process was the responsibility of one person who was an expert in that particular job. Union power ensured that no one who was unskilled or inexperienced ever put their hands on the equipment. Today many jobs in the industry are still very highly skilled (some of the new computerised equipment needs special technical staff who require constant retraining as the equipment becomes more sophisticated). But the widespread use of video which, in comparison to film, is cheap to use and in some ways simpler to handle, together with the reduction of union power, has led, as explained earlier, to multi-skilling (referred to more pejoratively as de-skilling or casualisation).

Multi-skilling simply means that the same person can do several different jobs. This has revolutionised the way the industry works, especially in video production companies. Huge crews are a thing of the past, except in big-budget feature films and some very expensive television dramas (which are increasingly less feasible financially). The boundaries between jobs have become blurred, as have the divisions between the various sectors of the industry, because video now produces a high-quality image.

Ten years ago any analysis of the production process would be dealt with under two separate headings – film and television – (the independent video industry being hardly mentioned since it scarcely existed). That division accurately reflected reality because the two sectors were very different, both in their working practices and in their culture. This is no longer so strictly the case and people now work in all sectors and even sometimes in different job areas.

For these reasons it is simpler (and more relevant) to view film, television and video production together as variations of essentially one overall process. Differences in methods which still exist between the various sectors are often the result of the dictates of the recording medium, whether film or electronic video. There are, however, specific traditions and practices (especially in the film sector), and these will be noted as we go along.

Case Histories

JOHN MORRIS

John Morris is twenty-eight and a freelance editor. Eventually he wants to move into direction.

Ever since I was at school I wanted to be involved in films and in television programmes. I went to the pictures three or four times a week and I watched loads of television. I even read books about directors, I was so keen. I asked the teachers at school about how you got into films, but the careers teacher knew nothing about it. Because of my working-class background, and because I come from the North East, they had nothing to suggest but going into a factory, a shop or on to university! I didn't want to go to university, so I left school and I did A levels at an FE college. The college had no film or television courses to offer, so I couldn't do anything useful.

But I was playing in bands all the time. I had a lot of odd jobs with bands, because I knew about sound recording. While I was doing this, I made pop videos by myself, some on Super 8 and some on VHS. I did everything myself. I was director, camera operator, sound editor. Things were very bad in Newcastle at that time, lots of unemployment, so the government put small amounts of cash into a number of community arts projects and, as a result, there were a few editing suites around with rather scrappy facilities. But you could practise on the equipment, which was very basic. I went on training myself as much as possible. I worked with bands, sometimes I had to go on the dole, sometimes I earned a little money, but all the time I was still really keen to get into real film work and I kept going.

Then in 1986 the North East Media Training Centre began. It was aimed at the unemployed and the working class. It was great, right on my doorstep, in my own home town. I couldn't believe it! I went along to see them with the bits and pieces I'd done and I was accepted on a 12-week introduction course, four weeks doing everything and eight weeks making a 10-minute film. I directed and edited a science fiction film which worked reasonably well. Then I managed to get on the NEMTC two-year course, which paid £50 a week in term time.

In the first year again we did everything. There were thirty trainees and we swapped all the different production jobs between us. In the second year I specialised in editing and a film I worked on, *The Waitresses*, won the Royal Television Society's best student film. Northern Arts and Channel Four both liked it.

When I finished the course I was offered two jobs. One was in a facilities house in Newcastle. I was taken on as junior editor for a year and I worked on commercials, documentaries and corporate videos. It was very machine-based and I like the creative side, so, after a year, I quit and set up as a freelance editor. I've managed to stay in work ever since, except for a three-week period. I've worked on corporate videos, union videos and recently I worked on *Little Richard Wrecked My Marriage* for Channel Four.

I love my job, although there is a lot of stress. I can't imagine doing anything else. I get so much real pleasure out of it. In my first job I was basically a runner and worked seventy hours a week for very little money, but it got me here.

What I really want to do is direct. In fact I want to write and direct. I'm working on two scripts at the present time. My ambition is to direct a feature film. Whether that ever happens remains to be seen. This summer I am making two low-budget 16mm films to build up my show reel and gain experience. I think the NEMTC course is great because it is not for white, male, Oxbridge-educated people, it is for people like me. I'd like to see more courses like that.

TONY TACKABERRY

Tony Tackaberry is twenty-three. He is presently working as a researcher for Hawkshead, an independent production company based in London. He began as a runner.

I left school at 18 after taking three A levels in politics, ancient history and history, none of which bears any relation to the television industry! I only passed one of them, so I went away for a year without really knowing what I wanted to do. When I came back, I sat around for two months still not really knowing what to do with myself, but I had one or two friends and relatives working in the industry and I had always been interested in film, so I decided to give it a try.

A friend photocopied some of the addresses in the industry's directories for me and I rang a lot of production companies and asked what they specialised in, and then I wrote a letter to each company which used the very basic information I had found out on the phone. My CV was very thin, so I felt that everything depended on the letter. Funnily enough, although I wrote about seventy letters, I actually got my job because a friend saw that Hawkshead was advertising for a runner's position in the ACTT's list of vacancies, so I sent my CV and a letter and was interviewed by the Production Manager and an administrative person. Then a week later, I was interviewed by Carol Haslam, who is a Managing Director of Hawkshead, and when I got home that night there was a message that they were offering me the job. There were about twenty-four applicants and I had been on a shortlist of four, so I was really surprised and pleased.

A runner does everything and anything. I made coffee and tea, I dropped film off at facility houses in Soho, answered the telephone, went out and bought things which were needed, moved desks and chairs, looked after the tape library. A runner should never say 'no' to anything. I always tried to do what I could without being too pushy and, as time went on, I got to do more and more things.

It's not an easy job being a runner. In fact in some ways it's a very tough job indeed, but if you can carry it off good-humouredly that's what they are looking for ... I suppose. You have to have the temperament and you have to try not to tread on anyone's toes!

Anyway, then Carol asked me to do some small bits of research for her and eventually I was given a job as assistant researcher on a series of ten-minute education programmes on careers for the BBC. I had to help find the people for the programme. The aim was to give the viewers a 'taster' of what the various professions and jobs were like. What is it like to be a construction worker, for example? They were really nice little films with good graphics and I really enjoyed doing them. I was really busy because I was still working as a runner at this time.

After that I worked as a researcher on pilots for a quiz show and then worked on two programmes which Hawkshead did for Channel Four in the *Without Walls* series. It was a French/English co-production about French and English intellectual life. The French team moved over here and the English team worked in France, so I worked with the French. The programmes were called *Tunnel Vision* and they were a great experience. The French were really laid back and it was great fun.

Then it was back to working on another quiz programme. This time it was a sports quiz and I had to find thirty-six sports journalists willing to appear on television. It was pretty nerve-racking because, as a group, sports writers on newspapers are not overenthusiastic about television. One team, which shall be nameless, pulled out at the last minute and the programme had to be rescheduled. That sort of thing can make you panic!

Last summer (1991) I worked on two Hawkshead programmes. One was a *South Bank Show* on Douglas Adams and the other was a drama starring Steven Berkoff called *Tell Tale Heart*. I was really pleased with the way those programmes went and I was given an assistant director credit, which was very exciting. At the present time I am working on a series about environmental issues leading up to the Earth summit in June.

I enjoy my job. In fact I am surprised how much I enjoy it, probably because of the immense variety of subjects I get to work on. In fact I am a bit wary about the industry taking me over! What I would really like to do would be directing, but it's difficult when you are like me, without any background training. I do get frustrated because of the lack of any coherent training framework in the industry. Hawkshead are very good and you can learn on the job to a certain extent, but there is a limited amount that you can learn that way and a small production company does not have the resources for extensive training. I really feel the need for some formal training. It's a real problem for the industry as a whole, at least that's how I see it.

9

THE STAGES OF PRODUCTION

Producing a film, television programme or video involves several distinct stages which are usually referred to as pre-production, production and post-production.

Pre-production

Pre-production basically means planning. It is the stage when all the components are organised and assembled in preparation for the actual filming or recording. The first stage in any production is the idea. A feature film may start with a producer's idea for a story. The producer may have purchased the rights to a novel or a play (which in the film world is called the 'property'). The idea for a television commercial may be thrashed out in the advertising agency which has received the commission to publicise a product. In television a scriptwriter might come up with a 'situation' for a situation comedy.

Once the idea has been thought of, however, it must have some physical reality: this usually means it has to be committed to paper. The film producer might ask a scriptwriter to come up with a 'treatment' or outline of how the idea might be made into a movie, and from that a script may be developed. In television a 'commissioning' editor might like the scriptwriter's comedy idea and commission a script. (Or it may be that the editor has come up with the original idea and then commissioned a writer to script it.)

Wherever an idea comes from, however, what it needs to be realised is money. After the brainwave must come the finance. Getting 'backing' has always been a nightmare for British film-makers. Often the only available backing is American, which leads to the question of how British a British film made with American money actually is. 'He who pays the piper calls the tune' has been too often the unfortunate experience of many British film producers – a situation which has also disheartened many young idealistic film-makers. Very few British investors have been prepared to back the home-grown feature film, which has always been thought a high risk. Neither has the government ever offered much support. As a result, British cinema has always faced an uphill battle, which explains why the support of Channel Four for the feature film industry was such a surprising development and such a big boost (see Chapter Two). However, one positive development in recent years which has offered hope to European film-makers is the increasing interest in 'co-production', where the money is raised in several countries and the film is given a more international flavour. Co-production, however, is also criticised in some quarters because the products of such co-operation have tended to be rather bland and 'unlocated' in a region or country.

In contrast to film producers, however, those in television were a protected species. In the old days producers in the BBC and ITV who had a brainwave for a programme only needed to secure managerial support. They did not have to hustle for money in the market-place. If a programme idea was 'accepted', producers were given a budget, with a principal obligation to produce the best programme they could while staying within budget. If behind the scenes, in managers' offices up and down the country, there were rows about budgetary shortages, nevertheless, on the whole, television producers did not have to dirty their hands by grubbing for money in the outside world: that was a managerial responsibility. The 1980s, however, have changed all that, and today even BBC producers have to face the cold breeze of market reality.

In practical terms what this means is that, in the future, 'the raising of the money' will be the key phase in the production process in television as well as film. This has already provoked a painful period of adjustment in television. In theory, the film industry, because of its own historical experience, should have no such adjustment to make, but it is a fact of life that young and talented film-makers in this country still find it difficult to trim their sails to economic and political reality.

As this book goes to press, Britain is in the grip of a major recession. It is extremely unlikely that, in such circumstances, the cultural arm of the government will give anything more concrete to encourage a more positive climate for growth and creativity. Cynical observers, in fact, doubt the government's long-term commitment to a serious cultural policy on film at all. If you want to work in this industry, therefore, be it film or television, the best advice is to make sure you know about money, how to get it, how to earn it, how to look after it and how to increase it.

The American film industry has always worked on the money principle. The British film, television and video industry will have to do the same, massively handicapped by the overwhelming odds in favour of the Americans. In practical terms, people who want to make films or good television programmes will have to learn how to talk to bankers and accountants. This will mean playing their game. It may mean wearing a suit rather than dungarees for a money interview (most bankers are highly conservative people and alternative styles of dress can frighten them off). Film and television are industries in the throes of a major transition. Those who have business acumen and a nose for money, in addition to creative talent, are the ones who will succeed. In Chapter Five, which looked at education, we pointed out the importance of financial training: accountants and business graduates should find no shortage of jobs in the industry.

Once the money for production is secured, the people, 'the talent', can be assembled and hired. The size of the crew will depend on the type of production. A feature film usually means a mass of people and so does a television drama production, whether it is shot on film or tape. Most television programmes, however, as well as pop videos, corporate and training videos, will need far less. Many independent production companies will try to get by on as little as possible. Most of the people working on a production will be freelance, hired on short-term contracts for as long as the production takes. During pre-production, once the crew is hired, locations (real places for outdoor and indoor scenes) are arranged and a budget and shooting schedule prepared.

On feature films the people hired will include directors, casting directors, performers, scenic and graphic designers, camera operators, make-up artists, production managers, directors of photography, property buyers, location managers, property masters, gaffers, the first, second and third assistant directors, script supervisors, boom operators, art directors, set directors and so on. All these jobs, with the exception of performers, are behind-the-camera jobs, and setting the standards of competence for these parts of the industry is the responsibility of Skillset (see Chapter Seven). Over the next few years it is expected that every one of these jobs will have N/SVQ qualifications attached to them.

Some of the jobs listed above are only found in the film world, or they are called something different in television. Part of the responsibilities of people participating in the NVQ workshops of Skillset, therefore, is to bring some order into job descriptions. When the film and television industries were more separated, as they were until the late 1980s, the fact that similar jobs had different titles was acceptable. As the industries draw closer together this can no longer be maintained, especially since, as we have seen, many freelancers will be working across all three sectors. It will simply be too confusing if they have to change job titles for what is essentially the same work.

Traditionalists hate to see some of the old job titles go, especially in the film industry, but the establishment of the NVQs will inevitably encourage the streamlining process since qualifications will be awarded by job function. It will be sad to see old names wither away, as the NVQ nomenclature becomes accepted, but it is the inevitable result of change and casualisation. The tight *esprit de corps* of the traditional film crew has been eroded and, although this may be regretted, it is unlikely that it will ever return.

In television, as far as the BBC and some of the Channel 3 companies (such as Granada and Yorkshire) are concerned, pre-production still involves a fairly high (but steadily decreasing) proportion of core staff. However, Channel Four and some of the new franchise holders (such as Carlton Communications) which take over in 1993 function as publisher/broadcasters. In other words, they do not themselves make programmes, but instead order (commission) them from independent film and video companies. These independent production companies function rather like the feature film companies in that they employ only a handful of permanent staff members, but hire extra people as freelancers when the need arises for production time only.

Although the BBC and those commercial companies which still function as producer/broadcasters will have to allot 25 per cent of their programming to the independents, their regular programmes, such as the evening news on the BBC, will still be produced, directed and organised by staff personnel. Increasingly, however, many of these people will be contract rather than permanent employees, although their contracts are likely to run for three- or five-year periods rather than for the few months which characterise the film and independent video sector. Make-up artists, graphic designers and behind-the-scenes journalists associated with the pre-production of these regular programmes will be what could be called 'semi-permanent' staff.

Production

Production is the actual recording or filming. For a feature film this can take months; for a television programme it might be an hour of high-pressure studio time (with or without an audience). Most behind-the-camera jobs will still be involved at the production stage of a film, although some, such as the casting director on a big feature film or a commercial or television drama, may have moved on at the end of pre-production. Production involves performers of all sorts: actors, stunt artists, presenters, journalists, news reporters, news readers and so on.

This is the high-profile, glamorous aspect where well-known stars and entertainers are involved and where the big money is made.

Most of the equipment used in the film industry is still very traditional, although it has become somewhat more compact and lighter and there have been impressive advances in sound using Dolby noise reduction systems. The size and format of the film varies according to what it is being used for. Most feature films are made on 16mm or 35mm film and some more recent productions have used 70mm for better resolution and clarity.

In pre-production the script has already been broken down into 'scenes' and a shooting schedule prepared which lays down which scenes will be shot on which days. For economy's sake all the scenes on one set or location will be filmed at the same time, regardless of the order of events in the story-line. If a film begins and ends in Paris, but takes place mainly in London, the Paris scenes will be shot together. A continuity person keeps careful notes to see that the actors' costumes and hairstyles look the same in scenes which are supposed to be close together in the story, although they may be shot weeks apart. Continuity also takes notes on the timings of every take. In television this work is usually done by the production assistant.

Scenes are dealt with as 'shots' and 'set-ups' when the camera is moved to a new position and the lighting is changed to accommodate this. Each shot may take several 'takes' to get right. For actors and actresses film work can be very technical, because they have to walk to exact marks on the floor and turn and gesture at the correct moment to suit the camera and the lighting. They also have to keep in character and maintain the appropriate emotional attitude in scenes which are shot out of sequence and may, from day to day, bear no relation to each other.

Electronic technology has had an enormous impact in recent years on television production. Film was once used a great deal in television, because of its high quality, but this is no longer the case (except for commercials, where film still dominates). Today, most day-to-day television programmes are recorded in a studio by as many as six electronic cameras operated by cameramen or women. These cameras are usually rather large and are supported on a pedestal on mobile mountings. The images are recorded directly on to videotape which is then taken to the editing suite to be crafted into a programme.

Some television programmes go out 'live'. They are not pre-recorded and then edited, but are transmitted directly without editing. These are mainly news and current affairs programmes and chat shows. Many live programmes also include pre-recorded and edited inserts which are sometimes referred to as 'films' (though nowadays this is increasingly rare). So-called 'film inserts' have usually been recorded electronically. Coverage of a by-election result, for example, will often include a live studio discussion and live reports from the constituency, but will also feature short 'films' describing the campaign and the constituency during the weeks leading up to the election.

Live shows are the high-risk area of television because so much can go wrong: a guest can be drunk or swear or slander someone, or the newsreader can give an introduction to an insert about cot deaths only for pictures of animals in a zoo to then appear: a juxtaposition which can jar the audience and deeply offend and hurt some of them. It requires a certain amount of coolness and nerve to cope with this type of problem, and those who can do so probably deserve their high salaries.

In the early days of television everything was live and many of the traditional procedures in television date back to that period. Live television means that the staff are usually on a knife-edge and have to be extremely efficient and alert. Pre-recording of programmes has meant a considerable relaxation of the emotional tension in television, to the chagrin of many of the people who now fondly remember the old days when television was 'real'.

In addition to the heavy cameras used 'in-house', outside the studios much use is now made of a small video camera which is hand-held and supported on the shoulder. Single video camera production (Portable Single Camera or PSC), sometimes referred to as ENG (Electronic News-Gathering) or EFP (Electronic Field Production) has revolutionised news-gathering because of its ease of use and speed of editing.

The ENG operator sums up the *as it happens* public image which television likes to present to the world. ENG operators from all the broadcasting companies of the world, camera on their shoulders, at the ready, squinting through the eyepieces, crowd together on the tarmac to record Boris Yeltsin as he descends the steps from an aircraft to greet President Bush in Washington. This is the all-pervasive image of television news recording today.

Some dramas are now recorded on small hand-held cameras, especially plays which aim at a gritty realism. The single-camera recording has the flavour of a news report about it because the audience has become so attuned to the technique via television news. *The Bill* uses this technique: policemen rush up and down corridors and in and out of offices with the camera operator following close behind. There are very few cuts and edits, which increases the sense of news coverage. A great advantage of this is that, besides being effective, it is also relatively cheap!

The most elaborate of all recordings in television is the Outside Broadcast (OB). The OB unit is essentially a mobile studio control room built into a van with a number of cameras linked to it. The OB is mainly used for state occasions, political conferences or sporting events. There are, however, an increasing number of smaller mobile units which use portable single cameras (PSCs).

Work in the industry is now no longer restricted to feature films, commercials and television. All types of independent companies are now producing programmes for television, but there are also companies producing videos for the corporate sector, for education and training and for the pop industry. These companies produce videos which are tailor-made for a particular audience and their distribution is therefore limited. They are not broadcast and the companies producing them are sometimes linked together as the non-broadcast sector.

On the whole companies which are part of the independent non-broadcast sector use less sophisticated equipment than those independents involved in broadcasting. Broadcast standards require highly sophisticated and extremely expensive hardware, and it would make no economic sense for a small company with a limited market to spend astronomical sums on such equipment. The quality of the hardware, however, does make a difference to the finished product. Non-broadcast production sometimes lacks the finished polish of broadcast television and feature films. Sensing this, many would-be newcomers sometimes turn up their noses at joining small video companies as a way into the industry. This is a mistake, because the technical and creative skills required in this sector are similar to those of broadcasting. It is a good place to learn about production and gain experience in a variety of jobs in order to see where your particular interests and talents lie. Multi-skilling is endemic in this sector and it is an excellent place to learn and get a view of the whole process of production.

A Word of Comment

In Britain we have become used to extremely high standards in our films and on our television screens. This is because we have had a long tradition of high standards in hardware and very sophisticated and well-trained craftspeople. As television becomes more fragmented, individual companies will have less money available for broadcast purposes. Unless people are properly trained, standards will fall and people will have to become accustomed to a lower quality of image.

In the United States, while high technical standards and professional skills have been maintained on the large screen, the small screen has

101

seen deterioration in certain areas. To some extent this may be because of the widespread presence in the United States of community television on cable. While community television is an extremely positive development in that it allows great public access, it may have 'softened up' the audience for less polished presentation in mainline television.

In Britain, when people talk about quality television they are usually talking about the content of the programme and this is often linked with the idea of public service broadcasting. However, quality television can also refer to the quality of the image presented. A multitude of different aspects – good design, camera technique, editing – have accustomed the British audience to very high technical standards. When an experiment in community television on cable was introduced in Bristol in 1975, research indicated that the lack of technical quality was one of the barriers to its acceptance. Lack of training, combined with fragmentation of the industry, could lead to a decline in production standards in Britain. It is a matter of conjecture as to how British audiences will react to this.

Post-Production

For both film and video the main task of the post-production period is editing. The completed production is then marketed and distributed. While pre-production and production are often the work of the same company, post-production is often done by a separate company which offers specialised editing facilities. Companies offering editing equipment and skills are sometimes referred to as facility houses.

By the post-production stage most of the people involved in pre-production and production have moved on and a group of new employees with new tasks takes over. Producers and directors remain throughout all three phases, but post-production sees the hiring of editors, dubbing engineers, composers, special effects engineers and graphic artists (to work on the titles and the credits). In future most post-production jobs will also be freelance (even in television) and qualified people will move between all three sectors of the industry. The possible exception to mobility may be film editors, as this job requires a highly developed physical dexterity which probably has to be exercised on a daily basis if quality craft skills are to be maintained.

Post-production of film involves the processing of the exposed film by a laboratory and the transfer of the sound tape to a magnetic tape. This is followed by editing and completion. The film editor, helped by assistants, assembles the pieces from the best takes into a 'rough assembly' which the director and producer view and comment on. This is tightened up into a 'rough cut' and then into a 'finished edit' or 'fine cut'. Editing film involves 'cutting' the picture and adding the soundtrack, opticals, titles and special effects. The fundamental difference between film and videotape is that film is physically cut in the editing process, and videotape is not. The film editor's hands actually touch the film which he or she cuts while viewing the film frame by frame on a Steenbeck (a film editing table).

A sound editor or dubbing editor puts together several different tracks, which are mixed at a dubbing session in a sound studio to make the final soundtrack. The tracks include the actors' dialogue, sound effects (sometimes created, but often borrowed from the sound effect libraries) and recorded music to match the timing and mood of the edited film.

In contrast to film editors, video editors push the buttons in an editing suite. Videotape editing requires extremely sophisticated electronic editing machines, but these are relatively easy to operate. The editor of a videotaped programme will view the original tape with the producer or the director and then the scenes which are to be retained for broadcast are selected. These are then copied on to another tape while the first tape remains untouched. Sound effects and music are added and the finished programme is ready for transmission.

The majority of programmes now seen on television are recorded on electronic cameras, as are most live programmes. Sound and pictures from the studio floor are routed to the videotape recording suite for editing. For many years film produced much higher quality pictures than video, although it was always very expensive. As video technology has improved, however, so has the quality of the picture. Therefore, for economic reasons and simplicity of use, video has become more widespread. There are still some people who claim they can spot the difference between a filmed or taped television programme, but for most viewers this is impossible.

Video has had a particularly dramatic impact on news production. Before electronic news-gathering (ENG), news events were recorded by film cameras and cans of film then had to be rushed back to the labs to be developed and edited for the evening programmes. This was a rather cumbersome system, and stories are still told of motorcycle messengers carrying the vital film coming into collision with a car and seeing the precious item for the evening news unrolling along the road and driven over by heedless drivers.

The post-production stage can be quite straightforward and short-term for most programmes, but it can take longer than the actual filming on feature films, pop videos and commercials, especially those with dramatic special effects. Pop videos have made a virtual cult out of the editing stage and most of the budget can be spent on this phase.

Exhibition and Transmission

For film, once the editing is completed, the finished picture and sound go back to the laboratories for 'combined prints' to be made for distribution to cinemas, where they will be exhibited. In television, once the video editor is finished, the programme will be stored away for future use in the appropriate spot in the schedule. The actual showing of a programme is known as transmission. Transmission control is part of the technical side of television and it is concerned almost exclusively with the day-to-day scheduling of programmes. Transmission controllers make sure that programmes go out on time and in sequence.

The public image of a television station depends considerably on this job being done well. If a television company puts out a programme at a time which is different from that listed, it irritates the viewer. Viewers are also used to a seamless sequence of pictures: blank screens can be very disconcerting and will alienate an audience. When a mistake is made that the audience sees, it is usually the transmission controller's fault.

A Word of Advice

These then are the various stages of production. Books which describe the production process in more detail are listed in the Appendix below. Particularly useful accounts of the production process in documentary film, corporate video and television programmes can be found in Robert Angell's *Film and TV: The Way In; A Guide to Careers* (BFI, London, 1988). In many schools media studies are part of the curriculum and more young people are following such courses at GCSE level. The information in this chapter is therefore familiar to them. Others, however, are at schools where media studies are not part of the curriculum. Such students are increasingly at a disadvantage when it comes to applying to study film or television at higher or further education level.

Another, more practically oriented solution is to buy tapes from the BFI, the BBC or the television companies which have been designed to help teachers and pupils to study the media. These provide information about the basic techniques. In addition, the British Universities Film and Video Council has a number of recent BBC Television Training Videocassettes which can be viewed free of charge at the BUFVC – but make an appointment first. Addresses and information are given at the end of the book.

Finally, anyone interested in the whole production process should try to visit: the Museum of the Moving Image, South Bank, London;

Granada Studios Tour, Water Street, Manchester; the National Museum of Photography, Film and Television, in Bradford.

Case History

GIANCARLO GEMIN

Giancarlo Gemin is twenty-nine. He went to the Bishop Hannon High School in Cardiff where he took six O levels and two A levels in Art and Spanish.

After school I went on to take a Diploma in Technical Theatre and Scenic Design at Mountview Drama School and I then spent six years working as a theatre director and designer. This was good experience. I worked mainly in opera production and I had jobs at the Theatre Royal in Brighton, the Tonbridge Arts Centre, the Brighton Festival and in Venice in 1983–4, but I always wanted to work in film and television. So I decided to take a BTEC HND in film and television at the Bournemouth and Poole College of Art and Design between 1988 and 1990.

The course is very practical and it involved a lot of technical experience. You do everything. I worked as a lighting gaffer, an assistant sound operator, assistant camera operator and assistant director on various video and film productions. One of the problems for me was that there was a heavy emphasis on writing and I'm not a natural writer. I found that really hard! In my final year I made a 16mm film called *Adagio*. The College has a graduate show at BAFTA every year and *Adagio* was shown. I was lucky because through that show I made contacts and got an agent.

Adagio was really my passport into the industry. My written qualifications were not that great, far less than many people I came across. But now I had something to show. Then it won the Grand Prize at the Bilbao Film Festival in November 1990. I never realised the level of competition in the industry until I started to try to find work. I made another film called *A Day in the Life of a Child* and was a director on a 25-minute documentary, *The Lowdown*, which was transmitted by the BBC. Then *Adagio* won best live action short at the Chicago International Children's Film Festival. But finding jobs as a director on films is a real problem. It's trying to raise the money that's difficult. I

105

had this idea for a film project for Help the Aged, but even for a charitable cause it was hard to find backers. I really wish I knew more about raising money. The problem is that, if the film is to be transmitted on British television the backers want a place in the credits and the sponsorship rules on television are still so strict. The big boys have the sponsorship contracts all sewn up.

I am passionate about directing. That's what I want to do, but finding work is very hard and the recession hasn't helped. What the industry really wants is ideas. If you can come up with an idea, you've got your foot in the door. If you've written the thing, then you've really got them. That's a wonderful position to be in. I'm glad now that the College encouraged me to write, because it's important to put your ideas across well. If you have an idea, my advice is to target individual producers who you think will be interested.

I know I am a good director and I want to make films. What I would like to see is some sort of financing body which would feed money to new film-makers on a loan basis. Film-making is an art form after all. At the present time I just keep plugging away trying to get commissions to do projects which interest me.

(Adagio *is the charming story of a boy who loves listening to opera on his personal hi-fi. A friend works in the library and lends him tapes. Then he gets into a fight and his personal hi-fi gets broken. He tries to steal another, but that fails. He can't get help anywhere and finally sneaks into the English National Opera. The film ends with the boy watching a performance of* The Pearl Fishers.

Giancarlo is waiting for Adagio *to be transmitted by Channel Four.)*

PART FOUR
THE JOBS

10

THE PRODUCTION TEAM

Film, video and broadcasting encompass many different jobs. In the previous chapter we looked at the way films or programmes are constructed through the creative and technical expertise of a production team drawn together to craft the final result. In this section we will look at the individual jobs more closely and examine the various options open to those who wish to work in specific areas.

Most career books start with a discussion of entry grades because they are obviously of great significance for new recruits. However, despite the elements of normal industrial production in film and television (which it is correct to stress), the world of moving pictures is not, and never will be, an industry exactly like any other. There is a special quality associated with the production of entertainment which makes the work more a way of life than a job. This is true for all aspects: technical/craft, artistic/creative and even administrative/management. In virtually all areas people can become hooked on the industry in a way which is quite unusual and rare in other jobs. They all share a sense of working towards the final result. In film and television it is virtually impossible to dig oneself into a bunker and take a blinkered approach towards one's own specific task area. A sense of camaraderie and a commitment to team effort is an absolute rule if a production is to be successful.

For these reasons it is unwise to view the job market only within the context of those areas which are of particular concern to you. As we have seen in the previous chapter, you ought to have an overview of the whole production process. This was the strength of the BBC training system and its reduction is almost universally regretted. Understanding the top jobs in the industry is vital: the men and women in those jobs put their stamp on the whole creative process. Even the humblest runner, hired for the summer by a film company to make the tea, should be aware of this.

The movie and television industry is always more than the sum of its parts. In addition, this is an industry at the cutting edge of massive change in employment patterns and technology. As we have seen, this has produced a shake-out in the old rigid job structure. While there can be no doubt that the industry is in a state of flux and that the employment market is not buoyant, there are clear opportunities for young entrepreneurs who want to make their own programmes and have the business skills to finance them.

Reference has been made at several points in this book to the campaign in the 1970s for 'more access' and the emergence of the 25 per cent quota. Make no mistake, despite the recession, these developments have widened opportunities for the individual within the entertainment business. Consequently, a few (a very few) young people of exceptional talent and ambition have managed in a very short time, and with great good luck, to go all the way to the top. Many producers in the pop video sector are very young and other young people are running independent film companies, and therefore getting their own programmes on television. Although many young people complain about the present situation, these successes would have been unthinkable even five years ago.

We will look first at some of the most important jobs in the industry. It is important to remember, however, that multi-skilling is now endemic and strict craft and professional divisions are no longer as rigorously observed as they used to be. This is especially the case in small video companies.

Starting from the top:

THE PRODUCER (creative/management/financial)

Film

'Once I became interested in stories and getting stories told, I realised I had to be a producer to get them told in the right way.' (Warren Beatty)

Producing is the key job in film or television. Producers deal with ideas, money and organisation, three vital ingredients. Many young people who do not understand the industry confuse producers and directors. The producer usually has the original idea, commissions the script, secures the finances, *hires the director* and is involved in casting, finding locations and hiring the crew. Producers animate everything else. (For a description of the director's role, see below.)

Producers are often also closely associated with the marketing of films. He or (increasingly) she is the organising supremo, the presiding genius. Producers need to be multi-tasking types; they need to have a

110

finger in every pie and must be highly disciplined and organised, because everything depends on them.

The best producers are highly intuitive. They must have a nose for a good idea and be able to sense the way the wind of public taste is blowing. They often take great financial risks and the best are prepared to back their hunches against the criticism of the cautious. They need to have either great personal charisma to win over the doubters, or an extremely good track record. Investing in a film is a risky venture and bankers are never overenthusiastic about putting their money into what, in financial terms, is a long shot.

Increasingly in the feature film sector, the dominance of the big studios has meant the production of formula films made according to a set pattern based on market research. The research indicates what audiences want to see on the screens (boy gets girl, sexy love scenes, no sad deaths, car chases, exotic location, good punch-ups, for example). Big money producers are often held captive by the studios and have to produce films which abide by the formula. These films are designed to make money – and many of them do – but their producers are rather alien to the film-making tradition. They are more like hard-headed accountants and grey-suited businessmen. Many people regret the disappearance of the buccaneer entrepreneurs of the past. There are many groans about 'Wet young punks with MBAs and fancy suits': one of the more polite descriptions offered.

Fortunately, there are still film-makers around who follow their own hunches and produce movies which might not have 'marketable' themes. Every now and again they confound the market researchers by producing a film (sometimes referred to as a 'sleeper') which everyone wants to see: *Field of Dreams* was one such case. The best producers combine financial wizardry with artistic horse sense (a rare combination).

To bring a story to the screen, producers surround themselves with the best talent the budget can afford. They have to keep a tight hold on the purse-strings while allowing talent to flourish. This can be very difficult in a world of competing temperaments and supercharged egos. The quality of the final film will depend on the quality of the people the producer employs, and he or she must ensure that the performers and crew function efficiently as a team and without too much aggravation and conflict. The result can be an artistic master-piece – or a flop!

Television and Video
In television drama the producer's job is similar to a producer's job in feature films. He or she is the main organiser and nowadays can also

bear the major burden of raising the money (this is always the case in independent production companies). However, on the whole, the production team in television is smaller than in feature films, even if the drama is actually filmed as opposed to recorded on tape. Once again the producer may have the original idea and assemble the production team, and it is his or her responsibility to ensure that a high-quality programme is produced on time and *within budget*.

Most television programmes are not dramas, however, and require nowhere near the same degree of complex organisation or financial commitment. Today many film producers start in television or in video companies or in companies making commercials. Producers of television programmes tend to be *interest*-oriented rather than business types (although this is changing), because different kinds of programmes call for different kinds of abilities. Thus producers of documentary programmes often have a background in journalism; producers of quiz programmes must have an instinct for light entertainment; producers of pop programmes must know about contemporary music and also about lighting and sound effects; sports producers have a fascination with sports and are sometimes themselves ex-athletes or ex-footballers, for example.

It is very easy to confuse the functions of producer and director in television and in small video companies, because people in these sectors of the industry do take on both roles: producer/directors are very common. In television, much more than in film, the producer is part of the creative team. Television producers can have a hands-on role in the studio and on location, particularly if they are also trained directors.

So How Do You Get to Be a Producer?

By working your way up and showing a flair for the job. There is no degree in production: you prove yourself by doing the job. (Although some colleges are now modelling their training on the actual production process.) In film some producers have a background in business, accountancy or law, because knowing about money has always been essential. Some film producers were originally agents and came to know the business that way.

In television some producers come up via the technical route as camera operators or directors. This is particularly true for light entertainment; documentary and news producers are more commonly graduates who have previously been employed as researchers to gain experience. In the past it was very unusual for anyone with a business background to end up in television production, but the move towards independent companies has changed this. More and more people will have the opportunity to move into television production because of their money skills. In fact in the independent sector it is often people with entrepreneurial talent who form their own companies and then produce programmes for the market-place. In that sense the independent production companies have a similar 'culture', though on a smaller scale, to the feature film industry.

DIRECTORS

Film

'Concentrate on the story, leave the details to others – and sit whenever you can.' (John Huston)

In feature films, as the name suggests, directors direct the performances of the actors and dictate the camera shots. Directors have the key creative hands-on role. They are responsible for deploying the technical and artistic resources in the best possible way so that the picture ends up in the can for developing and editing. The director's main concern is with production and post-production, although he or she usually has a hand in such pre-production tasks as location selection.

What the director does is to take a script provided by the producer (and the writer) and guide the actors through it in rehearsal. He or she must then draw good on-screen performances from the actors, so many directors have some knowledge of acting technique. They must also have technical knowledge of cameras, lighting and the eventual editorial process, because they have to communicate clearly the visual image they want the technical crew to provide. Directors must also possess a good visual sense: they have to be able to read a script and see in their mind's eye the end result in pictorial terms. They discuss the set with the set designer and the wardrobe with the wardrobe designer. Not surprisingly, many film directors come from a theatrical or visual arts background.

On the set or on location the director is there, on the spot, talking to the actors, instructing the camera operators, debating changes in the script. The producer can be thousands of miles away negotiating with the backers for money as the film goes over budget. (As Michael Caine is reported to have said, 'I'm not interested in directing. Now producing! I noticed when it starts to rain, the only person who goes back to the hotel is the producer.') The classic image of the director in the old Hollywood films is a temperamental individual with a megaphone, shouting his instructions here, there and everywhere.

At the end of a day's shoot film directors view the 'rushes' in a preview theatre to ensure that the required image has been shot. If things are not quite right they can retake scenes the next day, although this is expensive. A director's hours are long and the emotional tension and stress levels are very high, but it is also possibly the most creatively satisfying job in film. Really talented directors are always in demand and salaries can be very high indeed. However, it takes a great deal of skill to be a director and there is no substitute for experience.

On feature films directors are assisted by first, second and third assistant directors. In a sense the word director in these cases is a misnomer because they are in no way trainee or deputy directors. (There is usually only one director on a film set and he or she is *God*.) Assistant directors have responsibilities which are more analogous to producing than directing. In fact the career route for assistant directors may be towards production management rather than towards direction (see below for a description of the duties of a production manager).

Assistant directors are part of the organisational and administrative side of film-making, rather than the cinematic and creative side. The first assistant director carries out the director's practical requirements, such as supervising the discipline and general organisation of the daily shoot. In the pre-production period the 'first' will work with the production manager to 'break down' the shooting script and examine likely requirements and responsibilities. The first assistant will also work with the director to find out how the film is visualised.

The first assistant director usually hires a second and third and their responsibilities too are organisational. They keep the production running smoothly with the second assistant working closely with the production office, and the third assistant working on the set making sure that artists receive the calls and appear on time (minutes must not be lost in such an expensive activity as film-making).

In television the equivalent of a first assistant director's job is that of studio/floor manager (see below). In fact, when television goes out on location, studio managers can be renamed first assistants.

Television and Video

In television the programme director, like the film director, converts the script into the images and sounds which eventually appear on the screen. In television drama they must have an excellent visual sense and sound technical knowledge. It is directors who coax good performances from the actors and performers in drama and light entertainment. Directors in television are assisted by production assistants (PAs, see below).

114

Producer/directors who combine both roles are often found in television and they can be very powerful.

How Do You Get to Be a Director? '*Let Me Count the Ways*'
Most directors today work in all three sectors. They are mainly freelance, although there are staff directors in the BBC and ITV. The cutbacks in television have undoubtedly affected the training of directors and Skill Search identified this as an area where a shortage exists. The problem for the newcomer is that the shortage is mainly one of experienced directors. Many film and television directors come up through the ranks. They can be former camera operators or (especially in television) studio floor managers or editors. With modern video cameras, however, technical knowledge is probably less significant than it used to be.

Major drama schools, film schools and vocationally oriented colleges and universities which offer media degrees provide courses in direction, and some fortunate graduates with good track records and glowing references *may* get jobs immediately in the non-broadcast and pop video sector. However, no one should go to college or university expecting a job to fall into their lap: it won't. The industry does not work like that, and particularly not in a recession.

Increasingly in the new freelance world there are many privately funded short-term courses in direction available to those prepared to pay. The well-respected ones are nearly always for people who already have some experience or a job in the industry.

The National Film and Television School provides a National Short Course Training Programme (NSCTP) in all aspects of film and video, but this is mainly designed for experienced freelancers already working in the industry who wish to retrain or update their skills. An experienced camera operator wishes to move into direction? The NSCTP will probably have a suitable course for him or her. Anyone working in the industry who is interested in retraining should be aware of these courses. More information on other available courses can be gained by writing to the British Film Institute for their *Directions, A Guide to Short Training Courses in Video and Film*, published biannually by the BFI's Planning Unit. Beware! More and more short-term courses will spring up in response to the crisis in training. Check them out first for quality and industry acceptance.

PRODUCTION MANAGER (administrative/managerial)

Film
Production manager is a job category mainly found in the film sector, and less so in television and video. The production manager is the

producer's deputy and is actively involved in the day-to-day problems of filming. He or she prepares a detailed budget for shooting and a shooting schedule, arranges the hire of equipment and obtains permission to film in certain locations. On a large production the job can be divided into two: a line producer in charge of administrative tasks such as budgeting, crew hire and contracts; and a location manager responsible for finding locations.

Location managers are sometimes found in television. This is because major television dramas can be as complicated to make as feature films and require outside locations (that is, locations away from the studios). The location manager, in film and television, discusses the script in detail with the producer and the director and then tries to find places which will match what he or she believes the producer and director want. Location managers need imaginative gifts, as well as common sense and organisational skills. In choosing suitable places a variety of factors have to be considered, such as noise, aeroplanes passing overhead and so on. It can be very difficult to find locations for a pre-twentieth-century drama: one episode of a BBC drama about Renaissance Italy was reported to have aircraft trails in the sky! Viewers love to spot such errors and write in if an accidental anachronism occurs.

On their initial visits, location managers will take photographs of the possible locations and bring these back to the production office for discussion. If a location seems suitable, then the production team will visit it to see if it lives up to the location manager's promises. If everything is fine, location managers will arrange for terms and the drawing-up of contracts. The public can be paid if their houses are used (though this is not as much as the uninitiated expect!) Location managers have many liaison jobs to do in the course of filming. If a large-scale shoot is going to take place, both the police and the local authorities have to be notified in advance. They must also ensure that everything is left as it was before the film crew arrived.

How Do People Become Production Managers?
This is definitely not a job for new entrants. Production managers have to know the business very well indeed. They sometimes have a legal or financial background, but mostly they have worked in television or film for years and have developed a feel for the job. In small independent companies production manager functions will often be carried out by the producer or director – another example of the trend towards multi-skilling.

116

FLOOR MANAGER (organisational)

Television

The floor manager's job is mainly found in television and it is focused on the day of the recording. Before the recording date, however, the floor manager usually receives a copy of the script and he or she must then consider any problems that could come up. Floor managers usually attend the last planning meeting of the production team so that they know exactly what is going to happen on the day. They make notes about any changes and can bring up any problems.

Floor managers have two main areas of responsibility on the day of recording: they liaise with the programme director; and they manage what happens on the studio floor. Since the director sits in the control room above the studio floor, separated from the studio by a glass screen, he or she needs someone to handle events down below and this is where the floor manager comes in. The director has to concentrate on the monitors and the pictures he or she wants to go out to the viewers, so he or she needs a subordinate to communicate his or her wishes to the floor. He or she does this through talkback to the floor manager. If you visit a television studio as part of the audience, the floor manager is probably the person who is obviously in charge and who 'warms you up'. He or she will talk to you before the recording and tell you what to do: for example, 'When Mr Bruce Forsyth appears, please clap when I give this signal.'

It is the floor manager who gives the director's instructions to performers and who also gives cues and prompts. Floor managers co-ordinate and manage everything that happens on the set on the day of recording. They make sure performers know where to stand, and what to do, that props and microphones are in place, that booms and cameras are in their proper positions.

How to Get in

In the past floor managers started their careers as floor assistants, which were the equivalent of gophers and runners in the film industry. Now floor assistants hardly exist (because of job cutbacks), and floor managers are recruited from a wide variety of jobs within television. They are rarely recruited from outside unless they have similar experience in the theatre. There are no formal qualifications for a floor manager except knowledge of the job and the right temperament combined with organisational ability. I certainly know of one case where a doorman at the BBC worked himself up to floor manager. Floor managers have to be very cool and calm since the job can involve a great deal of aggravation: there are frequent last-minute crises which might cause panic in normal people! Floor managers must never panic.

Once the NVQ system is functioning it is likely that standards of competence will be established for this grade (as for all grades).

PRODUCTION ASSISTANT (Administrative/Organisational)

Television

Despite their name, production assistants (PAs) assist the television or video director as much as the producer. For many years the job was almost exclusively done by women with expert secretarial skills, who acted as the director's personal assistants. This description, however, does not do justice to the scope of the job. PAs, more than anyone else in television, need to have an all-round knowledge of the way it works – technically, administratively and financially. Anyone who knows television will acknowledge that the PA is often the key element in the success of a production. Feminists within television have long argued that, had the job been traditionally done by men rather than women, it would have had much higher pay and status. PAs bear a great weight of responsibility: they are the pivots of a programme.

Production assistants are usually assigned to a particular pro-gramme from the very beginning; they help to keep control of the budget and do most of the organisation. The PA is the main point of contact for all members of the crew and production team. They accompany directors to production team meetings which involve the lighting supervisor, sound supervisor, graphics, wardrobe, make-up, studio managers and others, and they keep records of these meetings. They also do the routine office work such as booking rehearsal rooms, technical equipment, hotels for performers, dressing-rooms, catering facilities and so on.

Sometimes the PA job is divided into location PAs, who assist the director on location, and studio PAs who organise recording sessions in the studio, but most PAs combine both roles. It really depends on the size of the production. Drama, for example, if it involves a great deal of location work, could have two PAs. When television uses film on location, location PAs may keep the 'shot list', which means making a record of each shot, noting the number of the camera roll, the sound roll, the length of the shot and the general description. The purpose of the shot list is to provide the editors with a written record of the film when it reaches the cutting room. This process has been simplified with the widespread use of video, but location PAs still have

118

to keep very accurate notes of what is going on and they take very much the role of continuity people in feature films.

On location PAs look after transport, lodging and food and ensure that everyone gets to the location on time. PAs must be able to absorb grouses from the crew about hotel accommodation, food and daily rates, as well as cope with temperamental directors. For example, if the weather misbehaves everything may have to be reorganised efficiently at a moment's notice. Woe betide the PA who fails to do so.

The studio side of the PA's job involves many tasks: booking the studio for recording; outlining which studio facilities will be required; specifying the number of cameras; reserving the dressing-room for performers and so on. PAs set up a final planning meeting about ten days before a studio date, and the lighting supervisor, sound supervisor, floor manager, set designer, make-up artist, wardrobe designer, vision mixer, graphic designer and director all get together for a final 'talk through' of the script. Scripts are changed all the time during pre-production and the PA has to note the changes and type and retype the script to take account of the alterations. Often changes are made at the very last minute, almost at the point of transmission, so they have to be fast and accurate typists.

On the day of recording PAs sit in the control room (or, as it is sometimes called, the gallery), at a long desk facing a bank of TV monitors labelled Camera One, Camera Two, VT and so on. The PA always sits at one end, opposite the time monitor and next to the director; on the other side of the director sits the vision mixer. PAs time the individual elements within the programme as well as the whole programme, so they have to be able to use a stopwatch – in fact two stopwatches. PAs remind the producer if the recording is running fast or slow; they count in the VT inserts ('Run VT'); and they also have to answer the phone in the gallery and pass on any of the director's final orders. The PA gives instructions to the camera operators via the talkback system, reminding them when they will be 'on air'. In a live programme timing is particularly crucial. PAs have to remain calm under pressure and be able to do several things at once. As there is no daylight in the control room, the atmosphere can be claustrophobic and tense. After the recording PAs also attend VT editing sessions and ensure that the programme is edited to time. In post-production they also have lots of paperwork to clear up, including, sometimes, paying performers.

The job of PA requires stamina. It is rarely nine-till-five and it can involve a great deal of time spent away from home. On the other hand, PAs meet all sorts of interesting people and are at the heart of programme-making.

119

How Do You Become a PA?

Again, PAs usually need to have experience in the industry. Most PAs start as secretaries in the television companies and then compete for traineeships. Competition for these traineeships in the BBC or any of the ITV companies is very intense. However, it is likely that television companies will continue to train PAs because the job is so vital and because PAs really have to be familiar with all aspects of production. Freelance PAs who have been trained by the BBC or ITV are very much in demand because they know the business so well.

A broad general education and secretarial skills are essential; often the ability to read music is required since there can be a great deal of work in light entertainment and PAs have to count the beat in the gallery. Character and temperament are important elements in the successful PA. The highly strung and the temperamental are not suited for the job. Very rarely small video companies will allow a secretary to carry out the functions of the PA. This is truly on-the-spot training!

This chapter has looked at the jobs which form the kernel of the programme-making process. Directors, production managers and PAs, however, could not do their jobs without the support of the technical/creative staff.

Case History

CELIA BARGH

Celia Bargh is thirty-eight and has worked in the industry for four years. She trained as a secretary.

I've always wanted to work in television. It was an ambition that bubbled under the surface, but I lacked the confidence to get started. I started my career late because I had a daughter who is now eighteen. I didn't go back to work until she was eight, when I worked for a brewing company. It was a means of gaining work experience.

I tried to get into the Beeb as a secretary, but my shorthand speed wasn't fast enough. I did get a job with the Arts Council, which seemed a good stepping stone. After about a year I started applying for jobs at London Weekend Television. I liked their programmes and thought the company seemed young and energetic. The BBC had seemed very bureaucratic, so I hoped LWT might suit me better. At this point I'd really set my mind on a television career and thought, 'Even if it takes a long time, I'm going to persist.' I applied for a number of advertised jobs at LWT but they just wrote back saying 'Sorry, no'. So I wrote back to say, 'Sorry too but don't forget me'. After about six months of this, they rang to offer me a temp. job which I accepted. Fortunately after a month I must have passed the test because I became a permanent member of LWT's staff.

I thought it was just great. I was working for the Head of Programme Staff as secretary/assistant. I decided that I would really like to be a PA as I wanted to be part of the creative team, making programmes. I stayed in this job for two years hoping LWT would start a PA training programme, but this was February 1988 and worries about the franchise were looming. I learned all I could by doing attachments, sitting in on studios, spending time on locations with PAs. I held on hoping for training but the training opportunity did not arise, no money available. It was all very disheartening.

During this time I did have an attachment to a PA on a sitcom and as Production Secretary (again on attachment, thanks to the generous spirit of my boss) on the Royal Variety Show. I loved it. I think the industry is great. I enjoy the teamwork, the people, and seeing a script come to life on the screen.

But I still wasn't trained and training was what I needed. Then a contract came up for a production secretary in the drama department on *A Perfect Hero*. Happily I was taken on, although it meant I gave up my permanent status at LWT. It was interesting and I learned a lot but I was still caught up in the office, manning the phones rather than learning about the cameras/acting/filming process. So it was very frustrating. I was then very lucky to get a job with Noel Gay as production secretary on a sci-fi comedy called *Red Dwarf*. I worked with a wonderful PA who helped me, and let me help her a great deal. Then with the same company I went on to become the production co-ordinator on a children's drama for Christmas 1991 called *Merlin*. It was quite different from *Red Dwarf* and, like *A Perfect Hero*, was shot on single camera. *Red Dwarf* was shot in a multi-camera studio, so, by luck, I had experience of both single and multi-camera programmes.

Then I decided I really had to have some formal training, so I went on a PA course at the National Short Course Training Programme of the National Film and Television School for two weeks. I paid for myself. And it was worth every penny. I got real experience in studio work. You really get practical experience of working as a PA through exercises in making drama, light entertainment, magazine and live programmes. I loved it. The adrenalin was there. It was bliss.

What also made it worthwhile were the contacts I made. The PA course runs in conjunction with a Directors' course and a Vision Mixers' course, so it was very interesting meeting other people and learning about their experiences. I did the course in November 1991 and then in December I did a continuity course with Avril Rowlands.

Feeling so positive about these training courses I decided, if I possibly could, to hold out and not do another production secretary-type job. As the industry seemed very quiet in January I continued my own 'training programme' – for example, I sat in on ITN's early morning news (the director has been a tutor on the NSCTP course).

Then, at the suggestion of someone else I met on the second course, I wrote to corporate video companies for work as a PA and as a result I worked on a pilot business programme as a PA!

I am now working for Alomo Productions as production co-ordinator on *Birds of a Feather*. They are well aware I want to be a PA, but this job will involve a certain amount of production management, so it will be quite a challenge and I will learn more about another side of programme-making.

You have to be persistent and professional in this industry. I really feel I would like more training, but now there is little of it around. The trouble is that you have to rely on the kindness and generosity of PAs to train you. And this is wrong. It isn't fair on them. It has got to the situation where the industry relies on PAs to train others to do their job. It really is 'not on' from their point of view. I have always been amazed by the professionalism of PAs. Watching them work makes you feel very inadequate. When PAs are good, they are just amazing. It's incredible what they do.

The industry is great. You either love it or are bored by it. I love it. I love being part of a creative team watching the puzzle come together. You have to be flexible, prepared to work long and inconvenient hours. And you have to be persistent!

11

THE TECHNICAL TEAM

In the previous chapter we looked at jobs in the industry which new-comers are unlikely to get. This chapter deals with technical jobs, most of which have a major creative element but which, at least in principle, are available to school and college leavers at the entry/trainee/assistant grades. At the top levels, of course – such as cinematographer on a film – recruitment is still confined to those with extensive experience and proven talent, which is how it should be.

Again, as this book has emphasised, in the absence of any wide-spread pattern or logic to industry training, degrees and diplomas with a vocational component are now more helpful to job seekers than they used to be.

In television many of the following job categories used to be perma-nent staff positions. Young people accepted by the BBC or ITV, for example as trainee camera operators, were given on-the-job instruc-tion. This still goes on, but cutbacks have affected employment oppor-tunities by reducing total numbers within these companies. This is especially the case for ITV (the future Channel 3), where the move towards the publisher/broadcaster model, as opposed to that of pro-ducer/broadcaster, has meant, and will mean, that far fewer perma-nent jobs are available. Consequently, camera operators, vision mixers, lighting technicians and other technical staff increasingly work as freelancers, many of them receiving their start in the non-broadcast sector. In the independent video sector employees often find them-selves doing jobs for which they have not been specifically trained. This, as we have seen, has changed the whole face of the industry.

At the time of writing, neither Skillset nor the Arts and Entertain-ment Training Council have issued standards of competence for the National Vocational Qualifications in the various professional areas. Once the NVQ standards are specified, however, the situation will become much clearer. If the NVQs succeed and become universal, they will stimulate people to train and retrain in several job categories as industry needs ebb and flow and shortages and surfeits become apparent. Remember, however, that it is increasingly clear that they will have to do so at their own expense. The government is proposing to encourage an atmosphere which promotes training, but it expects employers and employees to pay for it themselves.

The technical/creative sector of the industry was, and still is, heavily unionised and many job titles and job categories were associated with union traditions in specific areas, notably film. In the multi-skilled, cross-sector environment, many of these titles are becoming redundant and Skillset may reduce them further. Therefore, in the following sections some of the more specific film terms have been replaced with more neutral descriptions, such as technician or operator.

CAMERA CREW (technical/creative)
CINEMATOGRAPHER/LIGHTING CAMERA OPERATOR
LIGHTING DIRECTOR
EXTERIOR CAMERA OPERATORS
CAMERA OPERATOR
CAMERA ASSISTANTS
ROSTRUM CAMERA OPERATOR

Film, Television and Video
'You can't fool that 70mm lens. It's terrifying what it picks up. You can see what time someone hobbled to bed. You can see the germs having a party on his eyeballs.' (Peter O'Toole)

The camera crew is at the very heart of film-making and there are many traditions in the working practices which impart a particular flavour to their activities. Camera operator is the job which people immediately associate with working in the industry and for many little, and not so little, boys and girls it has been a dream occupation (rather like engine-driving used to be fifty years ago). In the past the crew were all unionised and almost invariably male. Some camera crews worked together over many years, moving from film to film, with the union providing a bond of brotherhood (although there was always a strict hierarchy in the jobs). There is a mystique about a film crew which, despite the vast social and economic changes of the past few years, still lingers on. It is closely associated with the almost legendary reputation which British film crews have earned for themselves.

The basic function of a camera crew is to produce, on the director's instructions, the best possible images in terms of artistic interpretation

124

and technical quality. The most senior job in a film crew is that of cinematographer/lighting camera operator.

Cinematographer/Lighting Camera Operator/Director of Photography

Cinematographer (sometimes called the director of photography) is a title usually associated with very distinguished lighting camera operators on high-budget feature films. Cinematographers can be as famous as the director – indeed some of them are also directors. Nicolas Roeg is one example.

The basic responsibility of the cinematographer/lighting camera operator is the supervision of lighting and camera angles in order to provide the film's visual 'mood'. He or she chooses the appropriate lens and filters to create this.

The cinematographer discusses with the director the way the cameras are to be positioned, the composition of the shots and how the scenes are to be lit for the best possible result. After consultation with the director, he or she draws up a pre-arranged camera script which gives the order of the camera shots and also sets out lighting details. Cinematographers rarely handle the cameras on a day-to-day basis, but they always have the camera operation experience so that they know how to instruct their subordinates to produce the right shots.

Lighting Director

Lighting director is the job in television which corresponds roughly to lighting camera operator in the film sector. Lighting directors work closely with electrical technicians but basically, as in film, most of them begin as members of the camera crew. Sometimes, however, they may have come in from the theatre, or have a background as an engineer or electrician, or they may have moved across from film.

Lighting directors use light to capture the atmosphere of a programme. If a drama is supposed to be set in evening light the lighting director arranges this. They decide the position and strengths of the lights and the colours (Redheads and Blondes) in order to enhance the creative aspect of the set and the general mood.

Lighting directors must work closely with the camera crew, the sound department, make-up and the set designers as well as the directors. They also need to understand and direct the work of the lighting electricians. In preparation for a programme, lighting directors design the chart indicating the lighting rig, that is, decide which studio lights should be situated where. Electricians use this chart to change the lights.

Trainee lighting directors are sometimes called lighting assistants.

They begin on programmes which are fairly straightforward and their work is supervised by a lighting director.

Exterior Camera Operator
Exterior camera operators do more or less the same work as the lighting camera operators but on smaller productions. This level in the hierarchy is now rapidly disappearing (see Sue Davis (ed.), *The Official ITV Careers Handbook*, Hodder and Stoughton, 1989, p. 62).

Camera Operators
Camera operators actually man the camera under the lighting camera operator's overall direction. In film especially they can have considerable artistic input because they know how to secure the best shots and angles. Camera operators produce the pictures, the basic raw material of a film, which means that their talent and ability is the kernel of a high-quality production. They are helped by camera assistants. In television, camera operators probably have less creative input since directors tend to determine camera angles and shots in pre-production time (see below).

Camera Assistants (Grip/Clapper-loader/Loader/Focus-puller)
The camera assistant's job has been aptly described as 'babysitting the camera'. The assistant does all the housekeeping tasks: watches the level of the stock; keeps the production team informed about the amount of film stock being used (so more can be ordered if necessary); does basic maintenance of the equipment; and is also responsible for the safety of the camera during shooting (any piece of technical equipment which is moved is liable to accidental damage and film sets are loaded with potential dangers). Assistants may also drive the camera car on location. If the film team goes abroad they are usually responsible for making sure the equipment goes through customs safely.

Newcomers to the industry probably do not take account of the basic administrative work which film crews crossing boundaries have to negotiate. Countries governed by dictators are often not too keen on having their inadequacies revealed and they sometimes use customs procedures as a means of slowing everything down and of just being plain awkward. Camera crews usually have a fund of stories about the delays they have encountered dealing with obstreperous customs officials, especially those who want to strip down the equipment to search for drugs!

Assistants set up the camera on location, load up the magazine with film, make sure that the lens is clean and check the focus. They prepare the clapperboard, which should bear the name of the film, the director, the date, and also operate the clapper, usually at the beginning, but sometimes at the end, of each shot. In addition, they make a written record of all 'takes'. After filming has finished assistants unload the magazines and check that they are accurately labelled. They prepare camera reports which should include special instructions about processing and also provide details of the lighting and filters which have been used. These go first to the laboratories and then to the editors along with the film.

All these assistant jobs can be painstaking and boring, but they are a vital training-ground and can provide evidence of suitability for the job. Although the industry is less hierarchical than in the past, junior technicians in all jobs in film or television are expected to 'put up or shut up'. It is an exaggeration to compare it to the army, but, although the situation is changing, juniors are still expected to have respect for senior members of staff. This can be quite a shock to people who have not worked in the industry before. It creates a curiously old-fashioned ambience, but is a direct result of the discipline and teamwork which were required in the past.

On small shoots one camera assistant will do all these jobs, but on a big shoot assistants are divided into jobs with strange and evocative names such as focus-puller, clapper-loader or grip. The focus-puller ensures that the correct lens is on the camera and that the distance between the subject and the camera is correct to get a shot in focus. The focus-puller needs considerable technical knowledge and must work smoothly with the camera operator. If the camera operator alters a shot while filming, it is the focus-puller who operates the focus ring on the lens. Sometimes the director wants the foreground of the shot to go fuzzy so that the viewer can concentrate on the action in the background, or the intention might be to have the foreground highlighted and the background misty: this is where the focus-puller comes in. Lenses are expensive and must be carefully handled.

The grip's duties are moving the camera and operating dollies and cranes (the mounts for particular camera shots). Grips sometimes even design special rigs and they build and lay tracks for tracking shots. They are responsible for the camera's safety; grips also drive the camera car on location.

The loader or clapper-loader loads the clapper and loads and empties film. He or she also notes equipment details so that the laboratory and the production office can be informed.

Camera operators in television mainly work with electronic rather than film cameras. However, as mentioned earlier, people often refer to events being 'filmed' when they actually mean they are being recorded on tape.

Studio cameras are fairly large and are positioned on pedestals supported on mobile mountings which allow them to glide smoothly over the floor. Studios can have several cameras in operation at one time and usually each one is operated by one person. Some studio cameras are mounted at the end of a jib on a motorised crane. The crane is used for very high and very low shots (within a few inches of the floor). It has to be driven and swung by camera crew members.

In a studio the cameras have long cables which attach them to sockets and, via the sockets, to the control equipment. The cables have to be constantly moved to allow the camera freedom. This is known as 'cable bashing': the cable bashers, who move and untangle cables, are usually very junior trainee camera operators.

Camera operators in television have less control over the shots than film camera operators: the artistic/creative component of the job is less dominant. In television the shots are usually decided by the director after discussion with a senior member of the camera crew at a planning meeting. The director provides the camera crew with a pre-arranged camera script giving the order of shots. During rehearsals for recorded programmes, camera operators practice the positions. At the recording proper, directors cue the shots from the gallery: 'Camera two', 'close-up', 'two-shot', 'zoom' and so on. In some very static programmes, such as news, the cameras are operated and positioned by remote control and there is no camera operator in the studio.

In outside broadcasts (OBs) the camera operator functions in the same way as a camera operator in the studio. The classic outside broadcast is a great state occasion, such as a royal wedding. This would be handled by an OB unit (indeed several OB units), basically a mobile studio control room in a large van to which the outside broadcast cameras are linked. The grey outside broadcast vans of the BBC are well-known and are likely to set off a flurry of interest whenever they take up residence in a street prior to a recording. However, there is a tendency these days for outside broadcasts on a smaller scale to be recorded by portable single cameras. These are used by the camera operators rather like film cameras. The great advantage is that on most modern electronic cameras the operator can immediately review the shots on a tiny screen, a practice now familiar to thousands of amateurs with domestic video recorders.

On the whole television camera operators lead a more prosaic life than film camera operators because there is probably less location work. The one great exception is the news camera operator, one of the hardest, most prestigious and most glamorous jobs in television. International news cameramen lead exciting lives; they have to be quick-witted people with a strong individualistic streak who know how to look after their own skins: they can, after all, find themselves on the front line covering wars and more than a few camera operators have died on duty.

Typical of the breed is Mohammed Amin, African Bureau Chief for Visnews, who recently lost his left forearm in an ammunition dump explosion when Ethiopian rebels seized control of Addis Ababa. This left him unable to focus the lens, but a special camera has been developed so that his right thumb can operate the focus. 'I want to be a cameraman again,' he says, 'and filming where there is danger is the only life I know' (*FTT and BETA News*, October 1991).

Increasingly, news camera operators work on their own and without directors. This is a big change from the old days when news crews could consist of several people. If in addition to pictures a report is required, the news team will consist of two people: the camera operator and the reporter. Independent news camera operators have to carry out a complex range of jobs: sound, lighting, simple editing and maintenance. They also relay their recordings through telephone modems and satellite links back to base.

Rostrum Camera Operator
In film, television and video anything which cannot be done by live action can usually be achieved by a fixed rostrum camera, which is used for superimposing animations, titles or effects. The most famous operator of all is Ken Morse, whose name must have been included in more credits than anyone else in television.

How Do You Become a Camera Operator?
The main qualification is familiarity with a camera, film or video. You should have a good general education with GCSE or A levels, perhaps in maths or physics, and have the right personality to cope with a non-routine job. Knowing about different types of cameras is important; a flair for, or interest in, photography is an asset and will help you to secure an interview. The interview will be quite technical, in that it will explore your knowledge of cameras, so be well-prepared. Make sure that you can actually describe, for example, the function of the lens. You may *know* what it does, but make sure you can explain it clearly. Practise by saying it out loud to yourself in the bathroom perhaps! We often think we know something in our heads and then fumble and hesitate when asked for a precise description.

Connections are still useful in the film sector. A course in photography at a college of further education and a knowledge of electronics is an asset for a prospective trainee. A BTEC Higher National Diploma in an appropriate area, such as lighting or optics, is another plus. Many film schools and art colleges have courses in cinematography, and it is included in a few media studies courses. If you specifically want to become a film camera operator, it is probably best to follow a college course in photography or cinematography and then try to get into a film company as a runner. From there, go for one of the assistant camera operator posts such as a clapper-loader. Working your way up on the basis of proven competence is still the best method.

The BBC still trains its own camera operators and there are also traineeships in some ITV companies which can be applied for (although how many of these will survive in the new Channel 3 era is an open question). Both the BBC and ITV take their pick of applicants, so your credentials have to be good.

Camera operators are increasingly freelance. Film camera operators are accustomed to freelance work, but the decline of union power has made the job more competitive. Today there are many more inexperienced (and unemployed!) camera operators around than ever before.

The best route in is probably via video companies or television. If you have a proven knowledge of video cameras, through working in a workshop for example, a small company might take you on. With experience in television, some camera operators move on to film camera work, although in the past many were not prepared to risk this because television camera operation was a 'secure' job and film camera work was less so. In the era of the freelancer this is no longer exactly the case. Television camera operators nowadays might do a short course in film (and vice versa), so that they can work as freelancers across all sectors.

When the NVQs are in place camera operators will be able to earn qualifications on-the-job and this should improve the present rather confused situation. Highly skilled, experienced camera operators will always be in demand.

Camera work can be quite stressful, so temperament is important. You are responsible for getting a number of details correct, such as the exposure, colour balance, filters, the choice of lens and film, the camera angle and so on. The need to remember everything can cause anxiety in the highly-strung. Physical fitness, stamina, good eyesight and hearing are all essential.

There are short courses available in camera operation, but these are usually open only to people with experience in the industry. Camera operation used to be a job area which was almost exclusively male, but this, like everything else, is now changing.

SOUND CREW
SOUND OPERATOR/TECHNICIAN/RECORDIST
BOOM OPERATOR
GRAMS OPERATOR
SOUND DUBBING EDITOR/MIXER

Film, Television and Video
Sound technicians record and mix sound during shooting and recording. On location with film or PSC/ENG they work with portable equipment; in a television studio a sound technician operates a sound desk in the sound control room next to the gallery (and is then sometimes referred to as sound supervisor, see below). In the past sound technicians who worked in the studio rarely worked out on location and, in turn, location sound crews were hardly ever studio-based. Multi-skilling, however, is having an effect in this area as in others, and it is now more common to find sound technicians who are prepared to tackle both aspects.

Sound technicians aim to obtain the best possible quality of sound and interpret the director's wishes to find ways of creating an 'atmosphere' appropriate to the style of the film or recording. They have to be aware of acoustics and problems with echoes. Sound has developed a great deal in the last decade with the advance of stereo and digital recording and, clearly, sound technicians have to be up to date with new technology. On pop videos sound supervisors are very important indeed.

Recording sound on location can be difficult: the sound crew has to ensure that the sound is authentic and that there are no inappropriate noises. It is surprising how often this presents a problem. Everyone else on set tends to be concentrating on the picture quality and only the sound technicians actually listen to the sound. If a police siren can be heard faintly in the background it is the sound recordist who has to notice (especially if the film is an eighteenth-century costume drama!) On location, after a scene is shot, the director asks the sound recordist if the sound quality is 'okay'. Everyone holds their breath at this point because, if the sound team is unhappy, there often has to be a retake. This can make the sound crew very unpopular indeed and diplomacy is an essential but often unmentioned aspect of the sound recordist's job.

On location, sound operators will also often record 'wildtrack', or sound which is not in synch with the camera but is instead intended for the background. Wildtrack will later provide necessary atmosphere ('atmos') over shots, for example, which do not include dialogue. Sound technicians on location make notes about the sound which are then passed on to the editor to help him or her in the task of editing.

The boom operator is a junior member of the sound team who controls the boom, a long arm with a microphone (mike), which pivots and responds to sources of sound. In a drama, for example, the boom operator will have to swing the microphone between the speakers, so he or she has to know the dialogue and be ready and alert when different speakers come in. The job looks easy but requires considerable skill; inexperienced boom operators can make the jobs of more senior members of the sound crew very difficult. Boom operators cannot thump around in hobnail boots! They have to wear quiet shoes and clothing. Boom operators must have good hand-to-eye co-ordination and possess some understanding of camera angles and lighting.

Sound technicians can sometimes be seen in outside broadcast interviews holding the gun mike, which is usually covered with a fuzzy woolly protector. Gun mikes are directional, which means that they only pick up 'atmos' sound at the sides and the back. This is very useful when there is a great deal of extraneous noise. Mikes are sometimes attached to performers' clothing; this often requires tactful handling because female interviewees are often embarrassed by male technicians fixing microphones on their chests!

Sound has to be compatible with the picture, or, in other words, quiet for distant shots and louder for close-ups. If two supposed spies are whispering secrets in the background, and the voices boom out, it subliminally destroys the scene for the audience. Sound and image have to be synchronised so that they match exactly. In film that is the whole purpose of the clapperboard (which is such a symbol of the film-making process). In post-production the editor synchronises the loud bang on the soundtrack (as the top of the clapperboard hits the bottom) with the exact frame of the film which shows the clapper making contact. This is to ensure that sound and image are 'in synch' and is the reason why each scene in a film should begin with the clapperboard.

With ENG and PSC cameras the sound is recorded onto a strip on the videotape: sound and image are not separate entities as they are in film. Sound quality still has to be monitored, however, and the sound operator works in conjunction with the camera operator, carrying the recorder which is connected by cable to the camera. In the Betacam system the actual sound recording equipment is incorporated into the camera (just like the home video camera). Again, however, the sound person is attached to the camera operator so that he or she can monitor sound quality. The sound operator does not have heavy

132

equipment to cart around as in the past, but often has only the mixer to transport.

Sound technicians often begin as trainees on the studio floor. Trainees learn about the various types of microphones (how to place them correctly), and are responsible for making sure that communication systems such as 'talkback' and loudspeakers work well. They also have to become familiar with the work of the sound supervisor in the sound control room.

The sound supervisor or sound mixer supervises programme sound and monitors and adjusts sound during a studio recording. He or she is responsible for the operation of the audio-mixer console or sound desk. This consists of a vast array of buttons each representing a sound source. The sound mixer has to fade the sound sources up or down and balance them to provide the right mix. This can be complicated: in one scene, for example, there may be people talking, the sound of rain falling and then the theme music in the background. They all have to be balanced correctly or the rain will drown out the voices and the music overwhelm everything. The job requires experience and an artistic sense of which sound is appropriate at a given moment.

One of the feed sources into the sound desk is from the grams operator, who has a library of sound effects and music. The grams operator plays in on cue sound effects and music which are mixed with, for example, an actor's dialogue on the studio floor.

Sound dubbing editors, or mixers, are concerned with post-production and are highly skilled and experienced sound technicians. They work on the edited soundtrack and mix dialogue and sound effects and add the music for the final soundtrack. Sound editors sometimes have to re-record parts of the track to fit in with the pictures.

The soundtrack of almost any film or television programme is made up of a variety of sounds which were recorded in different acoustic conditions. The dubbing editor must blend the sounds in such a way that the audience accepts the track as completely natural to the film. Changes of levels have to be ironed out or varied (to give the illusion of depth). The music must be added so that it contributes to the dramatic impact of the programme or film without overwhelming it.

There are all sorts of problems for sound editors to sort out in post-production, from dogs yapping in the background to a narrator whose voice in one scene sounds oddly different from his voice in other scenes (possibly because he had a cold and sore throat on one day of filming). It is a real skill to be able to cope with these problems without shifting the viewer's attention from what is being said to how it is being said. The bugbear of many television interviews in offices is the telephone which rings while the interviewee is in mid-sentence. For news, if the phone is picked up quickly, the soundtrack is generally left as it is and the interview is not reshot, but this is an indication of how distracting extraneous sound can be. Viewers begin to wonder if the phone will be answered and they do not hear what is being said.

On high-quality productions it requires considerable artistic flair to knit together the sound elements in a coherent and pleasurable manner.

How Do You Become a Sound Technician?

People enter sound with varied qualifications, not necessarily in science, although most television companies look for GCSEs or A levels in maths or physics. Television courses at college can be useful, as can a BTEC, a City and Guilds course or a degree in electronics, computer science, programme operations or communications. Proven flair in audio work is obviously helpful.

There is no particular pattern of employment. Some sound technicians stay in the job for life, but others see it as a first step towards camera operation, direction or production. The BBC and ITV still train sound technicians and this is probably the most professional way in.

People get into film sound either with experience in television or video or, again, through contacts. Beginning as a runner, and attaching oneself to a sound team (helping the boom operator, for example) is one way. Employers often look for someone who is interested in music and it is sometimes possible to get in by begging a sound operator in a video company to take on an assistant. Those with no qualifications but who have a passion for sound, who know a great deal about audio equipment and are very talented may be taken on by a small video company at very low pay and then work their way up. The chances of this, however, are pretty slim at the present time, especially in a recession when trained freelance technicians are looking for work. Some sound recordists begin by working voluntarily with amateur rock bands and go on from there.

The crisis in training has meant that there are untrained sound recordists around. Again, however, the NVQ system may help to encourage training and retraining in the future.

In addition to further education courses there are also privately funded short courses available for sound technicians. These have to be paid for by the individual and are usually open only to those with experience.

134

VISION MIXER

Television and Video

There are no vision mixers in film: it is a profession specifically associated with television/video technology. Vision mixers assemble the visual elements of a television production so that the images flow in a realistic and logical order. The expression 'vision mixer' is used to describe the person who operates the equipment and the equipment itself. A vision mixer sits in the gallery, on the other side of the director from the PA. The vision mixer equipment consists of a large electronic console panel with buttons, faders and knobs and the vision mixer's job is to ensure a smooth transition from one shot to the next.

Each camera in the studio has its own input into the mixer, as have telecine machines (which transfer films into a television tape format), digital video effects units, computers, electronic caption generators, colour bars, colour matte generators, slide photographs and so on. Outside broadcast materials from abroad via satellite may also have to be fed in at the appropriate time.

The vision mixer, under instruction from the director, cuts (perhaps a 'mix' or a 'wipe') between vision sources. The vision mixer can add captions and provide special electronic effects, in this sense having much in common with an editor in film. He or she must be able to respond instantly to the director's wishes.

The director may decide to start a programme with a presenter on camera 1, followed by shots of a pop group in the studio on cameras 2, 3 and 4 (light entertainment involves much directorial imagination), then there may be a call to 'run VT', perhaps a recording of the pop group touring America by bus. The viewer watches a collage of images from the American tour and hears in the background the band playing in the studio. Then the director may order a 'wipe' of the American tour image so that it slides off the screen in one direction, the image of the band in the studio following behind until it again fills the screen. Finally a slide photograph of the leader of the group with his girlfriend may appear as the band plays their hit love song. The permutations are endless; the vision mixer must make all these cuts from one source to the next at the right moment. As the vision mixer operates the controls the end result is recorded on videotape, or transmitted live: it depends on the programme. Live transmission can be harrowing.

Some modern vision mixer consoles are extremely sophisticated and can produce a multiplicity of technical effects, such as dividing the screen into multi-images or creating rapid zooms in which a small dot appears on the horizon and becomes larger and larger until it dominates the whole screen. This, however, is moving into the world of

special effects and there are certain companies and artists who specialise in this area (see Chapter 12).

A vision mixer must be able to anticipate when the director will give
a cue because exact timing is important from a creative point of view.
In music programmes the cuts must be made on the right beat: a cut at
the wrong time can spoil the mood of a light entertainment sequence.
Some experienced vision mixers have a more developed artistic sense
than many directors, and it is not unknown for the vision mixer to
carry along an inexperienced director.

It follows from the above that the job requires good visual and
artistic sense, quick reactions and manual dexterity. For light entertainment a sense of rhythm and a feel for music are essential. For
drama vision mixers have to be sensitive to the exact moment when an
image must be changed to suit the mood of the piece.

Temperament is very important. Vision mixers work long hours in
darkened control rooms. They have to concentrate for long periods
and work under immense physical and mental pressure – eye-strain
and fatigue are quite common. There can also be a curious restless-
ness, the result of sitting in the same place for hours. Vision mixers
have to be capable of a hair-trigger response to any change in the
overall programme plan. They must never panic – even if the director
does! All of which can provoke high stress levels in all but the most
confident and competent.

OB units have their own vision mixers; this is reasonable since an
OB unit is basically a mobile television studio.

How Do You Become a Vision Mixer?
Occasionally some television companies do take on trainee vision
mixers, but they are mostly recruited from existing staff. Video companies take on recruits from recognised college media courses. Some
colleges also offer production courses which are good preparation.
Video mixers are usually young and there are just as many women as
men.

ELECTRICAL TECHNICIANS (technical)
GAFFER
BEST BOY

Film, Television and Video
Lighting technicians (often referred to in Britain as 'sparks') are
responsible for the electrical safety of the lighting equipment and the

136

supply of power to it. Lighting technicians wire and set up the lights used for illuminating the studio or location set.

Lights come in various shapes and sizes and can be tilted at many angles. Lights may also be placed on portable stands at the side of the set. Sometimes electricians may have small hand-held lights for an interview on an outside broadcast. Electricians rig the lights under the direction of the chief lighting technician who, in film, is called the gaffer. The best boy is the traditional name of the second electrician working under the gaffer in film. (Be careful! Some people confuse electricians with lighting directors. They are not the same at all: the lighting director is part of the camera crew and he or she decides *where* the lights should go.)

In television studios the brilliance of the lights can be altered from a lighting console in the control room. The operator of the console may be an electrician. Most studios have a lighting grid: a crisscross structure of metal bars, overhanging the studio space from which the brackets holding the lights are hung. Some grids can be lowered, but often electricians have to work on the grid many feet above the ground. Sometimes lights are attached to a specially built scaffolding or to a gantry (a framework rather like the arm of a crane, from which lights, and sometimes cameras, are hung). Electrical technicians therefore should have a head for heights. Electrical work can be very hard physically and electricians have to be strong. It was, and remains, very male-dominated, but there are a few female electrical technicians and their number appears to be on the increase.

How Do You Get to Be an Electrical Technician?
For film and video the main route is to be a qualified electrician and have contacts. Electricians usually have a City and Guilds qualification from a further education college and then apply to the company (either film, video or television) of their choice. Some move into the industry from theatre and stage lighting and there is also movement in the other direction.

These are the main technical creative posts. There is an excellent book which deals in great detail with all these posts in the commercial television sector. It is called *The Official ITV Careers Handbook* edited by Sue Davies and published by Hodder and Stoughton. Anyone interested in working for Channel 3 should look for the updated version due in 1992.

Case Histories

KATHY FRIEND

Kathy Friend is twenty-nine and describes herself as a fledgeling camera operator. She is based in Glasgow.

I've got eight O levels and one A level in English. I did a typing course at school because my mum told me it would be useful. It made me realise I never wanted to be a secretary! After school I went on to do a course in stage management at the Guildhall School of Music and Drama and, after leaving there, I stage managed for five years.

In between theatre jobs I made short video dramas with a friend. He and I both applied to the National Film School and, after five years, he got in to do a directing course and I didn't. Anyway I kept persisting making videos and applying for various courses. Then, after three tries, I got on the Scottish Technicians Training Scheme. I did the course for a year and it was absolutely brilliant. I met lots of people and made many contacts. Before I went on the Scheme I knew no one in the industry. I'd write letters asking people for jobs as a trainee, but I wouldn't even get any replies. After I had been on the training course it was much easier.

After I left the Scheme I became a freelance camera assistant. I learned a lot as an assistant because I worked with some very good cameramen and they taught me a lot. I mainly worked on documentaries and it involved quite a lot of travel. In 1991 I went on an NSCTP one-week course for Steadicam operators. I was the first woman to go on the course and it was worth it.

Since 1988, aside from my professional work, I have shot one small 10-minute, 16mm film every year. I thought to myself, if I can't get into film school, I will do this as a way of compensation. After all, at the National Film School I would have made films, so why shouldn't I train by making films myself? I want to be a director of photography on a feature film eventually and the only way to learn technique is by shooting your own films. You must practise. I practise on my own films!

In my professional life I am just beginning to work as a camera operator, mainly on corporate videos, although it is broadcast work that I like. Although it has taken me six years to become a camera operator, the time hasn't been wasted. I've learned a lot professionally and I've also learned through making my own films. If you want something enough, you can make it in the end. I really love what I am doing.

DAN GOODHART

Dan Goodhart is twenty-six and is working as a music cameraman for an Italian broadcasting company.

I went to Durham University and read history. While I was there I played around with video cameras with friends and got interested. When I was at university I thought about going into advertising and when I left I went on a small business course. My idea was to set up a business making videos for estate agents, which I did. It coincided almost to the day with the collapse of the property market.

While trying the idea, however, I met someone at a duplication company who told me there was a job going as an assistant editor with an off-line editing company in North Kensington, run by a husband and wife team. It was an apprenticeship really. I worked there for a year. I was only an assistant, so I did a lot of administrative work, hiring out of off-line suites, that sort of thing. Occasionally I got to do some editing myself, but I really cut my teeth editing weddings which I had shot with my own camera. It was an S-VHS camera at the bottom end of the professional market, not a full-size ENG camera.

While I was working as an assistant I met a lot of freelance camera people and realised that I liked their job better than editing, which meant sitting alone in a dark room drinking too much coffee. So I worked quite a lot, here and there, gaining experience on cameras all the time, but I decided I needed some proper training, so I went on the NSCTP course to learn how to operate Beta SP cameras, which are the industry standard. I put a show reel together and I got a number of jobs from people I knew.

Then, after about six months, an advert appeared in the trade press for a cameraman for an Italian television music company. I applied and got it. It's great. I basically work as a one-man band. I'm camera, sound and lighting, all rolled into one. The programme is broadcast in Italy twice a day and is a news programme about music. I cover concerts, features and interviews for the London office.

At the moment I am also shooting a travel programme with them, so I travel quite a bit within Europe, which I enjoy. I'm really having fun. I like being out and having the freedom: you are your own boss in this job and it's creative. It's real on-the-job training because, in a set-up like this where you do most of it yourself, you are learning all the time.

For me, working with an ENG camera is like working with a big toy.
I love it.

ORIN BEATON

*Orin Beaton is twenty-nine. He started a JOBFIT course in September
1986 and finished in September 1988.*

I was in the third group to go through in JOBFIT's first year. I had
already attended numerous video and film workshops where I discovered my real interest was in sound recording. It was while I was on
one of these courses at the National Film School that a friend told me
about the JOBFIT scheme, so I applied. I didn't think I would be
accepted because there were about 1,500 applications for only fifty
placements. I also thought that my job at the time, as a nine-to-five
civil servant, would not endear me to the interview panel.

In the first year you work in as many departments as possible, in the
second year you specialise. I think the first year was very useful
because I gained a basic understanding of the workings of each department, which makes you more appreciative of other people's problems
when you are actually shooting. That still helps me.

In the second year I specialised in sound and my first placement was
on a film called *Who Framed Roger Rabbit?* Initially I was terrified by
the scale of the production and I also realised that there were social
skills involved in the job besides sound recording. You have to be able
to talk to everybody, from the tea lady to executive producer. *Roger
Rabbit* was very challenging, because the director requested that the
actors who were providing the off-screen voices of the cartoon characters should be 'miked' at all times, as well as the actors actually in
shot.

After I finished training I worked on commercial and pop promos.
My first film job was offered to me by the sound recordist with whom I
had worked on *Roger Rabbit*. In this way JOBFIT was useful because
it provided an 'in' with useful contacts. I have worked with many
different recordists since and it is the best way to learn. You have to
have a wide variety of experience, because every recordist has his or
her opinion and technique about how to get the best quality sound to
match the shot. This includes the recording of sound effects and various 'wild tracks' to help the editor in post-production.

My advice to anyone wanting to get into the film industry is to attend as many courses as possible and read up on the technical side. Then you have to start telephoning equipment hire houses, heads of departments and production companies to get your foot in the door. Forget the glamour, forget the 'big bucks' (there aren't any), do the job because you are really interested in it and want to make it your career.

12

DESIGN

Design jobs in the industry include set design, wardrobe and costume design, make-up, graphic design and animation. Skillset is establishing standards of competence for these areas, but new recruits and those already employed should note that there is an Industry Lead Body for Design which is also establishing broad 'performance criteria'. In association with this, the design industry is currently carrying out a mapping exercise of jobs. Despite initial resistance (typical of a creative workforce) even the cynics in the design industry are now admitting that this has turned out to be a very useful exercise. The whole idea of developing standards of competence on the basis of a functional analysis of jobs has won converts.

A specific section of the Lead Body for Design is concentrating on television and film (as well as theatre) in terms of sets, props and costumes. New recruits and those who wish to retrain should be aware of the work of this organisation (its address is listed in the Appendix below).

SET DESIGN
PRODUCTION DESIGNER (creative)
ART DIRECTOR (creative)
SET DESIGNER (creative)
SET DECORATOR (creative/craft)
PROPERTIES (creative/technical/craft)

Film, Television and Video
The designer of a film set is usually referred to as the production designer; in television the term set designer is more common. Art director is a term also used, mainly on feature films, to indicate the person with overall responsibility for sets and properties and everything related to the film's design 'look'. There is a certain overlap

between art director and production designer jobs: indeed, they can be indistinguishable. In any case, whatever it is called, set/production/art design is one of the most creative jobs in the industry and increasingly designers work as freelancers across all three sectors.

The set/production designer is usually involved in a production from the initial planning to, and through, production. If the programme or film is a historical drama, the set/production designer will research the period in detail to make sure that the design and props are authentic. If the film or programme is to be shot on location, the designer will go out with the location manager to find appropriate settings. The design team for a series like *Poirot*, for example, would have to scour the country looking for examples of 30s architecture unaltered by 'modernisation'. Designers are also often asked to attend actual filming in order to keep an eye on what is going on.

In the pre-production period the set/production designer draws a floor plan, constructs a working model and decides the content of the set. Set/production designers work in close co-operation with producers and directors. The director and the set designer discuss their ideas in detail and then the set designer will draw a 'storyboard', rather like a strip cartoon, which describes the progression of the story, and what the set will look like, scene by scene. (Storyboards of famous films are collector's items for real film 'buffs'.)

The next step is the production of simplified architectural drawings of the sets, which are then costed. Designers have to have a fairly good business sense, especially if they are freelance, because extravagant designs are unlikely to win approval at times of financial stringency. Nowadays designers often have training in computer graphics, and they may plan the sets with the aid of a computer.

Once the sets are agreed upon, the designer may construct scale models to be used in liaison work with the costume designer, lighting director, sound supervisor and so on. Designers must ensure that sets are practical for the equipment and this is where scale models come in. It is important that sets do not impede the cameras, throw malign shadows or sound hollow if they are thumped. On a recent sitcom, the author noted an actor putting a plate on the draining-board of a sink unit. The whole unit shook unconvincingly and its flimsiness was immediately apparent. This distracts and annoys most viewers.

During this pre-production period designers tell the craft and workshop areas what they want constructed. They discuss with the properties department which cushions, plants, rugs and so on are required to 'decorate' the set and, in some cases, they go out to select and buy those furnishings which the props department is unable to produce.

Designers are crucial to the atmosphere of a film or programme.

Television and film are visual media and the images which impinge on the viewer are important because they produce an emotional response. Set design can involve massive tasks, such as the creation of a medieval castle or a spaceship, or it can concern simple projects such as the choice of desks and furniture for a news programme. The latter, however, can be very important: chairs which look uncomfortable or bizarre can make the interviewer and interviewee look ill at ease. This can subconsciously alienate the audience and break down the feeling of confidence in what is being said. Television design, in particular, involves a wide variety of work, from the complexity of a major historical drama to the set for a chat show or a mobile for *Top of the Pops*.

Many film and television designers have a background in theatre design, but some come from architecture or interior design, or even from landscape architecture. Film or television design is more complex than that of theatre design because the audience sees the set from all angles and in close-up. Film and television screens produce images of great clarity and the set has to stand up to close scrutiny as the camera moves in and even lingers. Sets, of course, are illusions: they are not what they seem. The cold eye of the camera, however, can reveal the smallest inaccuracy and anachronism. This can jar the viewer's sensibilities and, at one blow, destroy the atmosphere which the director or scriptwriter has sought to create. Attention to detail, and an understanding of the cinematographic art, are therefore essential to the set designer's job.

DESIGN ASSISTANTS

Designers on complex productions are usually assisted by design assistants who help with the research and the preparation of drawings and models. In film the production designer is usually also assisted by the set decorator; the latter is responsible for the selection of props and also supervises the 'dressing' of the set. The set decorator works from plans or sketches provided by the designer and prepares prop lists. He or she works closely with the Props Department in organising the dressing and striking (taking down) of the sets.

How Do You Become a Set Designer?
Most designers in all areas of the industry have degrees in some aspect of design. Set designers have BAs in Interior Design, or Art and Design, or Architecture, or Stage Design. Many art colleges provide specialised courses in set design which confer an advantage on those

who follow them as far as employment is concerned. Prospective stage or set designers usually have an interest in furniture, fashion design and architecture.

The design area of the industry is probably the one where raw talent is most at a premium. It takes time to suss out an untalented director or camera operator, but people who cannot draw or design are easy to spot. Consequently designers, in all areas of the industry, can be very young.

It is quite common for a designer to start in the theatre and then move to film or television. Some very fortunate young people may get taken on as assistants by television or video companies straight from college. In film some young people start in the properties department, move on to become set decorators and move up from there.

Most designers now work across all sectors as freelancers. Of course it still takes time to become well-known, and set design like everything else has been hit by the recession. Standards of competence for set designers are being developed by Skillset and the Industry Lead Body for Design.

WARDROBE DESIGNER (creative/administrative)
COSTUME DESIGNER (creative/administrative)
DRESSERS

The costume or wardrobe designer is appointed during pre-production to assess costume needs. After consultation with the director, costume/ wardrobe designers plan, design and fit costumes in keeping with the look and spirit of the production. They are assisted by wardrobe staff who remain throughout the production to maintain the clothes and ensure that performers are dressed properly (buttons and zippers are closed, stockings are unwrinkled, for example).

The costume designer begins by reading the script and identifying the period in which the production is set. Designers must have a sound historical sense and know about the class and social details which are intimately connected with how people dress. If gentlemen in nine-teenth-century England never wore brown suits in town; if society ladies in the Edwardian period always changed into 'tea' dresses in the afternoon; if contemporary middle-aged British men wear socks with their sandals but sophisticated Frenchmen never do: then wardrobe designers must know about all these details, which provide clues to a character, and incorporate them.

Wardrobe is also connected with an intuitive understanding of personality. If the leading female character has a flamboyant personality, she will not be dressed like a governess in lace collars and long black skirts. Costume designers have to be alert to the emotional tone of the drama. Clothes are intimately connected with confidence and costume designers must therefore have considerable psychological insight. The English middle-class lady who always wears Marks and Spencer underwear is different from the upper-class call-girl who wears hand-made lingerie from an expensive French couturier. Somehow the designer must convey this – even if the underwear is never actually shown on camera!

Costume designers also have to know about lighting and lighting plans. At times directors and cinematographers may want to create a mood which lighting and costumes should enhance. If the production is to have a pale tone, with sepia overlays reminiscent of an old photograph, then a designer who produces a costume design in vivid scarlet would deserve to be thrown out on their ear. If the director wants to convey the style of an impressionist painting, the costume director must look at the clothes in those paintings and check that the materials are in the correct style, textures and colours.

In a film or programme with a contemporary setting many of the clothes are simply purchased from ordinary shops or hired from theatrical costumiers. On the other hand, historical drama means a great deal of research in libraries, museums, art galleries, print shops and similar sources. Designers do not usually make the clothes themselves, but they do supervise their construction. They should understand tailoring and dressmaking and they will buy accessories (for example, stockings, tights, gloves, hats, belts, ties, scarves, shoes, earrings, and leggings).

Actors themselves can be very involved with wardrobe. Most of them are sensitive about their appearance (their face is truly their fortune) and they can be obstreperous when it comes to wearing garments which they don't believe suit them. If the leading female actor does not like her costume, and thinks it makes her look ugly or fat (when she is supposed to be young and beautiful), her unhappiness can affect her performance and the quality of the production. The costume designer has to be aware of such pitfalls and deal tactfully with sensitive feelings. Costume designers usually have to keep control of the department budget and ought to have both administrative skills and business acumen.

During the production of a drama wardrobe designers will be assisted by staff (dressers) who help dress the actors and wash, clean and iron the garments. Washing and drying facilities can present a major headache on location; a costume can get torn and covered in mud one day and be required for the shooting of another scene on the next.

Dressers help performers in and out of their costumes. This is a job which calls for real empathy and human concern. Actors can become very tense during filming and they may let off steam with their dressers. Many dressers are retired actors or young would-be actors who enjoy working in film and television and understand how actors feel. They often provide a sympathetic ear for a tirade against an insensitive director and boost the ego of the actor, stressing how good they look in a particular costume. Dressers frequently carry out minor alterations to the costumes during filming or recording, so they should be able to sew quickly and do small repairs. They are also responsible for the care of the clothes, including the washing, cleaning and pressing.

How Do You Become a Wardrobe or Costume Designer?

Today costume designers often come into film or television from the fashion industry or from art school. Many of them have degrees in Fashion Design, the History of Art or even Museum Studies. Some have a background in textiles; some costume designers have taken degrees in drama with a special emphasis on costume or wardrobe. They must possess a knowledge of fabrics and style and an understanding of dressmaking. Many costume designers come in via the theatre, where they may have come up through the ranks after gaining experience in a theatre wardrobe department. Increasingly, however, wardrobe designers do receive specific training on courses in the former polytechnics (henceforth universities) and art colleges. Nowadays wardrobe designers are often freelance and work in all sectors of the industry. Skillset is currently preparing standards of competence.

How Do You Become a Dresser?

Dressers are usually mature people with experience of the industry who wish to keep working in an environment which suits and interests them. They have to have the right temperament.

MAKE-UP ARTIST (creative/technical)

Film, Television and Video

Make-up artists on feature films or television drama can have a very complex job indeed. They may have to make actors look older, younger, bald, hirsute, dowdy, ill, or attractive. Make-up has come a long way since the old Hollywood films in which female stars in a sixteenth-century romance about pirates pranced happily aboard ship in the heavy 'pancake' make-up of the 1940s. Today make-up must fit in with the 'look' of the production. Fashionable women in the 1960s wore heavy eye-liner, false lashes and white lipstick but no blusher; in the 70s sparkly eye-shadow and blusher came into fashion; lip gloss was the rage in the 80s; certain coral and pink colours were not available in lipsticks prior to the Second World War, when the fashion was for a bold red: all this the make-up artists must know. They have to study the fashion plates of the periods in magazines like *Vogue* and incorporate them into their work with a subtlety which will not offend contemporary taste in beauty.

Science fiction, horror or war movies call upon the creative resources of the make-up artist. There are some highly specialised make-up artists who make a great deal of money creating, for example, terrible facial or body wounds for a war film or, at the other end of the scale, the fantasy make-up for the Addams family. Highly skilled technicians work with latex foam and other materials to re-create or change the shape of a face. The more specialised make-up artists have to know about the chemical composition of plastic substances: they cannot put a chemical which eats away at the skin on the face of an unsuspecting actor. They also have to be aware of the dangers of fungal diseases which can be one of the unpleasant side-effects of being encased in foam rubber! In America film and television make-up is dominated by men, and this used to be the case in the film industry in Britain. However, the BBC and the independent companies trained large numbers of women in make-up and it is now a much more evenly balanced profession in this respect.

Much of the work of the average make-up artist in television, on the other hand, is not so dramatic. It is usually described as 'corrective', which means making people look better by 'correcting' their worst features. Make-up artists will apply powder to shiny noses, cover up acne or 'white out' areas which will look shadowed under the studio lights. It is said that Richard Nixon lost the presidency of the United States to John F. Kennedy because in the television debates his chin always produced a heavy five o'clock shadow which made him look sinister and jowly. When he became president, Nixon made sure that talcum powder was liberally applied to the offending area. Make-up artists in television usually also have responsibility for hairstyling and for keeping wigs and hairpieces cleaned. They may have to wash, set and brush hair out and colour it in period and modern styles.

Once again it is important for people who want to become make-up artists to have a rapport with people with whom, after all, they will work at very close quarters. They often deal with actors on an early call, which can be at six o'clock in the morning, when few people are at their physical best and when many can be very bad-tempered. The actors may be depressed about their appearance, they may fear that their looks are going, that their eyes are baggy and their wrinkles showing, and they may blame it all on the hapless make-up artist, who will have to tread very carefully indeed.

Make-up artist and client are often in one-to-one situations. One of the hazards of the job for female make-up artists may be sexual harassment in the form of propositions and fondling. This has to be handled in a mature manner so that it is clear that such behaviour is unacceptable. Timidity and shyness are not useful attributes for a make-up artist!

Make-up artists on a film or major drama production work closely with the directors, costume designers and lighting personnel. Lighting is particularly important where make-up is concerned: the wrong make-up can be disastrous on a brightly lit set.

How Do You Become a Make-up Artist?

The BBC and the independent companies used to train make-up artists, but here also there have been cutbacks in recent months. In any case, the competition for trainee make-up artist positions at the BBC was extremely intense, with thousands applying for the few available positions.

Some trainee make-up technicians take up the career after a training as a hairdresser or beautician, but others have degrees in Drama or Art and Design from art colleges and film schools. Art schools provide training in sculpture which can be important for some of the more skilled areas. The City and Guilds, and BTEC, both provide recognised courses in Make-up and Hairdressing and Beauty Therapy, and these can help candidates to get jobs when they are advertised. Very specialised make-up artists have sometimes received a training at Madame Tussaud's. There are private schools which provide training, such as the Stratford School of Film and TV Make-up and Hairdressing where students do a three-month course from 'Moustache Maintenance to Severed Limbs' (*Independent*, 27 December 1991).

Make-up is another area of the industry which is increasingly dominated by freelancers. It has been badly hit by the decline in training provision in the industry and it is quite difficult for students to secure the necessary financial support to follow courses. If you are very keen, it may be an idea to put together a portfolio of work and then knock

149

on the doors of the various television and video companies asking to be taken on for general duties.

GRAPHIC DESIGNER

Film, Television and Video
The work of the graphic designer in films or in a television company is extremely wide-ranging. It includes typography, lettering, doing simple credits, designing mobiles, weather charts, cartoons and animation. Graphic designers might also be employed making props for special programmes: passports, foreign money, ration books and other historical ephemera, for example.

Graphic designers are most usually associated with the opening (the 'titles') and closing credits on films and programmes and the work increasingly involves computer graphics. Computers have made enormous inroads in this area and graphic artists have to be up-to-date with all the latest techniques and software as they become available. The future application of modern technology to the screen will require graphic designers to be extremely flexible in their skills; they will have to be prepared constantly to retrain on new equipment as it becomes available.

The production of credits for feature films is a particularly specialised craft and there are companies which work only in this area. Graphic designers often work for these companies; the graphic designer could well be part of a company team which consults with the producer, director and set designer on a film to establish a continuity of theme and mood for the credits. Most cinemagoers and television viewers accept the credits unthinkingly and do not realise the great ingenuity and effort which is put into them. Yet they can be crucial in preparing the mood of the audience for what is about to follow.

In television the 'titles' of a long-running series can cue the audience in to a meeting with 'old friends'. One of the most successful credits in recent television history was for the *South Bank Show*: this combined computer graphics with a highly recognisable musical theme.

Graphic designers today do not, as they sometimes used to, prepare captions (the identification of a speaker in written letters at the bottom of a television screen). These are now usually the responsibility of a caption generator operator, who uses specialised equipment similar to a word processor. (Caption generator operators might have secretarial training or be assistant floor managers who have been roped into the job.)

How Do You Become a Graphic Designer?
Graphic designers are usually art college-trained, with degrees or diplomas in graphic design. Alternatively they may have a Licentiate of the Society of Industrial Designers. Some of them come into television via commercial art studios or have been trained in computing where they find they have a talent for designing with computer graphic systems such as 'Paintbox'. Others work with special effects video companies. Highly talented art students who are trained in computer graphics should not lack for job opportunities.

SPECIAL EFFECTS TECHNICIANS/OPERATORS/ARTISTS

'A few years from now if you can still portray a human being, you'll be quite a valuable commodity.' (Jack Nicholson)

Special effects are currently the glamour area of film, as one film after another tries to outdo rivals in the scale and imagination of the special effects. Every kid with a computer dreams about creating special effects. *Terminator II* included about fourteen minutes worth.

Film does present problems for special effects, however, because it is essentially a nondigital medium: it is 'wet, chemical, messy and more organic than mechanic'. Quantel has recently produced its Domino System, which may do for film what digital systems are already doing for video. Domino digitalises short sequences of film, dividing each frame of film into a grid or map of points. The computer measures the colour and intensity of the film at each point. Using these measurements, it can manipulate the image, move parts around the frame, make a montage of images, change colour, fade, mix and wipe. This opens up many possibilities for film special effects and shows the significance of technology even with such a traditional medium.

Traditionally special effects artists are highly specialised freelancers for whom there is no set career pattern. Nowadays they are divided into physical and computer special effects artists. Physical usually means sets which are constructed, sometimes in miniature, specifically to be set on fire, blown up or whatever the script calls for. There are all sorts of techniques associated with this type of work, many of which are handed down by word of mouth, although books about special effects are available. Pyrotechnic experts need to have a special licence from the Home Office because the work is dangerous and can affect the safety of others.

Special effects operators come from a wide variety of backgrounds as electricians, explosives experts, inventors, ex-soldiers and the like;

they may be scientists with an interest in robotics or may have worked at Madame Tussaud's. There is simply no particular background which can be said to be typical: special effects people 'emerge' by being fascinated with the problems presented, 'having a go' and proving that they can do it. Temperament, however, is important: special effects experts have to be inventive, ingenious and scrupulous about safety. There are also specialist special effects camera operators who invariably have a camera background.

One of the most respected special effects outfits in Britain is the BBC Special Effects Department. The Department has a long history and has built up an impressive knowledge of the field. In the United States special effects are very big business and some freelance experts earn a fortune.

In recent years special effects has been revolutionised by computer graphics. There are video effects companies which provide a specialised service to films, television programmes, television commercials, independent pop video companies and so on. Computer graphics machines produce a multiplicity of effects which, as we have seen, are used in titles and in credits, and in productions which have, for example, a science fiction orientation. Some computer graphics can be added live to television programmes. A video effects company can provide appropriate effects downline to a programme director in the studio control room. These appear on a monitor in front of the director, who adds them as appropriate.

This field is developing very rapidly indeed and young people who combine technical ability with artistic talent are in a very strong position. 'Paintbox' is the classic computer programme which requires artistic talent. If you can't draw, you can't do much with Paintbox, no matter how good you are at computing. The pen is sensitive to pressure and, once the technique is mastered, calls upon the same skill as any artist needs.

The problem with Paintbox is that it deals only with single static frames (it was developed for television programmes such as weather reports) and it requires fifty frames to fill two seconds of time. The modern advance, vis-à-vis paintbox techniques, is Quantel's 'Harry Machine', which has the ability to deal with sequences and frames. The operator can flip back and forth using a foot pedal or the left hand. The operator of this machine, the so-called 'Harry artist', is the king or queen of the computer special effects/design business at the present time. The operator combines great technical versatility (because he or she is dealing with such matters as time codes and colour gradings) with real artistic talent. Quantel runs its own training programmes for Harry artists and the places are snapped up immediately. (For a fuller article on special effects, see Mitch Mitchell, 'Invisible Effects', *Television*, February 1992. The article discusses the techniques used in Anchor Butter's *Dancing Cows* advertisement.)

How Do You Become a Special Effects Specialist?
Aside from studying computer special effects, no career path can be specified. People certainly do not leave school or college and go into physical special effects. They have usually worked elsewhere in the industry first.

On the computer side of the business, Paintbox and Harry artists usually have an art school background and knowledge of electronic engineering or computing. People who work in this area often have a passion for computers and a flair for design, a relatively rare combination. There are no job shortages for Harry artists: the industry is crying out for them and the pay is excellent.

ANIMATORS
CARTOONISTS

Film, Television and Video
Animation is now closely associated with special effects and graphic art and computing and yet true animation is, as one commentator described it, the 'Holy Grail'. The best animation is still done by hand and, although much research is being done on computer animation by companies such as Disney and Cambridge Animation, the problem of creating really natural movement in drawn figures has not yet been conquered. No computer software yet designed can render the muscles in a human face which express nuance of feeling and emotion. Artists do this instinctively and this is why the best animation is still hand-drawn. Human communication skills are infinitely variable and modern technology simply cannot mimic the slight changes in gesture and movement which are necessary if cartoon characters are to appear really 'animated'.

In the traditional method of animation the animator breaks down the action of the proposed cartoon character into very small movements which are drawn on individual sheets of paper and photographed. When the film is projected, it seems as if the characters are alive and moving.

In most animation companies there is usually a key animator, the animation director, who will do most of the creative work. He or she comes up with the idea, designs the scene, decides how the action will happen and the expressions and appearance of the characters. This role is equivalent to the director on an ordinary film. Animators will draw the characters and assistant animators will tidy up the initial drawings and do the minor characters. Assistants may also prepare instructions for the camera operator (sometimes known as 'dope sheets') saying how a scene should be shot and how many frames of each drawing are required. There may also be assistants known as 'in-betweeners', who do the drawings in between the important actions. Generally there is also a 'paint and trace' department which takes the completed drawings and copies them on to 'cells' (sheets of transparent material) before they are photographed.

Most animation studios make their money through commercials. Full-length animation feature films are extremely time-consuming and very expensive. One of the most interesting examples of animation in recent years was Robert Zemeckis' *Who Framed Roger Rabbit?*, which combined live actors with animated cartoon characters. Most of the animation for this film was prepared in studios in London – increasingly a centre of first-class animation.

Animation is so very costly because it is labour-intensive. Computers, however, are also an extremely expensive initial investment and they do not have the elegance and naturalness of true animation. They can, on the other hand, produce images very quickly and efficiently and, once the investment has been made, they are obviously cheaper in terms of wages and manpower. It really all depends on the type of image the producer of the film or programme wants to convey. Until computers can do what the human hand and eye can accomplish, however, hand-drawn animation will still be the Rolls Royce of the cartoon industry. Paintbox and computer graphics will be used for more run-of-the-mill work.

How Do You Become an Animator?
Mainly by going to art college and being good at rapid drawing and sketching. There are independent animation studios which make animated films for commercials and features. The would-be animator should take a video which illustrates their own work to the studio and try to get a job as a 'runner'. Studios will be looking for originality and creativity as well as artistic ability: there are many more people who can draw than there are who can draw *and* come up with original ideas.

Channel Four has provided a showcase for the work of young animators in recent years, and this has given a boost to the profession. Although the most famous animation studio of all is Walt Disney, most commentators believe that Britain now has some of the best animators in the world. Animators in British commercial studios

154

working on cartoons for advertisers can make a great deal of money. The European Community's CARTOON scheme provides funds for young animators to produce pilot videos, and this has been a positive contribution to the development of the skills of European animators.

Summing Up

Design areas encompass some of the most creatively exciting areas of the industry. The design industry has expanded in Britain in the last ten years largely due to the high quality of education and training in British art colleges, polytechnics and universities. It is a strange anomaly that Britain, which is somewhat philistine in its approach to art and design in daily life, produces some of the best commercial artists and designers in the world. The British film and television industry has benefited from this.

Case Histories

DENIS DEEGAN

Denis Deegan is twenty-two and was born and educated in Eire. He is presently working for the Richard Williams studio as an animator.

I went to school in Dublin. While I was at school I wanted to get into cartoons and comics because I like writing. I left school at sixteen and I went to work with the Sullivan Bluth Studio. I started doing cell painting, working on *An American Tail*. Then I went on to work as an in-betweener and eventually became an animator. One of the films I worked on while I was there was *All Dogs Go to Heaven*.

Then, when I was twenty, I decided to go to Germany, to Berlin, to work on *Werner*. This was a part live-action animated film and it was pretty big: made the most money of any animated film in Germany. German animation was only really beginning at that time and Berlin was a good place to be. I met my girlfriend there, so learning the language wasn't a problem and it was very good experience to see how animation is done in another country.

After Germany I moved to England and got a job with Spielberg's Amblimation studio and after that with Richard Williams. This is a very busy studio and I've learned more here than anywhere else. The quality of animation is so good in England. Channel Four has really helped independent animation studios to develop. It has broadened the audience's viewpoint of animation and that has to be good. The general public is now more knowledgeable about animation. Mind you, I think there are some bad films coming out also and I am not sure that anything will ever compete with Disney.

If you want to be an animator, my advice is to do lots of life drawing and get into a good studio as soon as you can, because basically you learn from other people. You don't have to have degrees or qualifications because, if you are willing to work long hours, people will take you on and you can learn from there. Some studios tie you down and limit what you can do, but here you can come up with ideas and make a contribution. I like to be given a segment of a film to work on so I can develop an idea.

I absolutely enjoy what I do. Eventually I'd like to make my own film and I am working on a couple of ideas at the moment. There are lots of grants around.

I think the film industry in Ireland and Europe is developing, but in England the government doesn't help very much. There is such a lot of talent here: some of the best animators in the world. If the government put money into the industry, the economy would benefit but, if they don't, the talented people are going to go to the States or Europe.

CAROL PHILLIPS

Carol Phillips is twenty-seven. She has just started to work as a make-up artist on a film.

I did a City and Guilds qualification in hairdressing when I left school and worked as a hairdresser. I worked myself up so that I ended up as a manager of hairdressing on a cruise ship, but I really wanted to be a make-up artist. In fact I always wanted to be a make-up artist. While I was still at school I went for an interview to be taken on for make-up training at the BBC. But the BBC wanted me to stay on and do A levels and I didn't want to do that. I wanted practical experience not book study, so I left school. I had to decide between hairdressing and needlework, so I chose hairdressing.

After ten years of hairdressing, though, I wanted another step up and I heard about the Stratford course in make-up from someone at HTV. I heard that Shelley Weber was giving the course and that she had worked in the industry and was very experienced, so I decided to do it. I concentrated on film and photographic make-up while I was there, because I already knew about hairdressing. There was a great deal to learn. We were taught about prosthetics and we had to do ear and nose alterations using latex foam. Also someone from the BBC's *Casualty* came and taught us special effects: how to do scars with liquid plastic and blood scenes using gelatine, food colouring, sorbitol and various chemicals.

After I finished the course I got a contract working at Twickenham Studios on a production called *The Golden Years* about the Spanish Conquest of the Aztecs. I was supposed to do the extras, but I got to do some of the principals. Everybody had to be made to look darker, especially the actors playing the Indians. They had to be dark-skinned. Some of the ladies were very blonde, so we had to do a lot of sun-tanning and there was a lot of wig work where my hairdressing came in. Since there were also lots of battle scenes, we had to do gun markings. Guns leave soot marks on the face. In one scene an Indian was shot, so we had to have a pipe in his clothes so the blood would spurt out. The work involved a lot of wigs, false moustaches and beards.

You have to watch the continuity, shooting a film. You have to be very aware of the story-line. The continuity has to be spot on. You have to make sure that the actors look dirty or clean according to the story-line and, since it's shot out of sequence, you have to remember that the actors have to be clean one day, then mussed up the next and then back to clean again.

You also have to keep an eye on the well-being of the actors, so that they don't get hot and sweaty under the lights. There was a lot of sand around on the set and people kept getting it in their eyes, so I had to keep giving them drops. The Aztecs wore very elaborate head-dresses which Costume designed, but we put them on, so we had to discuss with Costume how to put them on properly.

This is my first job and I've really enjoyed it. I want to do more films and travel around. I really am still quite naive about the film industry and I want to see more and do more. What I really want to be is a make-up designer. It's one thing to train, it's another thing to get a job. My theory is that you should approach designers directly, not the production offices. Everyone says, and it's true, that contacts are vital.

13

RESEARCHERS, JOURNALISTS AND WRITERS

There are many jobs associated with writing in film and television despite the fact that they are essentially visual media. Television is a great consumer of journalists who are required in many different staff grades, and films and programmes also employ scriptwriters for the dialogue or commentaries. Many journalists begin their careers as researchers.

RESEARCHERS

Television
In television the researcher's job is extremely varied and the post tends to be the catch-all grade for graduate entrants. The term 'researcher' can be confusing because it implies study of a rather academic sort; people tend to think research means delving into matters deeply. In fact there is little of this in a television research job. Researchers spend a great deal of time on the phone making contacts, setting up programmes and finding interviewees. Most researchers work in current affairs and have the same time limitations as journalists. In other words, they have to put items together quickly and work under pressure.

Researchers are expected to come up with programme ideas and they can help write scripts and news reports. They act as the producer's right hand. The nature of the job really depends on the producer to whom the researcher reports: some producers have a great deal of confidence in researchers, who then gain a great deal of experience; other producers like to do everything for themselves and give researchers very simple tasks. Most researchers want to become producers and indeed many of them do, or they move into journalism in the news room.

The job is immensely varied. Researchers can be based in the television offices one day and out finding people and locations the next. They sometimes do the preliminary preparation for a programme and talk to members of the public to decide if they have anything to contribute and whether they will be able to cope with the interview situation. Researchers therefore meet the public a great deal and must be able to win people's confidence and put them at their ease. If someone is researching for a programme on Aids, for example, they must know something about the disease and deal with people in a sensitive and understanding way. Getting a good interview will depend a great deal on coaxing people along, especially if they are under severe emotional pressure.

Researchers also go out on recordings and they assist the director by setting up interviews and chatting to people beforehand about what they are to say. Research may involve finding people to form the studio audience for light entertainment or audiences to participate in controversial debates, for example representatives of the pro- and anti-smoking lobby. When the tabloid press was having a field-day with the story of men being able to have babies, the present writer was given twenty-four hours notice to find a man who wanted to get pregnant so that he could participate in a studio debate! It is not a job for the shy or the easily embarrassed.

In some cases researchers will actually help with the editing, particularly if a director has only been hired to do the actual recording and is not interested in the subject of the programme. This is most appropriate if the researcher has had the original idea for the programme.

There are specialised researchers for specific types of programmes. Researchers will be hired for a science series or a series on anthropology or music and so on. A fair number of researchers are employed in educational programming. Film research for television is also a more specialised area, and especially so if it involves archival film. Researchers who work on series which cover the Second World War, for example, will probably have a detailed knowledge of old newsreels and a good historical knowledge of the War.

Programme research is the area where ambitious recruits are supposed to show their potential. Increasingly people are taken on by television companies on three-month contracts and have just that time to prove they can do the job. Nowadays a number of researchers will be hired on these very short-term contracts, but only a few will secure more permanent employment.

Film

Researchers in the film industry are usually experts recruited for particular films. Thus if a feature film is set in revolutionary Russia, the company could well hire a researcher to check up on particular facts. If a real person is being portrayed, the film company might want to know if he or she smoked, or was a vegetarian or was fond of children, all of which might be incorporated into the actor's performance to provide veracity.

How Do You Become a Researcher?

Most researchers are graduates because intelligence, ingenuity and flexibility are important and a degree is taken to indicate this. In general it is the first job which is hardest to get. Once you have experience in television research, you do usually get other contracts, even if these are mainly very short-term.

One way in is the obvious one: apply for the researcher jobs which are advertised. They do crop up in the trade papers (see Appendix), but remember there will be probably hundreds of other applicants. Many graduates think of programme research as a dream job and the competition is very intense. Another way is to target a programme which interests you. Watch it, try to think up ideas for the programme and then send these to the producer, care of the programme and the company. Finding research jobs demands the sort of initiative which the job itself calls for. Again, send in letters, even though most of these will go directly into the wastepaper bin. Knock on doors and say you will do anything. Many researchers only get jobs in television after they have worked in newspapers or radio. Some people quite brazenly cultivate contacts and not a few researchers have found jobs through 'knowing' the right people. Once in, you will be expected to work long hours. There are very few old researchers. It is a young person's job and most researchers aim to be producers by the time they are thirty. One of the most famous researchers in recent television history was Esther Rantzen and look how far she got!

JOURNALISTS
NEWS WRITERS
REPORTERS
CORRESPONDENTS
NEWS READERS
NEWS EDITORS

Television

Journalism has been discussed in some detail in the section of this book which dealt with media education. Journalists can work on-screen or off. They can work on news or current affairs programmes

160

and can also be very important in documentary programming. Many producers in current affairs are journalists.

One of the main focuses for journalists in television is television news. News journalists can work behind the scenes in the studio putting together news bulletins, they can appear on-screen in the studio as newscasters, or they may go out on location and send in 'filmed' reports.

News is a high-pressure area. Programmes have to be up to the minute and, if a major news story breaks, items can be changed even as the news goes out on air. Hours too can be awkward: if there is a major air crash at four in the morning, then reporters will have to go out and cover it and journalists on call will have to come into the studio to put the story together. News stories come from a wide variety of sources. Journalists always have a fat 'contact' book in which they list useful names and numbers: politicians, police, doctors, 'experts' in all areas.

Most television journalists start behind the scenes as 'researchers' or 'news writers' in the news room. They will try to find stories, check up on the accuracy of information received and write news bulletins. They might then graduate to reporter level, usually in local news, and be sent out with a camera operator or a camera crew to report on a local event.

The best way to learn about local news reporting is to watch it over an extended period. Journalists will report on hospital shortages, visits by politicians, a local row over the police, complaints about rubbish in the streets, football hooligans, the first new babies of the year who have turned out to be triplets, the old lady who has reached the age of 105 and still has all her own teeth and so on. Notice what shots are used. If it's the baby story, is there an outside shot of the hospital? Is there a shot which links in with the New Year theme (fireworks at midnight perhaps)? The reporter usually only has an hour or two to assess the story on the spot and decide how it should be presented. He or she may do one or two interviews with the people involved and then a 'piece to camera', in which the reporter reviews the situation and gives background information.

Once the reporter is satisfied there is enough material, he or she goes back to base so that the video editor can put the story together in sequence. At this point they might record a 'voice-over' as the camera pans across, for example, the rubbish-strewn streets. The reporter is his or her own producer and director, makes most of the decisions and also writes the script.

The job requires intelligence, quick-wittedness and an ability to get on with people. Not everyone welcomes the reporter with the camera

161

and there can be tricky encounters. After one of the so-called 'race' riots in the early 80s, local reporters in an inner-city area were often met by indignant residents shouting, 'We're not animals in a zoo. Get out of here.' People had been annoyed by bad publicity and insensitive reporting mainly by the national tabloids. It took months of patience and tact to restore the feeling of goodwill which is essential if a local reporter is to do his or her job properly.

After overcoming all obstacles, the story might be dropped at the last minute because something more important has come up. This is annoying to the reporter and it can be embarrassing if the interviewees have gathered all their relatives together to watch themselves being interviewed on the local evening news. Great diplomacy is required in this situation, especially if one of the 'dropped' interviewees is the obstetrician who has given half an hour in a very busy, highly pressured day to the interview.

The aim of most local reporters is to graduate to the national news, BBC, ITN or Channel Four, or to a prestigious news programme such as *Newsnight*. These news programmes have special correspondents who report from Washington, Moscow, the UN, or Brussels or have a specialist area of responsibility such as social affairs, parliament, industry, the law or the media.

News editors have a very senior job. They make the final choice on the content of the news programme and bulletins, as well as deciding the 'running order': that is, which item should lead, which should come second and so on. This is a very important decision and news editors can be subject to enormous political pressure, particularly in an election period. Political parties complain vociferously if their point of view on the National Health Service, for example, is not the lead item. Editors also have to deal with decisions about content – whether an item is libellous, for example – and they are also responsible for long-term planning, management of staff and budget control (in association with others).

Budgets are a very sensitive issue at the present time because television news costs have been escalating. Tiananmen Square, the Gulf War, the breakup of the Soviet Union have all been very expensive to cover and there have been criticisms within ITN, for example, about high costs. Audiences expect full coverage, however, and would be very critical if a big story is missed. News people themselves instinctively want to cover everything just in case a big story breaks. A news editor who decided not to cover John Major's visit to Bridlington could lose his job if Major chose to announce his resignation there.

News readers, news presenters and newscasters have the most glamorous jobs in news and can be very highly paid. They must have a pleasant appearance, good diction, a pleasant manner and be able to remain calm when chaos is breaking out all around them. In the past it was felt that only men had the *gravitas* to read the news and that women did not have credibility. Newspapers used to run articles about how the 'lightness' of women's voices made them unsuitable for serious newscasting. Fortunately this has changed dramatically in the past ten years. Some newscasters are experienced journalists and write their own copy, and some have their scripts prepared for them by other journalists.

People tend to confuse announcers and news presenters. News presenters are invariably journalists, while announcers are men and women of pleasant appearance and voice who provide links between, and information about, programmes (see Chapter 15).

How Do You Become a Journalist?
It is estimated that there are about 30,000 journalists in the United Kingdom. Most of them work for newspapers, but about 5,000 journalists work in television and radio and there are also about another 5,000 freelancers, some of whom may work in the industry at some time during their careers. Journalism has always been an insecure profession and the onslaught on the unions has had a significant effect on the National Union of Journalists, which is currently losing members. Managers are abandoning collective agreements and negotiating individual short-term contracts.

As explained in Chapter 7, the education of journalists presents a complex picture, with a bias towards workplace training. Many television journalists begin their careers in newspapers or local radio and a patchwork of different types of training is available. Increasingly, despite a traditional antipathy towards academic training, most new journalists are graduates, although not many have degrees in journalism. There are now, however, some degree courses in journalism available at undergraduate level and it is likely that there will be more, thanks to the current changes in higher and further education. There are also very well-established courses at postgraduate level.

Journalism training which is specifically geared to television is hard to find. The BBC has trained television journalists for many years on a variety of schemes, but at the present time its News Trainee Scheme for new recruits has been postponed until 1994. However, the BBC continues to do in-house training of journalists for people who already work for the Corporation. One interesting trend is the 'multi-skilling' courses on which, in addition to training in journalism, BBC employees are provided with training in production, camera operation and other areas. This trend is an indication of the changes in the industry which have been discussed at length in this book.

In terms of broadcasting in general, the BBC also runs a Radio Trainee scheme, the aim of which is to recruit reporters for local radio. The idea is to bring in 'new blood' and applicants must have no formal training and no experience on a newspaper. It is an open scheme for which there are no formal entry qualifications, although about three-quarters of applicants are graduates. Trainees receive a two-year contract and a training salary. They have an initial training period in London and then three different placements in local radio, after which they go on the local radio reporters' reserve list. Trainees must be prepared to move at a moment's notice. The scheme applies to trainees in England and the Channel Islands and is not confined to younger applicants. People who have worked in jobs outside the industry for many years are eligible. It is, however, extremely competitive.

ITV was criticised for many years for not providing training schemes and at one time the IBA exerted pressure, resulting in the foundation of a National Broadcasting School. Unfortunately it went bankrupt after two years. However, many people enter journalism through independent local radio, which provides excellent experience. ITN also has a few traineeships available which are sometimes advertised.

Skillset is establishing standards of competence in journalism and writing, and it will be interesting to see what these are and what effect they will have. If they encourage the idea of continuous training for journalists, as they should do, they will have done the industry a great service.

SCREENWRITERS
SCRIPTWRITERS
SCRIPT EDITORS
SCRIPT READERS

Film, Television and Video
Screenwriting is the specialist term used for writing scripts for the cinema. Screenwriters in the past rarely worked in television, but today writers find themselves working in film, television and the non-broadcast video sector. The former clear distinction between screen- and scriptwriting is therefore becoming increasingly blurred.

164

Script Formats

Despite this, however, scripts still fall into two main formats, depending on whether they are intended for film or television. The film (sometimes called the Hollywood) format uses the whole page and there are very precise rules to be observed in layout which allow the length of the script to be judged immediately. (Or even, it is often suggested, by its weight. It is not unknown for a producer to weigh a film script in his or her hand to estimate its length.)

The film format will set out the script scene by scene, with an across-the-page description of where the scene is set and what the characters are doing. The actual dialogue, however, is set out down the centre of the page, with plenty of room on each side for the continuity marks.

For a television script the page is usually arranged in two columns. In the left-hand column are the instructions which relate to visuals (shot numbers, camera instructions – pan, zoom, VT inserts, Colour Separation Overlay and so on). The right-hand column contains everything associated with sound, including the narration or the dialogue. This format is now used for television drama as well as for non-fiction, studio-based shows because of its great flexibility. News operations today often use elaborate computer software which produces scripts for news rooms in this format. Computerised news rooms can quickly produce scripts already cued to a particular performer's speaking pace!

Both film and television formats are relatively easy to produce once writers have experience in the industry. Sophisticated scripts, however, perhaps for a television drama, can take a long time to reach a final version. Drama production on television has to be extensively preplanned, because studio time is very expensive and must therefore be used to its maximum potential. The director and production team meet during pre-production and, with a copy of the script, plan camera angles, shots and so forth, which are then listed in the left-hand column and linked by a line across to the dialogue. There are not many opportunities for a change of mind on the day of recording.

The Writing Process

As discussed in Chapter Ten, screen- and scriptwriters can either approach a film or television company with their own idea or, more frequently, they are given an idea and commissioned by film or television producers to develop a script from it. Sometimes they may be asked to 'adapt' a book or a play for the screen: Granada's prizewinning *Jewel in the Crown* was an adaptation of a series of novels by the writer Paul Scott.

If the screen- or scriptwriter initiates the idea, he or she will produce a synopsis or summary (as brief as two pages), and then approach commissioning editors, script editors, producers, agents, directors, production companies, in order to sell them the concept. Presentation is extremely important. If they like the idea, the commissioning agency will ask for an extended outline or 'treatment', which can run from ten to forty pages or more. The treatment will usually include a description of the setting and style of the film or programme. If the treatment is accepted, then a shooting script is developed. Sometimes the director and the screen- or scriptwriter work on the shooting script together and there may be a number of rewrites.

Television producers who commission a script might only want a 'rough script', or they might want a complete script. Writers can be commissioned for one or two episodes of a serial or for a complete set of scripts — it all depends. Different scriptwriters can be hired at different stages of a script, and this is very common in film. Or there may be a stable of writers for an extremely popular television soap opera. Comedy writers tend to work collaboratively, although most other creative writers prefer to write on their own. The writer gives an estimated date for delivery, but writers, as a group, are notorious for missing deadlines and a certain amount of bullying by producers can go on at this stage!

Most writers are freelance and on occasion directors assigned to a film will work with them. In television, producers often write their own scripts; this is especially the case for documentaries, when the producer might have a personal point of view to convey. Also, if a programme is low-key and low-budget, there may simply be no money available to hire a professional writer.

Permanent positions for writers in the industry are few and far between. The only posts which are really staff-based are those for so-called script editors or commissioning editors employed by drama departments or by series (such as *The Bill*) to find writers and work with them in developing scripts. Script editors on soap operas often need good memories, because they have to remember what the characters did three or four or twenty years ago. If they make a continuity mistake, if they forget the long-lost child or husband, the audience will soon make them aware of the error.

Script editors have the difficult job of acting as mediators between producers and writers. Writers are often very sensitive and dislike having to make changes to suit the demands of the small or large screen. When a famous author is hired to adapt his or her own work it can require great resources of tact on the part of the script editor. Writers have maternal feelings towards their 'children' and they can be outraged by an unsympathetic producer or director who decides to kill

166

characters off because 'they make the story too complicated'. Older, revered writers, who are not overfond of television, often find the whole process very unpleasant, especially when faced by young directors who are, from the writer's viewpoint, 'wet behind the ears'. Smoothing over such personality clashes is the very stuff of the script editor's job.

Script readers are sometimes employed by the established film and television companies, some of which might receive dozens of scripts each week. They handle submissions and report if any might be significant or useful.

How Do You Become a Screen/Scriptwriter or a Script Editor?

Screen- and scriptwriters usually have some experience in the theatre, film, journalism or television, or they may have written novels or other books. Some start by submitting a play for radio transmission and move on into other areas such as television or film. The BBC Radio Drama Department has a distinguished record in encouraging new writers and many people receive their first break in this way. A few people manage to get directly into film or television by writing a particularly original piece.

Some writers seek out a reputable literary agent (a list of agents can be found in the *Writers and Artists Yearbook* published annually by A. & C. Black), but agents are very choosy and it is quite difficult to register with one for the first time. If a prospective scriptwriter does not have an agent, then he or she can join The Writers Guild of Great Britain, which will act as a negotiating body on their behalf. The Guild covers the areas of feature film and television drama writing. Similarly the BECTU writers' section can provide useful help in negotiation.

Script- and screenwriting are not particularly lucrative unless the writers are very well-known and experienced. One of the major complaints associated with all forms of moving pictures is that insufficient attention is paid to the script. There is certainly a tendency for the industry to be so visually oriented that it forgets that one of the cornerstones should be a strong story-line. The worth of a good script is immediately apparent. A comedy hit series such as *Yes Minister* owed a great deal to its writers.

Most screen- and scriptwriters work freelance from home and this can be an advantage for married women writers with children. In general the industry can be hard for people in this category because of the unstructured working hours and the need for location work away from home. Writing avoids these problems.

In the past there has been little training of any sort for writers in the industry, but increasingly there are short courses springing up, such as

167

those provided by the National Short Course Training Programme of the National Film and Television School. In January 1990 the Northern School of Film and Television, a joint venture between Leeds Polytechnic, Sheffield City Polytechnic (now replaced by Sheffield Hallam University) and Yorkshire Television offered the only full-time MA/Postgraduate Diploma in Scriptwriting for Film and Television (fiction). In September 1993 this course will be expanded to include documentary scriptwriting, in association with Granada Television.

Script readers are also badly paid and it is difficult to become one but, like scriptwriting, it has the advantage that it can be done at home. Here again, experience of the industry is a tremendous advantage.

Case Histories

GEORGINA LOCK

Georgina Lock is an actress in her mid-thirties. She is presently writing scripts for film and television.

When I was still at infant school I staged stories for anyone who would watch, rambling affairs in which I starred and wore the curtains. This led to school plays, the West Kent Theatre and to a joint honours degree in English and Drama from Manchester University.

I started acting professionally with a Manchester-based theatre company and toured Europe with them, then leaving to stay in Amsterdam and work with a Dutch music theatre group, a Japanese dance company and eventually with an international theatre research group, who took me back to England via Australia.

As I'd performed solo shows abroad (*The Handbag Show*, which I wrote myself, and a frivolous set of audience participation Shakespeares for cabarets) and had my press cuttings, Equity were impressed enough to let me have a card. Taking *The Handbag Show* to the Edinburgh Festival put me in touch with interesting people and led to bits of work in film and television. The healthier arts grants situation of the 1980s allowed me to form a new company, 'Strange Bedfellows', with which I acted, wrote and occasionally directed. In short, I was diverse and happy.

Then I had a dramatic bike accident which restricted me to writing and directing. So I wrote a play, *Vivian Rivers and Her Date with Fate*, which had a rehearsed reading with the Women's Theatre Group (but which still needs rewriting ... perhaps it should be a film!) I also directed for the playwrights' co-operative, which put me in regular contact with lots of other writers.

A year or so later, a student producer whose film I was acting in asked to look at my writing and suggested that it was good film material. So I adapted a short story into a shooting script (one step too far, but the only format I knew as an actress), and sent it to the BFI. When it came back from there I sent it to Warner Sisters for 'She Play', who were complimentary but sent it back too.

A year or so later I saw an advertisement in the *Guardian*. The Northern School of Film and Television were offering MA and Post-graduate Diploma Courses in Production and Screenwriting. I hesit-ated whether to take the Production course with a view to becoming a director or to go for the Screenwriting. I applied as a writer and then put it to the back of my mind to avoid disappointment, so far back in fact that I accepted a part in a play and had to arrange a day from rehearsals to attend the interview.

I'm so glad I was accepted. It was my first chance to formally train and concentrate for a year on one discipline to ground my writing and stop squeezing it between other events. I learned masses through dis-cussing other students' work and rewriting my own as a result of the seminars. I made particular friends with a woman with whom I am now writing a sitcom. I was lucky, because one of my short film scripts, *Pressing Engagement*, was one of seven chosen for production by one of the directors on the production course.

I finished my first draft of my feature film, which also meant I finished the screenwriting course, in January 1992 and started looking for places to send it, not just with a view to getting it done, but also as a calling-card to people who might offer me other work. Making contacts can be as hard as writing, but one contact leads to another and people are prepared to help if you are serious. It's particularly useful to be in touch with a script editor. I was delighted when a script editor at the BBC called back to say she really liked my feature film and would be happy to meet and talk about it. Of course we talked about a redraft. Everything needs redrafting (until, I suspect, the day when 'it's a wrap'). My trick to conjure up energy is to look forward to what a script might become.

Times are hard and slow at the present time for the British screen industry and so for me too. The important thing is to keep going and to remain optimistic. It may help to be a woman scriptwriter. There

169

aren't many women working in this area and producers and script editors, who are often women, are looking to redress the balance.

I'm glad I came into this in my thirties. Everything I have done so far has helped me, especially acting, which helps to develop the capacity to think visually. Actors know what doesn't have to be spoken because body language and situation already say so much.

ROSY CULLEN

Rosy Cullen is a playwright and screenwriter.

I came into films via the theatre. From childhood I've always seen writing as my career. But after university, the realities of making a living meant numerous odd jobs, mostly in and around theatre. Naturally I gravitated towards being a playwright and, after a festival commission from the Royal Shakespeare Company, I went on to write plays for companies as diverse as Solent People's Theatre and Contact Theatre in Manchester. I became particularly involved with theatre-in-education groups.

My interest in film developed by chance. A film director read the first draft of a novel I was writing and took an option on a screenplay adaptation. I wasn't familiar with film as a medium and I'd always imagined that the film industry wasn't very accessible. But the experience of adapting *Sand in the Rug* felt instinctively right in terms of my writing. Increasingly my focus turned towards the screen. Although theatre can be surprisingly flexible, what draws me to film is the breadth of the canvas and the chance to explore the visual subtlety in relationships.

I decided to go on the MA course in script- and screenwriting at the Northern School of Film and Television in Leeds, because I wished to build my confidence and extend my technical knowledge. One of the requirements of the course is to write a short film. My script, *Where the Cows Go*, was selected for production by one of the six student directors, Maggie Ford. I was fortunate in that our working relationship allowed me to become closely involved in the making of the film. Screenwriters are often excluded from involvement. Being able to follow the whole process was an essential learning experience for me as a writer of film. The film concerns an elderly woman, Lily, remembering her first dates in a psychiatric hospital forty years earlier. I drew on the experience of an eighteen-month creative writing residency with the psychiatric services in South Derbyshire to develop the script.

The film is now touring various film festivals. The festivals are essential showcases for new direction and writing in film.

Since the course I've received development money from British Screen Finance for a feature, *Shadowplay*, and I am now looking for production interest. I've also co-scripted a project with film-maker Karen Ingham, *Falling Through Blue*, commissioned by the British Film Institute. Currently I'm hoping to write for a new BBC drama series, having just submitted a commissioned treatment.

One of the difficulties for a writer is making the right contacts: you often feel isolated, reliant on agents and keeping your ear to the ground for openings in television. I've recently met with the First Film Foundation. They can act as creative foster-parents to people starting out in the industry and their encouragement is very welcome.

I know that I've been lucky up to now, because I've received development money for my feature scripts. Whether I'll ever see them on-screen, given the lack of finance in this country, is another matter. A lot of great film-writing talent is going to waste because of lack of opportunity.

14

EDITING AND ENGINEERING

EDITOR (craft/creative)
ASSISTANT EDITOR (craft/technical)
PROJECTIONIST (technical)

Editing is one of the key creative elements in the process of film and programme-making. Film editors usually work closely with directors (and sometimes scriptwriters), while video editors often work with programme producers. Both types of editors take decisions about the picture images which have been shot in production. They decide what should be retained and what should be discarded, so that the film or programme can 'come together' in a visual and stylistic narrative which audiences find appealing and which expresses the vision of the whole creative team.

The process of editing varies depending on whether the editor is dealing with film or video. Film, after it has been shot, is developed in a laboratory. Then, in the editing process, it is physically cut and reassembled. Video is more immediate: once a scene has been shot it can be played back immediately and assessed. Editing video usually consists of retaining the original tape (the master), and then selecting the desired scenes and images, which are copied onto a blank cassette on another machine. Editing techniques for both film and video are fairly simple to learn, but editing is much more than technique. The way a good editor puts together the images (and sounds) is the crucial final stage in the whole creative process. It takes talent and a great deal of experience to become really expert.

Film and video editing are still very separate professions, but freelance editors now do work in both media because, despite the different physical attributes of film and video, similar creative gifts are needed to edit them. Editors have to understand the techniques of telling a story and know how to create a logical and coherent narrative. However, film editing requires a specific manual dexterity unnecessary for video editing. In turn, video editing demands (or used to demand) some technical understanding of complex equipment while film editing does not.

Television companies used to carry out most of their editing in-house. Along a certain corridor would be rows of small film editing suites where editors worked away on different programmes. Usually quite separated from these, in another area, there would be a VT or VTR Centre where video editors (and also engineers, see below) were located. These still exist, but in recent years there has been a rapid growth of what are called 'facility' houses, which exist independently of television and film companies and specialise in various technical services including editing. An editing job today, therefore, is likely to mean working in a facility house, rather than in a broadcasting company. The 'Producers' Choice' initiative at the BBC, the growth of the publisher/broadcaster model at Channel 3 and the development of the independent sector have all promoted the development of these specialist facility houses.

Film Editing

Editors on feature films and important television programmes recorded on film are often hired at the beginning of the production period. They work on the film on a daily basis, doing a 'rough assembly' of the day's shots which the director and members of the lighting and camera crew can look at and assess each evening. This viewing of the day's 'rushes' makes final editing much easier, since the editor is aware of the day-to-day progress of the film, and is also able to draw the director's attention to poor material (and even, in exceptional circumstances, suggest reshooting a scene). If the editor is associated with the film from the beginning in this way, he or she is an important element of the creative team and acquires an intimate knowledge and understanding of the director's intentions.

The 'rushes' theatre may be a specialist dubbing or viewing studio or a very small private cinema with an experienced specialist projectionist to lace up the film and prepare the reels for the crew to view. A company in production may book such a preview cinema each evening for several weeks and the projectionist sees how the film evolves and how the editor cuts the film down to the final product. Not surprisingly, therefore, projectionists in this type of work often want to move into editing and they try to make the contacts which lead to assistant editor jobs.

The luxury of the preview theatre, however, is not the lot of most editors, but only of those who have very distinguished reputations and are engaged on major films. Most editors have no input at all at the production stage, but are faced with a *fait accompli* when the copy of the developed film arrives in the editing suite from the laboratory. There are no opportunities for second thoughts or reshoots, except in cases of dire emergency. Camera operators have been dispersed, performers are working on other productions and the editor is faced with the relatively lonely task of crafting the film into an acceptable finished article. Much grumbling and cursing about directors and camera operators can be heard emerging from the depths of the average editing suite as editors come to grips with this task!

The film does not, however, arrive in the editing suite in complete isolation. It is usually accompanied by a copy of the script and the notes which camera and sound assistants have made on location. There will also be laboratory report sheets including technical comments.

In the first stages of editing the editors and assistant editors work on a copy of the film (workprint or cutting copy) and the original picture negative is stored away secure and unmarked so that it is in prime condition for the final edit. The workprint, however, is still treated with great care: no dirt or grit must gather on the surface because this can damage the print. Editors often work with thin white gloves to keep the film as clean as possible.

The initial handling of the film is usually the task of assistant film editors. They do the preparatory work with the 'rushes'. Picture 'rushes' come from the laboratory, while sound 'rushes' often come separately from a sound transfer facility. Rolls of 'rushes' can be anywhere from 400 to 2,000 feet in length. The assistant 'synchs' them up, which means synchronising the sound with the picture. When in synch, the image and sound coincide properly; when out of synch, they are mismatched. (The appearance and sound of the clapperboard, as explained earlier, is the 'synch' point for both sound and picture.)

During the process of 'synching up', the assistant breaks down the film into manageable units of usually around 1,000 feet and each unit is clearly labelled with the name of the production, the roll number and other relevant information. Every shot has to be 'logged' in this way, because it is essential that written records are accurate. This is as true for rejected shots as it is for shots which are included, because there are frequent changes of mind at the editing stage. Nothing must be thrown away, because at some point the editor might decide to use scenes which were initially rejected. Scrupulous record-keeping and organisation are therefore an essential feature of the editing process; film edit suites will have hundreds and hundreds of strips of film hanging around the cutting room, and without proper records the whole process would quickly descend into chaos. Assistant film editors have to be meticulous and very well-organised.

Once the basic picture and sound footage have been synched up by the assistant editor, the editor takes over and, sometimes with the director's assistance, begins the process of editing the film. Scenes are viewed carefully and arranged in the proper order. Good shots are included and poor shots are taken out. The scenes are put together in a 'rough assembly', which is then tightened into a 'rough cut' and then into a 'finished edit' or 'fine cut'. The soundtrack is also cut to coincide with the picture and the sound editor puts together ('mixes') several different tracks (dialogue, music and sound effects) to make the final soundtrack of the film.

The edited picture and sound then go back to the laboratories for so-called 'combined' or release prints to be made for distribution to cinemas. Basically, 'combined' prints are exactly that: the sound and picture are combined onto the same piece of film. The magnetic soundtrack is translated into an optical one which runs alongside the picture at the edge of the film. This the film projector converts into sound when the film is projected onto the screen in a cinema.

Video

The video editor and the film editor basically carry out the same function, but the experience is different because the technology is not the same. Video editing is done electronically: the editor does not cut anything, but instead presses buttons on a console. With video, soundtracks can be mixed and synchronised with the pictures during the actual editing process. It is also easy to try out special effects with video (according to the capacity of the video equipment). In film, which is essentially a non-digital organic medium, special effects can only be accomplished by using complex and expensive techniques in the lab. (However, as explained in Chapter Twelve, there are recent developments which are likely to overcome this problem to a certain extent.)

When the producer and editor of a television programme have decided on the edit points, the sections of the tape to be used in the transmitted production are recorded onto another tape. In the past videotape editors often began their careers as engineers and technicians, because it was useful to know something about the equipment. However, there is now much more emphasis on the creative and imaginative side of VT editing. Videotape editors are increasingly emerging as the key people in the post-production phase. Electronic technology has resulted in a visual versatility which could once only be obtained by combining a film laboratory with a film editing suite.

Increasingly in broadcasting companies and in facility houses editors tend to be VT specialists. Freelance editors working across all sectors of the industry are more often people who initially trained as film editors, but who were quickly able to acquire the ability to edit VT (once the technology became more accessible). Freelance editors with distinguished reputations can make a great deal of money. However, it is more difficult for video editors to acquire film editing skills than vice versa, though there are courses available to enable them to do so. Assistant video editors make sure that the controls on the video machine are set up for use ('lined up'), and they do the general fetching and carrying of tapes. They watch the editors and learn from them.

PSC or ENG editing involves the same basic techniques as VT editing because the medium is tape. However, PSC/ENG tape is smaller. Also, on location, usually only one PSC/ENG camera is used and, as a consequence, there is much more out-of-sequence shooting. In other words, the actual recording of the item is carried out using techniques which are more similar to shooting on film than recording in studios, and this obviously affects the editor's work. PSC and ENG are normally used for news and therefore ENG/PSC editors often work against very tight deadlines. ENG/PSC editors are sometimes expected to be able to maintain and repair their equipment because they occasionally work away from base where no engineers will be available.

The Editing Experience

Editors usually work on more and more complicated films and programmes, gaining experience as they go. As we have seen, they must have organisational ability and they must be systematic. They must also have an aesthetic sense, a quality which is difficult to describe. Editing may be an innate talent, but it also develops through practice. Editors acquire an instinctive 'feel' for what will create the right effect and they have a sixth sense for when a shot should be cut or held. They will decide if a close-up is better in one scene than a long shot. They will know when to cut from one shot to another and when to slow the action down and when to speed it up. The pace of edits can have an enormous effect on the mood and emotional temperature of a scene. A jump-cut, for example, is a cut which takes place abruptly and draws attention to itself, and yet it may be appropriate in certain circumstances.

Sometimes editors work on a film or programme almost entirely on their own; at other times the director is very dominant. Editors have to be ingenious, because the very shot which would have been useful as a bridge between scenes may not exist or may not have turned out.

Problems must be overcome in such a way that the audience is not aware that editing techniques have been used to cover them up. This is where experience comes in.

Really experienced editors can cut a film in such a way that essentially unpromising material is put together in a manner which is appealing and unique. This is a rare talent and such editors are much sought after and highly paid.

How Do You Become an Editor?

Most people become editors by being taken on as trainees or assistants by broadcasting companies or as runners in post-production companies and facility houses. Some students from film schools and colleges, who have been trained in editing techniques, may be taken on directly as fully-fledged editors in the non-broadcast sector (or they might be if the recession had not hit the industry so badly), but this is still relatively rare. Film people tend to believe that editors are born not made and that they have particular imaginative and creative gifts which cannot really be taught; that the best training for editors therefore is to be taken on in the humblest of jobs, where they gradually acquire the necessary skills through watching the experts and through hands-on experience. Gradually innate talent will then emerge.

There is much truth in this, but aptitude can be developed. Also there is a danger inherent in the industry's anti-formal education bias, especially as far as video editing is concerned. Technological hardware is becoming ever more complex, and in future there will be a need for skilled editors who will understand and keep abreast of developments and who will be prepared to train and retrain as new technology comes along. Although deep technical knowledge is not necessary for VT editing, it does have a place, particularly in an increasingly technological world. Far too many employers (and employees) in Britain are hostile to formal training, which is why the workforce is so notoriously unskilled and untrained. One commentator has suggested that it is more correct to compare the post-production business in film and television in the 1990s to the computer industry, rather than to the film industry of the 1950s (Mark Bishop in *Televisual*, June 1990). The warning makes sense: film and television are intimately connected with technological developments and the workforce has to be aware of the significance of this.

Traditionally, however, educational qualifications have not been particularly important for editors, although, to be taken on by a broadcasting company in the first place, trainees must have a good general education with respectable GCSE passes. The most important qualifications up to now have been a passion for film and television and an obsessive interest in editing, together with a willingness to work long hours for miserable pay in order to acquire the necessary experience.

There is considerable competition for jobs as assistant or trainee editors. Many people with editorial ambitions learn the basic skills and practice by joining workshops or community groups which make films and videos. They also attend colleges and courses. They may then edit their own film or tape, which they take round with them in the search for jobs. On feature films, editors have a big say in who they have as their assistants, so they should be approached directly. A list of editors' names can be obtained from BECTU or from trade directories such as Kemp's *Film and Television Yearbook*.

Although formal education has not been an important element in the work experience of editors in the past, the growing technological complexity of the industry is likely to require more technical training and understanding in the future, especially for those who wish to reach the top. Would-be editors should take account of this: this is an area where qualifications are going to be increasingly important.

ENGINEERS
TECHNICAL ASSISTANTS
TECHNICAL OPERATORS/TECHNICIANS

Broadcasting

Broadcasting depends for its success on its engineers. Without the technology, broadcasting and video would not exist. Service and research engineers keep everything running smoothly.

As has been discussed often in this book, we live in an ever more technically oriented society. Broadcasting has witnessed extraordinary advances in the past decade, thanks to, among other things, the micro-chip. As the technology of the industry has become more complex, there has been a greater tendency to employ more qualified people on the engineering side and graduates have become more common. This is especially so in specialist research areas within the BBC and the independent companies. In the past the BBC or ITV would recruit would-be engineers with A levels and then train them. Today gradu-ates in electronics, electrical engineering and applied physics are increasingly taken on for direct appointment as engineers.

There are many categories of engineers in broadcasting and they often have different titles in different companies. On the whole, how-ever, operational engineers look after the technical facilities which make broadcasting possible. Operational engineers can be found in

178

studios, on location with outside broadcast vans, or at transmission sites. They are concerned with the operation and maintenance of the networks, with radio links for outside broadcasts, with actual recording, with news-gathering, and with transmission.

One of the most important areas of operational engineering work is vision control. Very precise standards are demanded of broadcasters in Britain and engineers are necessary to make sure these are enforced. Vision control or video engineers sit in control rooms and ensure that each camera in the studio is correctly adjusted so that it matches the others and the exposure settings and the colour balance are right. It is no use for the presenter's face to have a green tinge on one camera and a red tone on another. Every camera should produce pictures of a consistent quality or viewers will be distracted. In the past the job of matching cameras to each other was complicated, but this function is now largely computerised. Nevertheless video engineers still need to adjust and align cameras during operation. In some companies vision control staff also carry out maintenance work on the cameras, while in others this is the responsibility of maintenance engineers.

Engineers are also found in the VT or VTR Centre, where all the videotape and telecine machines are kept. As we have seen, VT editing is carried out in this area, but VTR work includes many other jobs, such as recording the programmes being made in the studio, replaying recorded inserts into live programmes (such as news), replaying completed programmes for transmission and using the telecine machine to transfer ordinary cine film or slides to tape so that they can be viewed on the television screen. Cine film is not easily adapted to the television screen, and telecine staff, with the help of sophisticated electronic processors, have to overcome many problems posed by, for example, the variety of film gauges and different screen widths. It was partly because VT editing was carried out in the area where many associated engineering functions went on that engineering technicians with an interest in the creative side of programme-making moved over into editing.

Engineers are also required to monitor and correct the technical parameters of all video and audio sources within the station and are responsible for incoming signals from other centres.

Outside broadcast engineers carry out many of the above duties, but their job is more varied and they frequently have to deal with emergencies which call on their initiative and ingenuity. They often have to repair malfunctioning equipment at very short notice and with highly agitated production staff breathing down their necks. Outside broadcast engineers meet the public much more than ordinary engineers in television stations.

179

Engineers are also required for maintaining, servicing and repairing equipment. Microtechnology has resulted in more complex equipment with built-in automatic correction circuits, so there is less hands-on repair work but instead a greater need for expert technical knowledge of electronic circuitry.

Senior experienced engineers are also required to plan new technical developments and to develop new systems. They play an important role in assessing the new equipment and new technology which constantly come on to the market and they provide advice and make decisions about purchase and installation. Engineers in these areas also require financial acumen and must be able to write technical reports which communicate difficult scientific information succinctly and clearly.

Engineers are helped by technical assistants or trainee engineers and technical operators or technicians (different companies use different titles). Assistants set up, align and maintain broadcasting equipment and in some cases operate it. Technical operators are more junior members of the team who help with the preparation and operation of equipment.

How Do You Become an Engineer?
Trainee operational engineers usually have a BTEC Higher Certificate or Diploma in Electronics with Television and Communications, or a City and Guilds or Higher National Diploma or Certificate in Engineering or Electronics or Telecommunications. Sometimes they have a degree in Engineering, or Electronics or Telecommunications. Specialist engineers almost invariably have a degree in Engineering, Electronics or Telecommunications. Technicians must have good general education and usually Maths and Physics at A level. They may also have a BTEC or City and Guilds in Electronics or Computer Science. Virtually all technical people now are expected to be able to use computers and, in certain cases, to carry out computer programming.

For a more detailed discussion of an engineering career in independent television see Sue Davis (ed), *The Official ITV Careers Handbook*, Hodder and Stoughton, 1989.

Case History

JACKIE VANCE

Jackie Vance is twenty-eight. She works as a freelance film editor.

After school I worked for two years and then went to the Bristol Old Vic Theatre School although I was really interested in film, but somehow I thought you went into the theatre, then into television and then into films. I guess I was rather naive! At the Old Vic I set up a video course for myself, because I saw all this video equipment there and wanted to use it. I wondered: 'What happens when you put this and this together?' I grabbed other students who were interested too, but basically I was very much on my own. I really wanted to work in the movies because I love film, so when the time came for attachments I'd ring up editors and say: 'Can I come into the cutting room and watch?'

Through watching I got the basic idea, although they wouldn't let me touch anything. An Australian editor and his assistant were really helpful when they saw I was keen. They gave me a list of all the cutting rooms in Soho, and I walked around with that list and tried to find someone who would take me on. It was really demoralising. I hassled everyone who offered any sign of a job. Then a post-production company in Dean Street mentioned that the industry was setting up JOB-FIT, so that really interested me. Meanwhile I got taken on as a trainee by a documentary editor and he was fantastic. A really good teacher. I learned a lot from him. Then I heard that Thames TV had an editor's course, so I thought, 'Here's my chance', and applied for that. I really thought I had a good chance of getting in, and then they stopped the course! As I say, it can all get pretty demoralising. Then JOBFIT actually started. They took on four groups at staggered intervals and I was taken on in the fourth group!

On JOBFIT there were college courses covering everything, sound, camera, artwork and so on, and many attachments in different types of jobs, so that you learned all about production, not just about what interested you. I knew I wanted to get into editing. I was interested in production and how it worked, but editing was what I really wanted to do. Everyone else wanted to work on camera, but I avoided the camera like the plague. Well, that's not quite true! I did some work on camera, but I knew it was not for me.

In my second year of JOBFIT I specialised in editing and I had some very good attachments. One of the chaps I worked for asked did I want another attachment. I knew they were getting ready to work on a series and I knew that I would be finishing on JOBFIT about that time, so I said 'Yes'. I was lucky this time, because I got a job as Second Assistant Editor and the wonderful union card. At that time (1989) you could not do anything in the industry without a union card. Now you can walk in without one.

Well, since then I've worked freelance and never, except for a period of about two months, been without a job. I would like to get more

181

senior jobs, but I want to stay in work whatever happens. I would really like to work in features, but most of the feature people now work in television. Actually that has done a lot for television technique in my opinion. Television is becoming more experimental. I suppose film people want to make sure that when the features industry comes back to life again they will still have their hand in. I've worked on a feature film called *Chicago Joe and the Showgirl* and I've also worked with Mike Leigh on *Life is Sweet*. Working on something like that is why I came into films. Mike Leigh will actually ask you at a screening of the rushes, 'What do you think?' – even when you are at the bottom of the ladder as a trainee or a second. When someone like that asks you for your opinion, it is really great.

To do this job you have to be interested in film. Why do such a ridiculous job with such long hours if not? It's a long, hard haul, but it's really worth it!

15

PERFORMERS

'The Talent'

Most of the people we see on the small and large screen can be described as performers who exercise their professional skills in the provision of entertainment. In feature films virtually everyone we see is an actor by training and by profession. On television and video, however, the 'faces' which appear on the screen include actors, musicians, dancers, singers, stunt performers, as well as journalists, newsreaders, presenters, announcers and members of the public.

Television viewers often do not distinguish between the various categories, but lump everyone together as 'stars'. This is incorrect: there are sharp distinctions between the various categories. Newsreaders, as we have seen, are not actors, but journalists who happen to appear on-screen. Announcers are usually not journalists, but instead are personable public relations-type people employed by television companies to provide links between programmes and inform the public about the station. In this Chapter we will look at the jobs which make up the various aspects of life in front of camera.

PERFORMERS (creative) including

- Actors
- Musicians
- Stunt Artists
- Dancers

Very few performers ever have permanent jobs. Acting, dancing and making music are not very stable professions. On the large screen major stars, and indeed all actors, are contracted for a particular film during the production period only, and are sometimes referred to as 'the talent'. In the old days Hollywood studios kept a 'stable' of actors under contract. Contract players were paid a regular salary, for perhaps a five-year period, and were drafted into films as the studio bosses saw fit. In this system actors had little control over the films in which they appeared. If they did kick up a fuss about an inappropriate role, they would find that they were not given any further parts and, when their contracts came up for renewal, they would be dropped. This system, which did offer something in the way of guaranteed employment, no longer exists. Today film actors are freelancers who work on a film for a certain length of time and then move on. They usually employ agents to help them find work and to negotiate their fees. In the United States actors can make a living solely out of film, but in Britain most actors need to work in the theatre and on radio and television if they are to survive.

In every sector, as already mentioned, they are usually employed for the period of performance only. Actors in a feature film or a television drama are hired only for the number of days on which they are required. Television companies do not employ performers on a staff basis. Even if actors are important characters in a long-running soap opera, their contracts will be regularly subject to renewal, perhaps every year. Indeed it is not unknown for a character to be written out of a series if the individual actor makes a fuss about money or is perhaps involved in a real-life scandal which may 'reflect' on the character in the drama.

As a result there is little financial security. The only possible exceptions are certain categories of musician working for the BBC. The Corporation continues to maintain orchestras and, although these are constantly threatened with extinction and are always subject to cutbacks, they do provide a form of regular employment for musicians. Also, because music and light entertainment are an important feature of television (and radio), the BBC, and some independent television companies, employ Musical Directors or Heads of Music to advise on the musical content of programmes, the arrangement of music and the contracting of composers. These are experienced people with vast knowledge of performance and management. Musicians employed by film, television or video companies are generally members of the Musicians' Union.

In the past it would have left a false impression to include a description of performers in a book about 'careers' in British film or television because, despite their vital role, they were never part of the career structure of television, nor part of the core of employees who earned their living solely in film. They were rather 'hired in' as necessity demanded, often from the theatre, and they moved in and out of the industries as opportunities opened and closed. As film, television and video have drawn closer together, however, and as freelancing has become the more common pattern of employment across all sectors, the experience of actors and performers is not so different from that of all employees on temporary, short-term contracts.

In general all actors in film, television or video are members of the British Actors' Equity Association, the actors' union. Although the reality is that most actors spend far more time unemployed than working, acting is a very attractive and glamorous profession and new recruits therefore constantly clamour at the door. If everyone who wished to act were allowed into the profession, it would be swamped and many newcomers would be willing to work for very little pay. As a result, Equity tries to protect its members from too much competition by imposing limits on the numbers who may enter the profession in certain areas each year. The quota system which sets the limits is heavily criticised for its exclusivity. On the whole, however, the criticism comes from outside the profession rather than from within. The simple fact is that there are not enough jobs round for all the people who wish to act; if the doors were opened to anyone and everyone, the acting profession would be overwhelmed by amateurs wanting to 'have a go'. Salaries and fees would fall and standards would drop.

It is in order to avert this danger that Equity has made special agreements with many employers who agree to employ only 'professionals'. Newcomers, therefore, cannot enter the profession through West End theatre, the National Theatre, films, television, commercials or radio. Only artists who already have professional experience, and who are also members of the union, can be employed in these areas. Equity does, however, grant recognition to a certain quota of new entrants each year in certain sectors and jobs. Newcomers can qualify for union membership by securing jobs as performers or assistant stage managers in a subsidised repertory company or in theatre-in-education or a young people's theatre company. They can also join pantomimes, fringe companies and summer season companies, all of which make them eligible for Equity membership. The Royal Shakespeare Company at Stratford-upon-Avon and the Chichester Festival Theatre can take on a certain quota of new recruits, but competition for these places is extremely fierce.

Ambitious young actors who come in via these routes serve what amounts to an apprenticeship, learning their trade. Drama graduates, or those who have done courses in stage management, usually find their way in by this means. Once they have become members of Equity, they can work in film or television.

Most actors and dancers obtain further work by signing a contract with a theatrical agent. The agent then seeks work for the performer. When film or television producers or casting directors want actors they usually approach agents or scan through casting directories such as *Spotlight*, which includes a photograph of the performer and a description of their work to date. If a producer is looking for a 'type' or a look-alike (in a historical drama, for example, casting directors might want someone who looks like Churchill), the photographs can help in the search.

Singers and dancers are usually granted Equity membership once they have secured employment, as are directors, designers and choreographers employed in the theatre. Professional broadcasters in television or radio can also sometimes obtain membership of Equity on the basis of their experience in non-acting areas. Thus a presenter might wish to become an actor and his or her experience on television may help to gain Equity membership.

There is no easy or classic route to becoming an actor or dancer in film or television. People with ambitions in this direction should follow a drama course at a college or university, or go to one of the leading drama or ballet schools. Training, talent, hard work and luck are all essential requisites. Performers have to be versatile, and those who are successful will work on the stage, in film, in commercials, on video, on television and on radio as opportunities arise. It is no use thinking 'it would be nice' to act in *EastEnders* and writing to the BBC to apply. Acting is a hard profession to enter and an even harder profession in which to make a living. This is particularly so for women: Equity has been criticised recently because women actors generally earn less than men, even when they are better known.

There is a common belief that would-be actors without a union card can start work as an 'extra' or 'walk-on' in television or as 'background', 'crowd artist', 'double' or 'stand-in' in films and commercials, and that such work will be considered as professional experience by Equity. This is not the case. Equity does not recognise that such jobs amount to a 'professional' portfolio and, in any case, such work is usually given to union members first. Only when sufficient Equity members are unavailable are 'walk-on' jobs offered to 'amateurs'. It is virtually impossible, therefore, to break into serious professional acting in this way. On the other hand, working as an extra is one way to find out about the profession of acting and also how film and television work. It can provide insight into the way the industry functions and what the various people do. Advertisements sometimes appear in the journal *Stage* for these types of jobs.

One of the in-front-of-camera jobs which always attracts interest is that of stunt performers, artists or 'arrangers'. Stunt performers in film and television must also be Equity members and be listed on the Register of Stunt Performers. Only professional actors or performers can join the Stunt Register. This is because many stunt people in the course of their work actually double other artists, so they have to be able to act!

There is a variety of expertise under which stunt performers can register, including Fighting, Falling, Riding and Driving, Agility and Strength, Swimming and Sub-Aqua. In most of these categories there is also a variety of subdivisions. In Falling, for example, stunt artists can be qualified in trampolining, diving or parachuting. They must have achieved, for instance, the elementary Gold Award in Trampolining; or a Silver Standard in Highboard or Springboard Diving from the Amateur Swimming Association to qualify for inclusion in the Diving subdivision; or a Category 8 from the British Parachute Association with a 'c' license (minimum of fifty jumps) for the Parachuting subdivision. (Full details can be obtained by writing to Equity.)

It is not easy to become registered as a stunt performer, which is sensible, since doing and arranging stunts can be dangerous. As we have seen, very high standards of physical and sporting skill are required. To qualify for the Register it is necessary to be a full member of Equity and to be aged between 18 and 30. Stunt performers have to serve a probationary period of three years on the Stunt Register, during which time they can only work under the supervision of a Full Member. After that time they qualify as an 'intermediate' member and are free to take work performing and arranging their own stunts, but they cannot arrange and supervise stunts for other people. Only after another two years are stunt performers fully registered, at which point they are then free to arrange stunts for fellow performers or actors.

Standards of competence for actors, dancers, musicians, performers and stuntpersons are presently being developed by the Art and Entertainment Training Council in association with such bodies as Equity, the Musicians' Union, the National Council for Drama Training, the Council for Dance Education and Training, and the Association of British Orchestras. For further information see the address of the Arts and Entertainment Training Council at the end of this book. For information about Dance and Drama courses write to:

The Secretary
Council for Dance Education and Training, 5 Tavistock Place, London WC1H 9SN

The Secretary
The National Council for Drama Training, 5 Tavistock Place, London WC1H 9SN

PRESENTER
ANNOUNCER
CONTINUITY ANNOUNCER

Television
Presenter is the term used for people who 'front' programmes. They act rather like a host or 'Master (or Mistress) of Ceremonies' within a programme. Presenters introduce programmes and often provide the verbal links between items. They sometimes also interview guests. On very popular programmes the presenter *is* the show, which may be named after them. The programme is then a vehicle for the presenter's own personality.

Presenters are frequently well-known personalities who have come into television after winning a distinguished reputation in another sphere of activity. In other cases, television has 'made' them. In North America personality presenters tend to have a relatively short public life, but in Britain an innate conservatism has ensured that some presenters have been around for many years.

Personalities 'emerge' and there is no way of predicting who will end up a success and who will not. Producers searching for new faces will sometimes seek out presenters. A television company will sometimes hear of an athlete who is attractive, articulate and quick-witted, and who is on the point of retirement, and offer them a job in sports presenting. A producer planning a new show on cookery will contact various well-known chefs and ask them if they would like to front the programme. Anton Mosimann, for example, became a household name, but his professional training was as a chef; television was only an incidental interest for him, at least at first. In the same way, academics are sometimes asked to present programmes like *Timewatch* and scientists may, on occasion, be invited to introduce *Horizon*. Presenters of documentaries are often distinguished journalists, and political programmes are sometimes hosted by ex-MPs. Quiz shows are often presented by actors or comedians who have had a career in clubs.

In other words, presenters often have a notable career apart from broadcasting and very few people actually set out to be television 'presenters'. If they do, they are unlikely to succeed. Presenters are important because they can make or break a programme. *Blind Date*, for example, is identified with the personality of Cilla Black, but she too made her reputation first in another area, pop music.

For all the above reasons there can be no description of a presenter's typical career path. It is a matter of chance, but being a celebrity in other fields is probably an advantage. In any case, presenting is not,

188

for the most part, a long-term job. Many presenters only appear on television for one series. Presenters who do become identified with a long-running show, however, are often able to earn considerable amounts of money from public appearances, opening fêtes, supermarkets and the like.

Announcers are employed by television stations to provide the link between programmes. They are sometimes called continuity announcers because they provide the atmosphere which ensures that the programmes flow smoothly and continuously one after another. In recent years on-screen announcers have been a feature of the commercial sector rather than the BBC, which has tended to use voice-overs. ITV companies use announcers to give a 'face' to the station. They may have a touch of a regional accent so that viewers can identify with the personality, who should never appear remote.

Announcers inform viewers about the evening's schedule. They announce the next programme or programmes and refer to any changes or delays. It all looks very easy, but there is more skill than first appears. What the announcer says may influence the viewer's decision to continue watching or to change to another station. They therefore have to deliver their material (and many of them write their own scripts) in such a way that viewers are persuaded that the next programmes will be exciting and interesting. In this sense the announcers are part of the sales team of television. They work to keep the viewers watching their station.

They can also play a very serious role. One of the strengths of local and regional television (and even more so of radio) is that it can respond quickly to an emergency and often has a highly respected profile within the community so that viewers trust what it says. If a major catastrophe happens in the region, the station will interrupt programming and an announcer will appear to provide information in a newsflash. If there has been a major road crash, for example, and the police wish motorists to avoid a certain area, it is the duty announcer who will appear on-screen to relay the police information. If there has been a leak of poisonous fumes from a chemical factory, and the police want an area to be evacuated, they will inform the local television station. Again it is the duty announcer who will appear on the screen to tell residents what to do. At such times announcers have to be calm and sensible: they have to keep the viewer from panicking and ensure that accurate information is conveyed so that the emergency does not become blown out of all proportion.

Announcers, therefore, have to remain calm in a crisis. They also have to be able to ad lib, since there may have been no time for a script to be written and they have to provide correct information without benefit of notes or an Autocue. In some areas announcers are also journalists and participate in local news and regional programmes as presenters.

Announcers represent the public face of the local television station. They can become very well-known and instantly recognised on the streets. As a result they are often asked to help with local charities or, like presenters, to open local supermarkets, fêtes or shows, and this can earn them considerable sums of money in addition to their salaries. Since announcers represent the station, they have to be careful about their public image and must not offend viewers by cantankerous behaviour in real life. This 'always being on show' can be quite a strain for some temperaments.

Announcers can work very difficult hours, since many stations broadcast seven days a week, twenty-four hours a day. This is not conducive to a normal social and private life. They must also be well-groomed and keep themselves looking smart and alert no matter what pressures they may be under. Most announcers are good-looking and dress in a conventional way, since most television viewers are not yet ready for alternative clothes styles. Television stations want to woo, not alienate, their audiences.

How Do You Become an Announcer?
Advertisements for trainee announcers do sometimes appear in the press and the television company is then snowed under with applications. Most television stations are actually looking for people with experience and newcomers are rarely employed. It is the sort of job which looks easy and glamorous, and people who dream of fame think that they could do it just as well as the person on-screen. In fact, most announcers have had some form of drama or speech training and they may even have acting experience and be members of Equity. Most importantly, they must have an ability to get on well with people in all walks of life and genuinely enjoy meeting people. They must not be hostile or aggressive, but have warm and expansive personalities. They are usually intelligent and well-read and are able to talk easily on any subject. Announcers have a natural charm and a good speaking voice so that people are both interested in them and enjoy listening to them speak.

If you feel that you have all these rare qualities, and you still have a burning desire to be an announcer, it might be an idea to write a script and prepare a videotape of yourself as a 'mock' announcer. This would provide you with the opportunity to spot the verbal mannerisms or facial ticks of which you may not be aware, but which would be a constant irritation on-screen. Only when you think you have a professional 'look' should you send the tape to a television station.

Announcers, as we have pointed out, are part of the sales team of television. The whole marketing side of film and television has become increasingly important in recent years and in the next chapter we will take a brief look at this side of the industry, where opportunities are currently burgeoning.

Case Histories

DAVID BRADFORD

David Bradford is a voice-over announcer at TVS. He is twenty-six and has worked in the job for three years.

I was always interested in the entertainment business and I used to work in hospital radio as a hobby. I worked for Radio Bedside in Bournemouth for about six or seven years, but my ambition was always to get into radio proper. Then, when I was twenty-one, I was offered a job by Plymouth Sound, the local ILR station for the South-west and I abandoned my secure job immediately. I did two shows for Plymouth Sound, playing middle-of-the-road music combined with chat and a friendly atmosphere.

Then the boss of Ocean Sound, another ILR station, was driving through our area and heard me on the radio and he offered me the breakfast show on Ocean Sound North, the FM station, with a full-time contract for six months. I worked on the breakfast show from 6 a.m. to 10 a.m., six days a week. It had a middle-aged, middle-income audience, so I had to change my style to some extent.

After that I went freelance as a presenter. I enjoy working freelance because I don't like to be tied down. You never know what's around the corner and as a freelancer you are always ready for new opportunities. The freelance market is precarious, but it does give you freedom. You can do as many things as you want. At one point I was working for three ILR stations. I lived in Bournemouth and at the weekends I would present a show in Bournemouth, drive to Brighton for another show and then back to Bournemouth to present an afternoon sports programme.

Then a friend told me that someone was leaving TVS. It's not easy

191

to get into television. It's not even easy to talk to someone. On two or three occasions I knocked on doors and was turned away. Then one day I managed to get past reception at TVS by saying that I wanted to buy something, and when I got into the offices I knocked at the door of the Presentation Department. I was really lucky, because someone had actually just resigned, so they asked me to do a tape and then took me on.

I shadowed a more senior announcer for a while and he showed me what to do. You have to understand the television vocabulary. There is such a thing as 'TV speak'. Anyway, once you get the hang of that, the rest is down to experience. It is important to be able to edit material in your head as you are speaking. You may have 15 seconds to go, or 10 seconds or 11 or 9, and you have to fill in the time with meaningful speech and finish up exactly on time. At the beginning this is very, very hard, especially if something goes wrong. And things do go wrong, and then it is all down to you to make things 'good'. You have to have the ability to fill in at a moment's notice.

Here at TVS announcers are not in vision. The station policy is that this provides a more streamlined look. I want to work 'in front of' camera and I have presented a late-night programme three times and that was excellent experience. Eventually I would like to move into presenting chat shows or quiz shows.

My advice in this business is don't expect the job to come to you. You have to put yourself out and, if you are freelance, you have to be available when they want you. If you have personal commitments, and a job comes up, then you have to change your commitments. If you are good, you shouldn't be out of work for long, once you have experience, because nine-tenths of finding a job is people knowing you and your work. I haven't any major family commitments, so I can move as I want to.

I really enjoy what I am doing, but you have to be a perfectionist. You have to keep setting targets for yourself and aiming at them. In the entertainment world there is always something to aim for. This winter I shall be working in panto, which I enjoy, and acting is very good experience for presenting. I was lucky I got my Equity card when I was working as a broadcaster.

BEVERLEY ASHWORTH

Beverley Ashworth is in her thirties and has been working for five years as a continuity announcer for Granada television in Manchester.

192

I was working as a video producer and scriptwriter with a corporate company when Central Television asked the company I was working for to prepare videos of prospective continuity announcers. People kept saying to me that I should do one myself and so I decided I would. I thought to myself: I like this job! In fact I did not get a job at Central, but two years later I saw an advert in the *Guardian* for a continuity announcer at Granada and I sent an audiocassette and some photographs and got an audition. There were hundreds of applications. I was staggered by the amount of interest and I didn't think I had a chance. Then I was appointed.

As an announcer you have to be yourself. You have to be natural. It's not like acting. In fact it's rather an odd position to be in, because the public come to feel that they know you personally, not in a role. Sometimes in the street people come towards me, they know my face and they think that I must be a friend. They go to say 'Hello' and then they realise they don't know me. It's quite funny really. Actually most people are very, very nice. They come up to me and say they like what I do, but mostly they are not intrusive. I'm not bothered by the attention, because most people are polite. After all, I put my face on the screen in the first place!

There is no formula for this job and no way really you can train for it. There is no RADA course for announcers! It's all very much to do with image and who you are in yourself. It's no good if you are not secure, because it's a very subjective business and you can get criticism. I can't possibly appeal to everyone and I have to accept that. Some people love you and some people don't. I do receive some very appreciative letters and, as long as they keep coming, I feel I am doing my best.

You must be enthusiastic and you must look as if you are enjoying it. You can't afford to have an off-day. I try to make my 'pieces' interesting. It's all live, so you have to be able to fill in the gaps quickly and accurately, rather like Polyfilla! You have to be quick-witted, because the time you have to fill can be very elastic. The public are not supposed to realise when there are problems, but sometimes it's unavoidable. And then there are the crises. I was on duty the day of the Lockerbie disaster and you have to be able to say the appropriate words before you switch over to ITN. I can remember another time when I had to report a newsflash about a bank raid in Preston. The information was being faxed to me in bits and pieces, seconds before I went on air! Yet it's all supposed to look seamless.

I came from a newspaper/creative writing background, which was obviously useful, but you can't really prepare for this job. I like the job very much and I like the odd hours because it means that you can do other things. It doesn't take 100 per cent of your time. Sometimes, for example, I start at eleven at night and finish at six in the morning, but then I am free for several days. It means that you can combine the job with other interests. I am still writing and presenting corporate programmes, which I find a satisfying and refreshing contrast to broadcasting.

16

SALES AND MARKETING

The entertainment industry has always been about audiences. Theatre and film have always been concerned with the 'bums on seats' factor: customers keep the industry working. Film, especially, stands and falls, in the first instance, by the profits accrued from tickets sold at the box office.

Television, for most of its history, was largely protected from the market-place. BBC viewers paid the Licence Fee which provided the money for radio and television, but licence holders had little control over what they were offered. They must have been fairly content because, surprisingly, there was never any mass demonstration against the programmes which were transmitted. Only a very few people refused to renew their licences, perhaps because anyone who did not pay was not only deprived of the BBC but also of ITV.

ITV was also only fairly obliquely concerned with the audience as far as revenue was concerned. The main focus of ITV companies was selling air-time to advertisers, because it was the advertisers who kept the commercial sector going. Channel Four's minority programming was protected from the full rigours of the market-place by the simple expedient of having a large part of its income derive from a subscription paid by the ITV companies to support Channel Four via the IBA. In return the ITV companies were allowed to sell advertising space on Channel Four in their own regions.

The 1990 Broadcasting Act, however, pushed ITV and Channel Four into the colder climate of market economics. Part of the intention of the Act was to put the various ITV companies on to a more level pegging, as far as revenue was concerned, with satellite and cable. What that has meant in practice is that marketing and retailing have become very important elements in the economics of television, just as they always were for film.

The film industry has always had to cope with the market-place. Costs are only recovered by effective distribution, and distribution depends on marketing and advertising. Today television is joining film and becoming more dependent on people with selling, retailing and financial skills. Here, as elsewhere in the industry, there is cross-employment between sectors.

SALES AGENT (administrative/legal/financial)

Film

Once a film has been made, it has to make money to recoup its costs. The transfer of film from the production phase to the market-place is often the work of the sales agent. Sales agents represent film producers and negotiate sales agreements with distributors. Sales agents are usually people with vast experience of, and enthusiasm for, the film industry and who understand finance and contracts. Some sales agents are lawyers, but even those who are not must have some legal knowledge, even if it is only gathered second-hand. Sales agents are very important people indeed because, if it is difficult in the first place to raise money for film, this second phase of the money-making process is even more crucial. Sales agents must recover costs and make a profit for the backers, otherwise the film industry would collapse.

DISTRIBUTORS (administrative/financial)
SALES AND MARKETING

Film

Distributors are specialists in the exploitation of film in a particular territory. Most distributors in this country deal with American film because that is where the big money is made and many distribution companies are in fact American-owned. In the eyes of supporters of British film-makers, this is one of the main problems facing the home-grown industry. The distribution system is very effective in delivering mainstream Hollywood films to British audiences. It is less effective in distributing British or European films to the same people. Critics of the distribution system are also irritated that marketing is mainly directed at audiences in the big metropolitan areas. Filmgoers who live outside the big cities have often to wait for mainline films to be released on video. As far as European or minority films are concerned, the small-town cinemagoer is even worse served (unless there is a film society or club locally), since many of these films are never released on video. The whole system, say the critics, is so geared to American film that audiences cannot broaden their tastes and develop an interest in other types of film. They are restricted to consuming the 'Hollywood diet'.

Distributors negotiate the rights to show a film in cinemas and now, increasingly, on video or television. One distributor has remarked, 'Television rights are absolutely vital. I wouldn't be interested in taking on a film without them.' (*BFI Handbook*, 1991, p. 33)

Distributors also orchestrate the number of prints required and the advertising campaign to promote the film. Film advertising is becoming increasingly expensive (especially for blockbusters like *Who Framed Roger Rabbit?* or *Batman*), but it is very important to a film's success. Producers can feel betrayed by distributors who do not market a film effectively. Sales agents, of course, should make sure that they extract guarantees about the way the film is advertised before they sell the rights, but problems can nonetheless develop. Sometimes distributors have put up part of the cash to help a film to be made and they then do a deal ensuring they receive the film at a cheaper price. Escalating advertising costs have led some distributors to believe that eventually producers themselves will have to pay a share of the advertising and marketing costs.

There are five major distributors in the UK market: United International Pictures (UIP), which distributes films from Paramount, Universal and MGM/United Artists; Warner; Columbia TriStar; 20th Century-Fox; and Rank. In addition there are small independent distribution companies such as Oasis, Virgin and Contemporary Films. (A full list can be found in the BFI's *Film and Television Handbook 1992*, ed. David Leafe, London, 1991.) The independents tend to concentrate on non-mainstream foreign films (less than 1 per cent of the market), and they often have great difficulty finding cinema spaces for their films. For this reason several of the independents also own their own cinemas.

A job in distribution means working in sales, marketing/advertising, or publicity. There is also a great deal of administrative work of a routine type. A public relations qualification is often a help on this side of the industry, as are financial and accountancy skills, sales, marketing and business diplomas and degrees. Sales and marketing people are usually extroverted, self-confident and thick-skinned. They have to be: distribution is a tough business.

The distribution sector of the film industry is very open and there is none of the emphasis on 'family contacts' that exists on the production side. Once in, however, the new recruit will find that distribution is a rather close-knit sector and people know each other very well. There is much toing and froing between rival companies as jobs come and go. On the whole, however, there is little chance of moving from distribution into production (although it has been done, since distributors do make contacts with the film-making side of the industry).

Anyone with sales, marketing, organisational or public relations skills who has a burning desire to get into film distribution should look out for advertisements in the trade press. They could also look up the names and addresses of distributors in the BFI *Handbook* and write a letter of enquiry.

EXHIBITORS (financial/administrative/marketing/retail) SALES STAFF

Film

Exhibitors are the owners or operators of cinemas and they negotiate terms with distributors for the exhibition of films. Distributors generally receive about a third and exhibitors two-thirds of box office receipts. There is concern about cinema attendance at the present time. One of the traditions of the film industry is that it does well when times are bad because in a recession people want to escape from the depressing facts of life into the fantasy world of the cinema. This was certainly the case in the Depression of the 1930s. However, the situation is not quite the same in the 1990s, since cable and satellite television now provide round-the-clock movie competition for the cinema. This could cut cinema attendance if times become really tough.

One of the major developments in exhibition in recent years has been the spread of multiplex cinemas. Over 30 per cent of all cinemas in the UK now have five screens or more, as compared to 1 per cent two years before. The UK's multiplexes now take around 35 per cent of the total box office generated by mainstream releases. They are proving very popular, and especially with women, whose attendance at cinema is increasing possibly because of the brightness and cleanliness of the foyer and the unintimidating character and comfort of the smaller-scale auditoriums. Jobs in exhibition include directors of operation, theatre managers, box office managers, ushers, kiosk attendants, concession and box office sales staff. These posts are usually advertised in local newspapers.

Increasingly exhibition staff are trained in presentation and good customer relations. Most multiplex cinemas have in-house training courses. Box office and retail staff are also trained in the use of

198

computers, since pre-advanced booking is an important part of modern cinema exhibition.

PROJECTIONIST

Film

Traditionally the most sought-after 'technical' job on the exhibition side is that of projectionist. *Cinema Paradiso*, a recent Italian film, beautifully illustrated the romance of the job in the days when the cinema was the only moving image mass medium. Modern projection is increasingly automated and 'high tech'. There is also no longer the risk of fire associated with nitrate film which used to give the job its rather daring image more than fifty years ago. Large exhibitors train their own projectionists, and again advertisements appear in the local press.

Anyone interested in this side of the industry who wishes to pre-empt advertisements in the local press should write to the exhibitors listed in the BFI's *Handbook*.

SALES CO-ORDINATORS/NEGOTIATORS/EXECUTIVES
(financial/retail/administrative)
MARKETING EXECUTIVES (managerial/financial)
MARKET RESEARCHERS (research/administrative)
TRAFFIC/MAKE-UP STAFF (administrative)

Television

The main activity for sales and marketing staff in television used to be interesting advertisers in the programmes on offer. Advertisers naturally like popular programmes, but in the past they were not allowed to associate the name of their product with a particular programme. They could say where they wanted an advertisement placed but, for most of the history of independent television, direct sponsorship of particular programmes was strictly forbidden. Such rules helped to protect programme-makers from too much interference by advertisers and this probably helped to promote more experimental, adventurous, innovative programming than conventional advertising agencies would initially have liked. Together the BBC and ITV produced what many regard as the golden age of British television.

Developments in technology, however, have ended the era when the air waves were a limited resource, protected and watched over by governments. The advent of cable and satellite has meant the multiplication of stations and channels and television has moved briskly into the market-place. Satellite and cable television stand and fall on their ability to sell their equipment and services to subscribers who are 'customers': the viewer pays for what he or she watches. Satellite and cable also derive revenue from advertising and they now compete with ITV in this area.

In the past decade ITV and the BBC have also acquired considerable additional revenue from the sale of their programmes overseas. High-quality British programmes are in demand, especially on so-called 'public' television channels in the United States. Overseas sales have become a lucrative source of extra finance and BBC Enterprises, for example, employs marketing and sales staff in this area. Some ITV companies run similar 'Enterprise' organisations to exploit their pro-grammes. There is in addition considerable money to be made from marketing the spin-offs of popular series through video and book sales.

All this has meant the expansion of the sales side of television. There are many more jobs than ever before for people who have been trained in accountancy, retailing, public relations or marketing. Moreover the development of the European dimension in television (and film) has also led to greater demand for people with skills in foreign languages. This is particularly so in the era of co-productions.

What Do Sales People in Television Actually Do?
In ITV, cable and satellite advertising sales co-ordinators/executives/negotiators (they can have different names in different companies) negotiate the sale of air time. They take bookings and see that com-mercial breaks are filled so that there is no empty space within or between programmes. They spend a great deal of time on the phone talking to advertisers and refer constantly to computers which display details of available air time.

In principle working in television advertising sales is similar to working in newspaper advertising, in that the aim is to recruit clients. The actual details of how television advertising is bought and sold, however, are more difficult to grasp, because of the problem of peak and off-peak viewing. Advertisers have to decide where to place an advertisement so that it is most effective. They have to determine which spot in the schedule gives the best value for money for their type of advertising. Off-peak times are cheaper than peak viewing times and very cheap spots are often 'pre-emptible'; that is, an advertisement can be withdrawn at the last minute to be replaced by one paying a higher rate. Costs increase the more precisely an advertisement is placed. If an advertiser wants to place an advertisement in the break

200

between the two halves of the ITN News, this is certainly possible, but at a price. If the advertiser is content with a 'scattergun' approach, by which the advertisement is shown many, many times but randomly at the station's discretion, then costs can be reduced considerably. This is because the television company prefers to retain flexibility over the scheduling of advertisements. Sales staff have to be familiar with all these details and they discuss the problems and the opportunities with the clients.

Sales staff in ITV and the advertising side of cable and satellite have to know the company schedule. They also have to know which advertising companies will be interested in particular types of programme. Computer manufacturers might not want to advertise during a game show, but they may be interested in a programme on a scientific topic because it will attract viewers who are likely to be customers for the product. Certain seasons of the year appeal to some advertisers more than others. Companies selling lawnmowing and gardening equipment may not, for example, find November a particularly attractive month!

Sales staff have to be articulate, outgoing and also good at numbers, because they have to calculate very quickly the different rates of advertisements. Most companies train their own staff according to their specific demands and needs.

Marketing staff are responsible for attracting new business. They are top-level management people who usually supervise sales staff. They visit customers and manufacturers all over the country and try to persuade them that television is an effective advertising medium. Increasingly marketing staff are concerned with the sponsorship of programmes, a recent development in commercial television. The *Inspector Morse* series, for example, is sponsored by a company that produces stout – which the Inspector himself could easily drink. Linking an advertisement with a character in a series like this used to be considered immoral and illicit, but this point of view now carries little weight. The increase in sponsorship means that marketing people have to know much more about the content of programmes in order to know what will appeal to potential sponsors. (The sponsorship rules are still fairly strict and uneven. There is some resentment in the industry because of this.)

In addition to marketing and sales staff, there are also sales research employees who do market research into the effectiveness of an advertising campaign. They produce data about the audience's reaction to advertisements on television and interpret it for clients.

Researchers also play an important role in examining the audience figures for particular programmes and in this case they are usually called audience researchers. Broadcasting organisations have always been anxious to find out how many and what kinds of people watch certain programmes. They want to know which programmes are popular so that they can repeat successful programme formats. They also want to discover the types of people the programmes attract: are they working-class, women, men, pensioners, young people? ITV, satellite and cable all need this information so that they can charge advertisers appropriately. The BBC needs such knowledge so that it can justify the licence fee.

The Broadcasters' Audience Research Board (BARB) is a company owned jointly by the BBC and ITV which carries out research into how many millions of people watch each programme and what they think about them. Audience research is an increasingly sophisticated profession and market researchers often have a background in statistics, computing or psychology.

So-called traffic staff monitor the composition (make-up) of commercial breaks and arrange for the receipt and delivery of advertisements, usually a few days before transmission. They also handle any last-minute bookings, and number the advertisements in the correct order of viewing. It makes it easier for transmission staff if all video-tape advertisements and all film commercials are collected together.

Anyone interested in the sales side of the industry should look up the addresses of the various television companies in the BFI *Handbook* and write to them for more information. As far as ITV is concerned, they should consult *The Official ITV Careers Handbook* (ed. Sue Davis), Hodder and Stoughton, 1989.

Case Histories

GARY PERRY

Gary Perry is thirty and is Sales Group Head for BSkyB sales.

I went into the army after school, but when I left I was looking for a job. I wasn't really sure what career path to take. My sister was in the industry on the advertising side and she thought that a job in sales would suit me. She had worked for Thames TV and TSW.

I started with Central in 1983 as a sales trainee. Basically, to begin with I logged sales executives' bookings, but then I actually started selling space on television myself. Mainly at that time I was on the phone and the job was very administrative, but as you climb the ladder there is more actual selling and less and less administration. You go out of the office, meet clients and visit advertising agencies looking for business. I enjoyed that. Eventually I became a Sales Executive with Central and stayed there for five years.

I then joined TVam as a Sales Group Head and then took this job. I am responsible for a group which sells air time. I have a lot of managerial responsibility, because I have to set and meet targets. It's an exciting job and well-paid. The industry keeps itself to itself, but it is very sociable within the industry. There is a fair amount of stress because of having to reach targets and the competition with other companies.

Selling is an area where you have to be very fast and it's a young person's job. You need to progress very quickly because there is a lot of pressure and you can be burned out by thirty-five. When I joined the sales side of television, the job had more to do with personality, common sense and the ability to get on with people. This is still necessary, but there is more emphasis on qualifications today. Many of the new people have degrees in media or business studies. You need goods maths qualifications and English.

I've always enjoyed the industry. You make a lot of friends. In fact my social life is my working life.

PHILIP MOORE

Philip Moore is twenty-six and works as a sales agent for Swindon Cable Television.

I went to college after school and did engineering, but I didn't like it very much. I decided I didn't want to be an engineer. You couldn't earn very much and I didn't like getting dirty. I could make more money as a salesman. I started selling cars when I left school and then I went to Germany and sold books door-to-door. I came back and worked with a furniture company for a while and then I took a year off working in Spain in nightclubs. When I came back again I heard about this job through a friend. I didn't know anything about cable, but I did know about sales. I actually thought that cable was dying and that satellite had taken over! I didn't know anything about the industry and I hadn't realised the changes which had taken place.

The company trained me for two weeks and it was a tough course.

We learned all about the company's package, how to demonstrate it, the channels, service, installation. Then we went out door-to-door.

I really like the money, and working in the afternoons and evenings suits me. I like meeting people and I like the people I work with. The company is very well-run and well-organised. I just like selling and this sort of life, I suppose, and cable is interesting to sell.

POSTSCRIPT
Archiving and Film Research

There is a limited number of jobs available to people who are passionate about the preservation and history of film and television. The main area of employment is in the National Film Archive (NFA), which was founded in 1935 to maintain a national repository of films of permanent value, but there are other archives around the country which also employ film archivists. (For more information about archives and collections see *The Researcher's Guide to British Film and Television Collections* published by the British Universities Film and Video Council.) The NFA's moving image collection now comprises more than 175,000 titles dating from 1895. In the mid-1950s the NFA also began to acquire television programmes, the recording and preservation of which are now a major part of its work.

Archive work involves several stages: acquisition, preservation, cataloguing and dissemination. Since there is no law of statutory deposit for film and video production in the United Kingdom (in contrast to books), the acquisition of material for the NFA Collection is mainly through donation. The Acquisition section is divided roughly into three areas: feature films, documentary and non-fiction films, and television. Keepers working in this area have to seek out possible donors and diplomatically persuade them to contribute to the Archive's holdings.

Preservation and restoration, which is a highly technical and specialised activity, is carried out at the J. Paul Getty Conservation Centre in Berkhamsted, which is the main storage site for safety film and video. Nitrate film is kept at a specially equipped site in Warwickshire. Nitrate film decomposes as it ages and becomes highly inflammable (there was a disastrous accident because of nitrate film at the Mexican film archives some years ago). The 140 million feet of nitrate film in the NFA's collection are systematically being copied on to modern safety film as part of the process of preservation. Berkhamsted

205

has an international reputation for film preservation and conservation and it trains people from all over the world.

The Cataloguing section of the NFA is based in London and has the Herculean task of indexing, cataloguing and analysing all the films and programmes in the collection. Film cataloguing has to be very detailed, because it is not possible to scan a film as one can flick through a book. Film researchers are therefore very dependent on catalogues for detailed information about a film. Also film can be damaged through frequent projection, so it is particularly important, if a film has not been copied on to a video viewing-copy, that only bona fide researchers are given access. This can annoy people who do not understand the fragility of film and who wish to view the collection: staff in this section of the NFA have to be extremely tactful. The Cataloguing section provides an excellent service for film researchers and the Production Library provides film-makers and television producers with extracts of films for use in compilation films and documentary programmes.

The training of film and television archivists used to be somewhat haphazard. Some keepers/curators had archival qualifications at postgraduate level, but many archive courses focus on historical documents and written material and do not include training in the preservation and archiving of the moving image. In the past, therefore, film archivists tended to be people who were passionately interested in the history of film, but who had to learn the techniques of preservation and conservation on the job. As the work has become more technical and professional, however, the need for specialist training has increased. In response to this, the University of East Anglia established the first postgraduate MA course in Film Archiving in 1990. Based within the East Anglian Film Archive, the course has about six places available each year. The course will provide fully qualified and competent recruits for this important section of the film industry over the next decade and will be one of the best qualifications for people seeking a career in film research.

APPENDIX
Applying for a Course or a Job

The basic rule in applying for a course or a job is to follow the instructions to the letter. When you apply for a position in film and television, or for a course in the media, the competition will be fierce. Therefore if the application form asks that you type your answers, do not write in pen, pencil or biro. One employer told me that for one job she had over 500 applications. Faced with so many letters and forms, she immediately rejected those which had failed to follow instructions. Into the waste-paper basket (unread) went all applications written in red or green biro, because candidates had explicitly been told to use black. *Rule Number One: if you cannot follow basic instructions, you are of little interest to the industry.*

Rule Number Two: do some research. Don't wait passively until you see a job advertised. Very few jobs are ever advertised, since most of them are filled internally. This is a very hard fact for newcomers to grasp. If you want a job, as a runner for example, you have to hustle. You have to find out about the employers: film and video companies, the BBC, ITV, satellite and cable companies. Ignorance will get you nowhere. Read the trade magazines so that you are well-informed about what is happening in the industry. Employers are impressed by people who have taken the trouble to find out about them.

Rule Number Three: make your own opportunities. When you feel you know something about the industry, then you should write to, telephone and visit the companies, again and again. Try to find the name of someone in a company who might be prepared to see you. Ask everyone for advice. And remember you must be able to take rejection: it requires persistence to get into this industry and there will be very many disappointments before you make any headway. Forget any nonsense about overnight success. Getting in will test your perseverance!

Rule Number Four: live and breathe the industry. In other words: watch films and television over and over again. Think about what you see constructively and analytically. What are the films and programmes saying? How do they get their messages across? Try to think up new approaches and ideas as you watch. Employers are looking for an enthusiasm and passion for the industry. The dilettante approach is fatal.

Rule Number Five: produce a portfolio of your own work. As explained earlier in this book, the advantage of formal coursework is that students are usually provided with the opportunity to make their own films and videos. They put together examples of their practical work to show prospective employers, who after all need something by which to judge you.

Rule Number Six: construct an effective curriculum vitae (CV). A CV is a description of you, and should set out your skills, abilities, personality and experience. People are incredibly lazy about their CVs. Once they have done one, they send it out indiscriminately in all directions. In fact CVs should be tailored to suit each individual job. Companies specialising in corporate videos have different interests from companies specialising in pop or educational videos. Think about what the employer might be looking for. Emphasise that part of your experience which is relevant to the particular job. For this reason it is always worth trying to put your CV on a word processor so that it can be easily adapted and updated. Make sure that there are no mistakes in grammar or spelling: employers can be very particular and some of them are insulted by poorly prepared CVs or letters of application. There is nothing charming about the casual approach.

Rule Number Seven: if you get the longed-for interview either for a course or a job, show your enthusiasm, but don't show off. As explained in this book, making moving pictures is a joint effort and employers are looking for people who can fit in with a team, especially at the beginning. When you are producing or directing *the* British film of 1995 you can afford to throw your weight around a little, but not before! The key personality traits which employers say they are looking for are: the ability to be a team worker, common sense, curiosity, good communication skills, attention to detail, a willingness to work long hours, the enthusiasm to keep a project going, commitment, physical stamina, practical skills and lateral thinking.

Remember there are many more people than there are jobs!

Useful Names and Addresses

Vocational Qualification Councils

National Council for Vocational Qualification (NCVQ)
22 Euston Road, London, NW1 2BZ
Tel: 071 387 9898

SCOTVEC
Scottish Vocational Education Council
Hanover House, 24 Douglas Street, Glasgow, G2 7NQ
Tel: 041 248 7900

Vocational Qualifications: Awarding Bodies

The Business and Technology Education Council (BTEC)
Central House, Upper Woburn Palace, London, WCIH 0HH
Tel: 071 413 8400

City and Guilds of London Institute
76 Portland Place, London, W1N 4AA
Tel: 071 278 2468

Royal Society of Arts
RSA Examinations Board
Westwood Way, Coventry, CV4 8HS
Tel: 0203 470033

Industry Lead Bodies

Skillset
c/o Channel Four, 60 Charlotte Street, London, WIP 2AX
Tel: 071 927 8568

Arts and Entertainment Training Council
3 St Peter's Buildings, York Street, Leeds, LS9 8AJ
Tel: 0532 448845

Arts and Entertainment Technical Training Initiative
The Cockpit Theatre, Gateforth Street, London, NW8 1NB
Tel: 071 262 7907

Industry Lead Body for Design
29 Bedford Square, London, WC1 3EG
Tel: 071 631 1510

Industry Training Organisations

Skillset (formerly Broadcast, Film and Video Industry Training
Organisation)
60 Charlotte Street, London, W1P 2AX
Tel: 071 927 8568

Arts and Entertainment Training Council
3 St Peters Building, York Street, Leeds, LS9 8AJ
Tel: 0532 448845

Photography and Photographic Processing Industry Training
Organisation
British Institute of Professional Photography
Fox Talbot House, 2 Amwell End, Ware, Herts., SG122 9HN
Tel: 0920 464011

Unions

British Actors' Equity Association
8 Harley Street, London, W1N 3TD
Tel: 071 636 6367

BECTU
Broadcasting, Entertainment, Cinematograph and Theatre Union
111 Wardour Street, London, W1V 3TD
Tel: 071 437 8506

Union Recognised Pre-entry Courses

Seven schools and colleges are accredited by BECTU as providing
recognised practical training for the industry. Graduates from these
full-time courses may apply for union-graded jobs and, if selected,
receive full union membership.

Bournemouth and Poole College of Art and Design
Wallisdown Road, Poole, Dorset, BH12 5HH
Tel: 0202 533011

London College of Printing
Film and Video Division, 6 Backhill, London, EC1R 5EN
Tel: 071 278 7445

London International Film School
24 Shelton Street, London, WC2 9HP
Tel: 071 836 9642

National Film and Television School
Beaconsfield Film Studios, Station Road, Beaconsfield, Bucks,
HP9 1LG
Tel: 0494 671234

University of Westminster
18–22 Riding House Street, London, W1P 7PD
Tel: 071 911 5000

West Surrey College of Art and Design
Falkner Road, The Hart, Farnham, Surrey, GU9 7DS
Tel: 0252 722441

University of Bristol
29 Park Row, Bristol, BS1 5LT
Tel: 0272 302204

There are many other courses offering qualifications in film, television
and video. The British Film Institute publishes a list of available
courses entitled *Film and TV Training: A Guide to Film and Video
Courses*. There is also a BFI list of courses in higher education entitled
Studying Film and TV (see bibliography).

For information on short courses consult the BFI publication *Directions: A Guide to Short Training Courses in Video and Film*. The BFI
is currently compiling a comprehensive computerised database of
training courses. This is available from mid-1992.

Professional Associations

PACT
Producers' Alliance of Cinema and Television
Gordon House, 10 Greencoats Place, London, SW1P 1PH
Tel: 071 233 6000

PACT publishes a journal entitled *Impact*.

IVCA
International Video Communications Association
Bolsover House, 5/6 Clipstone Street, London, W1 7EB
Tel: 071 580 0962

IVCA is the professional association for visual communications users
and suppliers. It has a student/trainee membership category and publishes the *IVCA Magazine*.

Writers' Guild of Great Britain
430 Edgware Road, London, W2 1EH
Tel: 071 723 8074

British Kinematograph Sound and Television Society (BKSTS)
547–549 Victoria House, Vernon Place, London, WC1B 4DJ
Tel: 071 242 8400

The Royal Television Society
Tavistock House East, Tavistock Square, London, WC1 9HR
Tel: 071 387 1332
For further names and addresses consult the BFI Handbook.

Journals

The following are useful magazines and journals for information
about the industry:

Audiovisual	*Stage and Television Today*
Broadcast	*Studio News*
Impact	*Television*
IVCA Magazine	*Television Week*
Media Week	*Televisual*
Producer	*Time Out*

Screen International   *TV Production International*
Sight and Sound   *Viewfinder*

The Media pages of the *Guardian* (each Monday) and the *Independent* (Wednesday) are also useful.

Jobs are advertised in:

Audiovisual	*Observer*
Broadcast	*Screen International*
Campaign	*Stage and Television Today*
City Limits	*Sunday Times*
Daily Telegraph	*Televisual*
Evening Standard (London)	*Time Out*
Guardian	*TV Production International*
Independent	*UK Press Gazette*

Videocassettes

The BBC publish television training videocassettes which can be bought from the BBC or viewed at:

The British Universities Film and Video Council
55 Greek Street, London, W1V 5LR
Tel: 071 734 3687

Titles include:

Writing Commentary: Television Continuity:
 Part 1 An Introduction
 Part 2 Tricks of the Trade.
Making a Drama of It.
Making of the 'Six' (about the making of the Six O'Clock News)
Language of Film:
 Part 1 Lenses and Light
 Part 2 The Soundtrack
 Part 3 Actors and Camera.

BIBLIOGRAPHY

Allen, J., *Careers in TV and Radio*, 3rd edition, London, Kogan Page, April 1990.

Allen, J., *The Kogan Page Guide to Careers in the Media*, London, Kogan Page, 1989.

Alvarado, Manuel and Buscombe, Edward, *Hazell: the Making of a TV Series*, London, BFI, 1978.

Alvarado, Manuel and Stewart, John, *Made for Television: Euston Films Limited*, London, BFI, 1985.

Angell, Robert, *Film and TV: The Way In*, London, BFI, 1988.

Bernstein, Steven, *The Technique of Film Production*, London, Focal Press, 1987.

Davis, Sue (ed.), *The Official ITV Careers Handbook*, Sevenoaks, Hodder and Stoughton, 1989. The *Handbook* is currently being updated.

Elliot, Geoffrey and Foss, Hannen (eds.), *Video Production Techniques: A Handbook for Television, Film and Audiovisual Programme Makers*, looseleafed handbook which is updated. Published initially by Kluwer, Brentford, Middlesex, now by Longman (from 1992).

Kemp's International Film and Television Yearbook, 1990/91, London, Kemp's Printing and Publishing Co.

Ostrov, Rick and McCord, Bill, *Careers in Film and Video*, London, Kogan Page, 1989. (Third edition due out in July 1992)

Ross-Muir, Anne, *Women's Guide to Jobs in Film and TV*, London, Pandora, 1987.

Winston, Brian and Keydel, Julia, *Working with Video*, London, Pelham, 1987.

Writers' and Artists' Yearbook, published annually, London, A. & C. Black.

The British Film Institute's *Film and Television Handbook 1992* is an

214

indispensable source of information on all aspects of the industry. The *Handbook* is published each year and, in addition to annual reports on cinema, television and radio, it also provides up-to-date information on courses, organisations, production companies, television companies, workshops, film societies, preview theatres, distributors, cable and satellite companies, studios, video labels and so on. The *Handbook*, like other BFI Publications, is available from BFI Publications, 21 Stephen Street, London W1P 1PL.

The British Film Institute also publishes lists of courses in film and television training. They include: *Film and TV Training: A Guide to Film and Video Courses*, a comprehensive guide to courses which include practical work with film and video or photography, either as a major component or as a subsidiary element. The booklet includes sections on Undergraduate courses; Postgraduate courses; Higher Diplomas; Diploma and Certificate courses; Film and Video Workshops and Short courses. Price: £4.25 (£4.75 including postage and packing).

Studying Film and TV, compiled by Lavinia Orton and published by the BFI, is a companion to film and television training, and is a guide to courses of more formal study. It contains information on universities and colleges offering Film and/or TV Studies. Section A lists those institutions where film is the major part of the course; Section B where film comprises 25–45 per cent of the course; and Section C where film and/or TV studies are less than 25 per cent of the whole course. Part Two lists postgraduate courses available in the UK. Price: £4.25 (£4.75 including postage and packing). Both publications can be purchased together at a reduced price of £8.00 (£8.75 including postage and packing).

In addition there is a BFI guide to short courses, *Directions: A Guide to Short Training Courses in Video and Film*, published biannually by the British Film Institute's Planning Unit. It contains information on production training and articles on current practices and issues around training. Price: £3.00 (£3.50 including postage and packing).

Source material for some of the film quotations in this book come from Crawley, Tony, *Chambers Film Quotes*, Edinburgh, W. R. Chambers Ltd, 1991.

215

Media Course Guides from the BFI

Updated annually, BFI course guides provide all the necessary information for anyone seeking training in the media, whether academic or practical.

Film and Television Training   198 pp   £4.75 inc. p & p
A comprehensive guide to colleges, polytechnics and workshops offering practical courses in film and video production.

Studying Film and Television   124 pp   £4.75 inc. p & p
A guide to academic courses in higher education. Gives details of both undergraduate and postgraduate courses offered by universities and polytechnics in which film or television is a major, substantial or minor component.

Directions   98 pp   £3.00 inc. p & p
A guide to short practical training courses run by and for the independent film and video sector. *Directions* also includes some short courses run by further and higher education colleges.

Copies of these publications and the BFI Media Education catalogue are available from:

> BFI Publishing Services
> 29 Rathbone Street
> London
> W1P 1AG
>
> Tel: 071–636 3289
> Fax: 071–580 9456

Index

217

219

220

221